Sanskrit Studies
Vol. 1, Saṁvat 2061-62
(CE 2004-05)

Sanskrit Studies
Vol. 1, Saṁvat 2061-62
(CE 2004-05)

edited by
Kapil Kapoor

Special Centre for Sanskrit Studies
Jawaharlal Nehru University
New Delhi

in association with

D. K. Printworld (P) Ltd.
New Delhi

Cataloging in Publication Data — DK
[Courtesy: D.K. Agencies (P) Ltd. <docinfo@dkagencies.com>]

Sanskrit studies vol. 1, Saṁvat 2061-62 (CE 2004-05)
/ edited by Kapil Kapoor.
xxiv, 288 p. 23 cm.
Contributed articles.
Includes passages in Sanskrit (roman)
Includes bibliograhical references.
Includes index.
ISBN 8124603480

1. Sanskrit philology — Study and teaching.
I. Kapoor, Kapil, 1940-

DDC 491.25 22

ISBN 81-246-0348-0
First published in India in 2005

Published by:
Special Centre for Sanskrit Studies
Jawaharlal Nehru University
New Delhi - 110 067.

in association with

D.K. Printworld (P) Ltd.
Regd. Office: 'Sri Kunj', F-52, Bali Nagar
New Delhi-110 015
Phones: (011) 2545-3975; 2546-6019; *Fax*: (011) 2546-5926
E-mail: dkprintworld@vsnl.net
Website: www.dkprintworld.com

Printed by: D.K. Printworld (P) Ltd., New Delhi

Editorial Advisory Board

Contents

Acknowledgement

WE gratefully acknowledge the generous research/ publication grant given by UGC that has facilitated this first volume in the proposed series.

I thank the scholars who have contributed to this volume. We acknowledge with thanks the helpful guidance of the Advisory Committee of the Centre for Sanskrit Studies, JNU and the support of the Editorial Board.

I am grateful to my colleague Dr. Rajnish Kumar Mishra for his help in finalizing the manuscript and for the cover design.

My Ph.D. student Shri Tulsi Das Majhi deserves thanks for his help in reading the proof and for preparing a scholarly index.

I must acknowledge the great support extended in this first volume by Dr. Shashiprabha Kumar, Head, Special Centre for Sanskrit Studies, JNU, New Delhi.

Finally, I thank Shri Susheel ji of the D.K. Printworld for his personal and deep interest in this publication and for taking care at every stage to ensure quality in printing and production.

Key to Transliteration

VOWELS

अ *a*	आ *ā*	इ *i*	ई *ī*	उ *u*	ऊ *ū*
(but)	(palm)	(it)	(beet)	(put)	(pool)
ऋ *ṛ*	ए *e*	ऐ *ai*	ओ *o*	औ *au*	
(rhythm)	(play)	(air)	(toe)	(loud)	

CONSONANTS

Guttural	क *ka*	ख* *kha*	ग *ga*	घ *gha*	ङ *ṅa*
	(skate)	(blockhead)	(gate)	(ghost)	(sing)
Palatal	च *ca*	छ* *cha*	ज *ja*	झ *jha*	ञ *ña*
	(chunk)	(catch him)	(john)	(hedgehog)	(bunch)
Lingual	ट *ṭa*	ठ* *ṭha*	ड *ḍa*	ढ* *ḍha*	ण* *ṇa*
	(start)	(anthill)	(dart)	(godhead)	(under)
Dental	त *ta*	थ *tha*	द *da*	ध* *dha*	न *na*
	(path)	(thunder)	(that)	(breathe)	(numb)
Labial	प *pa*	फ* *pha*	ब *ba*	भ *bha*	म *ma*
	(spin)	(philosophy)	(bin)	(abhor)	(much)
Others	य *ya*	र *ra*	ल *la*	व *va*	
	(young)	(drama)	(luck)	(vile)	
	श *śa*	ष *ṣa*	स *sa*	ह *ha*	
	(shove)	(bushel)	(so)	(hum)	
	क्ष *kṣa*	त्र *tra*	ज्ञ *jña*	ळ* ḷ	ॠ* *ṝ*
(*kṣatriya*)	(*trishūl*)	(*jñāni*)	(*play*)		

अं (ं) *ṁ anusvāra* (nasalisation of preceding vowel) like *saṁskṛti*

अः *ḥ* (*prātaḥ*) *ḥ visarga* (aspiration of preceding vowel)

ऽ 'Avagraha' = consonant #'consonant (like:- *ime 'vasthitā*)

ꣳ (*guṁ*) = ꣳ

Anusvāra at the end of line is presented by म् = m (not ṁ)

* No exact English equivalents for these letters.

Introduction

I

ANTI-SANSKRITISM having been promoted, along with anti-Brāhminism, as a part of casteist and communal politics, the Sanskrit space has been shrinking in the last four decades to the great detriment of Indian culture and civilization even in major institutions of learning. JNU characteristically took a major remedial step when in 2002, the Special Centre for Sanskrit Studies was set up through sustained effort. With an assumed erroneous equation of Sanskrit and Hindu, Sanskrit has been opposed on several, often unstated and invalid, assumptions that one need not spell out here. Suffice it to say that the "social engineering" that has been politically structured in this country since 1947 that seeks to "modernise" India requires not just the exclusion of "Sanskrit Culture" but a positive opposition to it. As a consequence, the Indian society has witnessed the collapse of social and personal values, spread of materialism and consumerism, social conflicts, lawlessness and a general moral vacuum. These are all intangibles to begin with but in course of time their deleterious consequences for the very survival of the Indian polity shall be all too apparent.

With the given plurality of Indian reality, the Indian mind has always searched for synthesis and transcendence just as the Hebraic mind driven by its monistic/monotheistic imperative has searched for "difference," an ethnographic construct that informs the contemporary social, economic and political theory. The contemporary Indian mind, in the absence of sufficient space for Indian thought in the mainstream education, is totally derivative and subjugated by this ethnographic Western thought which, over the last three decades or so, has often proved divisive and disintegrating.

It is this state of the Indian mind and education that needs correction through a balancing thought structure and that is available only in Sanskrit intellectual texts. For this reason, it is wrong to consider Sanskrit as just another language — something like what Aṅgad had forcefully pointed out to Rāvaṇa in his court.

The Supreme Court of India had debated this whole question of Sanskrit and its place in Indian life and education in 1993. That 1993 Judgement is a historic statement about Sanskrit Studies in India. [We reproduce it in its entirety in Appendix for it not only argues for Sanskrit but also underlines the not so inexplicable anti-Sanskrit attitude.]

II

In that historic but overlooked judgement, the learned Judges say — and we quote verbatim (with ***emphasis supplied***) —

"So far as ***"We, the people of India" are concerned, they have always held in high esteem the cultural heritage of this ancient land. And to foretell our views, learning of Sanskrit is undoubtedly necessary for protection of this heritage. The stream of our culture would get dried if we were to discourage the study of Sanskrit,*** and that too on the most untenable ground that if the Central Board of Secondary Education (for short 'the Board') were to do so, it would have to make facilities available for learning of Arabic and Persian — these being also classical languages, which is the ground advanced by Additional Solicitor General, Shri Tulsi, appearing for the Board, in it not being in a position to accept the prima facie view expressed by us on 19.7.94, when these cases had come up for hearing that Sanskrit should be included by the Board as one of the elective subjects in the syllabus along with Assamese, Bengali etc. which are the languages specified in the Eighth Schedule of our Constitution, mentioning about Sanskrit being also an Eighth Schedule language. ***The desire to keep Sanskrit out does not stop here***, as the submission also is that if Sanskrit comes, the Board shall have to bring in languages like French and German. This is not all, as it is contended by the Addl. Solicitor General that the Board feels that arrangement may have then to be made for imparting education even in Lepcha, a language whose name many of the Indians might not have even heard."

"4. ***We fail to appreciate at all the stand taken*** by a responsible body like the Board, who has been entrusted with the onerous duty of educating the youths of this country "in whose hands quiver the destinies of the future," as the same is wholly untenable. ***Without the learning of Sanskrit it is not possible to decipher the Indian philosophy on which our culture and heritage are based.***

We may now advert to the broad framework of our education policy as accepted by the Central Government. For our purpose it would be enough if we refer to the policies as formulated in 1968 and 1986. Here again, we would confine our attention to what was stated in these policies regarding Sanskrit. **In the 1968 policy** the following found place qua this language:

"***Considering the special importance of Sanskrit to the growth and development of Indian languages and its unique contribution to the cultural unity of the country facilities for its teaching at the school and university stages should be***

offered on more liberal basis. Development of new methods of teaching the language should be encouraged, and the possibility explored of including the study of Sanskrit in those courses (such as modern Indian philosophy) at the first and second degree stages, where such knowledge is useful."

9. **The 1986 policy** has to say as below, in this regard, in para 5.33:

"Research in Indology, the humanities and Social Sciences will receive adequate support. To fulfil the need for the synthesis of knowledge, inter-disciplinary research will be encouraged. Efforts will be made to delve into India's ancient fund of knowledge and to relate it to contemporary reality. This effort will imply the development of facilities for the intensive study of Sanskrit." (Emphasis supplied)

"Indeed, our constitution requires giving of fillip to Sanskrit because of what has been stated in Article 351 in which while dealing with the duty of the Union to promote the spread of Hindi, it has been provided that, it would draw, whenever necessary or desirable, for its vocabulary, primarily on Sanskrit. ***Encouragement to Sanskrit is also necessary because of it being one of the languages included in the Eighth Schedule."***

III

With all this in mind, anguish not different in its intensity from that of the Ancient Mariner in Coleridge's celebrated poem, strenuous efforts were made to give Sanskrit its due place in JNU. Thus it is that through a generous grant by the University Grants Commission the Special Centre for Sanskrit Studies finally came to be established with the express purpose of imparting Indian knowledge systems to the bright young JNU students.

There is a strong reason why our young people should have access to classical Indian thought. The Indian mind differs from the Western, and the two cultures differ in their "drivers," in the way their members are "programmed." It is important to know our own foundations even for a proper appreciation of the products of the powerful Western intellectual tradition. The contemporary man is situated on the crossroads of the East and the West and it is imperative for him to know from where the roads come and whence they are headed to if he (or the human society) has to chart the right path of survival and happiness. One is convinced that our young minds must be given this Indian alternative to Western thought and an awareness of the difference between these two cultures of knowledge.

It is apparent that there are two knowledge cultures in the world of ideas — the Hebraic and, call it what you will, the Vedic, the Indo-European or the Pagan. The Hebraic subsumes, with internal differences, the Judaic, the Christian and the Islamic sub-cultures, all *Theo*-centric — marked by a belief in a personal God. The Pagan is represented by the R̥gvedic culture and subsumes, through a variety of inter-relationships, the Hindu, the Buddhist, the Jaina and the Sikh, the Iranian and the Greek sub-cultures. The Hebraic-Vedic opposition is characterised by the Hebraic notion of the One Formless Personal God presiding over a separate material universe as the object of knowledge (and devotion) — an unqualified monotheism — as against the Vedic notion of polytheism, of an informing principle immanent in the material universe that takes numerous forms as so many "gods."

At the end of the second *kāṇḍa* of his *Vākyapadīya*, Bhartr̥hari (fifth century CE) says, "the Mind acquires critical acumen by interacting with the other traditions. What does he know who knows only his own tradition?" A beautiful thought of an intellectually confident India but sadly, today, with our systems of knowledge having been marginalised and excluded from the mainstream education, we have to ask, instead, *what does he know who does not know his own tradition*? I put myself at the head of the post-1947 "lost generation" of young people who at best are ignorant and at worst have contempt for themselves. Herein lies the answer to the question why one should study our own traditions of thought.

India has continuous and cumulative intellectual traditions in many domains of knowledge. This tradition begins with the *Ṛgveda*, the first attested Indo-European document, and continues to be alive in life, practices and learning of the Indian people. As a mechanism of transfer and evolution of ideas from one generation to the next, the tradition is comparable to the perennial flow of the river Gaṅgā — *bhāratīya jñāna paramparā sanātana gaṅgā pravāha.* The power and pertinence of knowledge systems in this tradition are attested by the existence of innumerable texts and thinkers that continue to be a subject of study in major contemporary Western universities as well. Thus, for example, besides the powerful texts of philosophy, Pāṇini's celebrated grammar is being studied in the Departments of Computer Sciences and Systems all over the world and the new consciousness studies in the Western universities are being founded on the texts of Śaivism, Tantra and Yoga.

There is a need to expound major Indian knowledge systems and produce and make available authoritative statements that articulate their validity for the contemporary Indian and Western reality. Above all, we need now to look at these knowledge systems in the modern perspective. The disciplines/domains of knowledge include Logic,

Philosophy of Language, Technology and Crafts, Polity and Governance, Ethics and Sociological texts, Architecture — the Outer Sciences, Poetics and Aesthetics, Law and Justice, Mathematics and Astronomy, Agriculture, Trade and Commerce, and Medicine and Life Science.

The Sanskrit Centre proposes to re-examine, in its teaching and research programmes, Indian thought systems and relate them both to the contemporary Indian reality and the contemporary western thinking. This is to be achieved by (i) translating and making available to young students and scholars the primary intellectual texts of the tradition, (ii) expounding the thought systems and by (iii) applying the Indian theoretical frameworks to contemporary Indian and western realities.

As a part of this project, it was also envisioned to institute a research journal/publication that should encourage primary and comparative research. The present volume is the first — it lays no claim to any completeness or comprehensiveness of discussion of various issues pertaining to Indian Knowledge Systems. What it promises is a continuous commitment to Indian Knowledge Systems, their validity and value. We are fully aware that there are innumerable gaps in the discussions but we hope that every succeeding volume shall improve upon the preceding one. We hope this publication shall over a period of time build a team of young scholars with reverence for the tradition and a commitment to exact scholarship.

Articles in the present volume deal with diverse themes.

The first essay by Professor George Cardona discusses three logical issues that the Indian grammarians confronted. With his characteristic precision, Professor Cardona illustrates from *Aṣṭādhyāyī* the handling of the three issues:

(i) restricted domain of a rule versus non-applicability in a domain; (ii) use and mention of a term; (iii) posited concepts denoted by *laukika vākya* versus "true reality" denoted by *alaukika vākya*. This is one example of the close relationship that obtains between grammar and philosophy in Indian thought.

In the essay "Indian Logic and Modern Information Technology," the two scientist-authors argue that classical Indian texts such as Śāstras and Vedāṅgas are "a goldmine" for information technology and knowledge systems. They show that *Mimāṁsā, Nyāya, Śikṣā* and *Nirukta* can provide "a new conceptual basis," an alternative basis, for knowledge representation. To that end, they argue that Indian logic may be used to develop IT tools and products for conducting administration, business and educational activities in the Indian multilingual environment. They also show some of the applications and give examples of Petri Nets to show the usefulness of concepts of Indian logic in this area.

Dr. Rajnish Kumar Mishra in the third essay, "Buddhist Theory of Meaning" explains that mainly the logicians of the *Sautāntrīka-Yogācāra* schools take up the questions of meaning as part of Buddhist epistemology. *Śabda*, for them, is subsumed under inference. Along with other means of knowledge, it brings about cognition of the universal through difference and cannot touch the unique particular. In this respect, *apoha* is a major thesis supported by all the four philosophical schools of Buddhism. Dr. Mishra expounds it at length and contributions of Diṅnāga, Dharmakīrti, Śāntarakṣita and Ratnakīrti towards a greater understanding of this concept are explicated. Attention is drawn to the process of exclusion and also to the limits of verbal evocation as argued by the Buddhist thinkers. It is noted that the Buddhist thought, including verbal denotation, subscribes to *akhaṇḍa pakṣa,* the non-partitive view, and its implications for Buddhist logic are also hinted at. Finally, the critique of *Apohavāda* by grammarians, philosophers and Mimāṁsakas and the Buddhist rejoinder are discussed.

Dr. Upendra Rao in his essay on Keśakambali's philosophical position locates him in the intellectually turbulent period in world history between eighth and ninth century BC when a galaxy of thinkers in Greece, Persia, China and India were articulating their several, and often, competing systems. A near contemporary of Buddha, Keśakambali represents the heretic stream of Indian philosophy that is sometimes related to the hedonistic Cārvākas and at other times to the austere Buddhists. His views are quite radical — he rejected after-life, the existence of *ātman,* the merit or demerit of deeds and the Brāhmanic ritualism. Dr. Rao brings to bear on Ajita's views the critiques of Jaina and Buddhist thinkers and concludes by saying that Keśakambali could not correctly be called a hedonist and that his philosophy is also ultimately rooted in the Upaniṣads.

The next essay, "The Paraśurāma Narrative" by Professor Randhir Singh is an unusual study. On the pattern of Saussure who at the time of his death was trying to decode Ṛgvedic symmetries, it is one of those few studies that look upon some of India's Vedic and epic texts as repositories also of encrypted statements that contain highly significant knowledge, including scientific knowledge and demonstrates how such texts may be interpreted to yield that coded knowledge. Dr. Randhir Singh in this essay establishes that the legendary Paraśurāma narrative recounted in a number of texts is in fact coded mathematical knowledge. Dr. Singh convincingly demonstrates that the narrative codes the value of π, *pi* (*/par*) and the related recurring numbers. In the process he explains that the familiar names such as Kurukṣetra, Śoṇitasarovar and Samantapañcaka while being names for real places that exist even today with the same names also denote equally real mathematical numbers and values. In this context it is pointed out that interesting questions about history, archaeology and discourse are involved in this kind of research. In particular the scholar cautions the readers that the Hindu narratives are not to be read as mere stories and that all of them may be fruitfully searched for the embedded meanings.

Professor Rama Nath Sharma in the paper "Some Thoughts on *Vipratiṣedha*" describes the two types of exceptions, *saṁjñā vipratiṣedha* and *saṁjñetra vipratiṣedha*, and explains the conditions of application, both shared and independent. Professor Sharma gives several examples from Pāṇini of "situation(s) of conflict" between rules and explains how in the tradition such conflicts are resolved by taking into account factors such as domain, scope and conditions of application of rules. The essay shows how Pāṇini's 4000 rules constitute a single statement (*ekavākyatā*) and in the process articulates the tremendous systematization involved in *Aṣṭādhyāyī*.

The concept of *Brahman* in the three schools of Vedānta is the subject matter of Professor K.T. Pandurangi's article that comes next in this volume. The learned professor dwells on the concept of *Brahman* in the context of the Indian mind's search for origins, for the source of the universe, its order of evolution and its purpose. This concept has been analysed in the *R̥gveda* itself, we are informed, and had evolved through various Smr̥ti systems. Nāsadīya-Sūkta and Viśvakarma-Sūkta, we are told, define *Brahman* in their characteristic twilight language of apparent contradictions. However, the seed thought contained in them is developed and explicated in the major schools of philosophy — Sāṁkhya, Yoga, Vedānta,

Vaiśeṣika and Nyāya. Pandurangi ji focuses on the three schools of Vedānta — *Advaita, Dvaita* and *Viśiṣṭādvaita* — and points out that the concept has three dimensions — metaphysical, epistemological and theological — and two levels, the functional and the ultimate. The basic question of relationship between mind and matter, he says, generates the need to posit the concept of *Brahman* as an explanatory construct. With this question in mind, the three schools of Vedānta formulated their ontological position on this fundamental category and its status as the source of creation. In *Advaita, Brahman* is the only and ultimate reality. *Dvaita* considers the mind and the matter as distinct and yet *Brahman* as the ultimate cause of *all* cause. In *Viśiṣṭādvaita*, the mind and the matter constitute one complex whole.

Professor R.P. Goldman in the next article compares *Mahābhārata* and *Rāmāyaṇa* from the standpoints of nature, scope and philosophy. He points out that though *Rāmāyaṇa* is also sometimes referred to as *itihāsa*, it is not self-evidently an *itihāsa* as *Mahābhārata* so obviously is. *Rāmāyaṇa* is more a *mahākāvya* with an exemplary person as its protagonist. *Mahābhārata* is much more inclusive in its scope being a virtual encyclopaedia of history, law, cosmology, mythology, science, theology and philosophy. It has been instrumental in the dissemination of Hindu culture and thought all over South-East Asia and constitutes the foundation of that vast and complex edifice we call Hinduism. Professor Goldman then dwells at length on the significant differences, apart from generic, between the two epics. Apart from showing the comparatively restricted philosophical content of the *Rāmāyaṇa*, Professor Goldman argues that the crucial philosophical difference between the two epics is the contrasting conceptualisation of the two *avatāra*s, Rāma and Kṛṣṇa who appear as central figures in the two epics — one self-aware of his divinity and the other, Rāma, unaware of his divinity. It is concluded that this crucial difference determines the two different epic discourses.

Dr. Shashi Prabha Kumar in her article "Ecology and Conservation in the Bhūmi-Sūkta of *Atharvaveda*" foregrounds the fact that Indian thought has always been remarkably sensitive to the ecological concerns. The Vedic literature reflects so very often on the deep inter-relationship of this earth's ecology not only with humanity but with all life. In the Bhūmi-Sūkta, too, there is extensive meditation on the three dimensions of ecological thinking, of ecology as an interface of life forms, as conservation and as the equipoise between man and the resources. Dr. Kumar concludes that Indian thought, particularly Vedic thought, holds the right lessons for the contemporary ecological crisis.

In the next very evocative and comprehensive essay, Dr. Lokesh Chandra charts over time and space the interflow of art between India and Japan. The learned author painstakingly details how triggered by the massive wave of Buddhist thought and inspiration Japanese sculpture, painting and architecture blossomed, proliferated and found perfection from the sixth to the seventeenth century. He divides the history of Japanese art into eight phases. The first three phases are the age of founding of monasteries and temples and of clay and bronze images. The Aśoka period, 538 CE to 644 CE, is marked by clay sculptures of Avalokiteśwara and Bodhisattvas marked by a certain simplicity of line but shown to be endowed with miraculous powers. The Tempyo period, 711-781 CE, is the age of Hindu gods — whole pantheon of Hindu deities is sculpted in this phase. Lakṣmī and Saraswatī images predominate. The Jogan period, 782-897 CE, is a period of symbolic representation and *maṇḍala*s come to be created depicting sages and deities. There are multitudes of figures and designs in this prolific age. The Fujiwara period from 898 to 1184 gave a fresh impetus to the establishment of monasteries and saw the rise of theory and model books came to be composed about iconography. The Kamakura period, 1185 to 1332, saw the creation of scrolls, of the *Lotus Sutra* for example, and is marked by the Unkei style of sculpture inspired by Vijñanavāda school of Buddhism. This age is also marked by the rise of Zen Buddhism. The brief Nambokuchu period, 1333-1391, saw the expansion of Zen thought and art and is known for the rise of art forms such as Koan, Ikebana and Haiku. The Muromachi period saw the rise of Suiboken paintings and style influenced by Zen and marked by a certain austere beauty. Finally the last great age is identified with and named after a master imagist, Koppa-Batsu Euku (1632-1695) who carved or painted one hundred thousand images of Buddha in 28 years. Professor Lokesh Chandra concludes that this Japanese art inspired Indo-Japanese art form characterized as "frozen music of forms" and there is marked evidence of this in Tagore's work.

In his four-section essay on "Aesthetics and Ideology," Professor Makarand Paranjape argues that the aesthetic value of art is real and cannot be ignored or side stepped for the good reason that a merely ideological reading necessarily ends up as a partial reading missing out, as it does, on so much that affects and attracts an ordinary auditor. The two, the aesthetic and the ideological, have to go together and that is the marker of literary hermeneutics. Commenting on the position of Professor D.D. Kosambi — a progressive intellectual who exercised no mean influence on the growth of left academics - who while granting the aesthetic value of *Bhagavad-Gītā* argued that it has no social value as it offers nothing for social reform, Professor Paranjape cites the clinching example of the massive *Svādhyāya* movement of Sri Panduranga Sastri Athavale, a movement that drew its inspiration directly from the *Gītā* and was instrumental in effecting wide-spread social reform. On this fact, he grounds his conclusion that in this highly determined world of "economic paramountcy," "whatever little authority the aesthetic may retain is also the last resort of criticism."

In the last essay, Professor Kapil Kapoor deals with India's continuous, cumulative, hoary textual traditions of knowledge and describes how in its long history it has seen several times the cyclical process of loss, recovery and renewal of texts. He notes that all cultures have central texts, codes of knowledge that inform its civilizational institutions. Over a period of time such texts tend to become assymetrical with the immediate context and unless the society re-contextualises them they may be lost forever. Living cultures do not let their central texts die and that is true of India. Professor Kapoor traces several episodes of loss and recovery from the Purāṇas down to modern European Indology. Beginning with post-Mahābhārata War recovery of the texts by the sage Vyāsa, he brings the narrative down to Max Müller who in his own time "recovered and renewed" the *Ṛgveda* along with so many other Sanskrit intellectual texts. The whole process is linked to the forces of subjugation that create a pressure on the mind to abandon its own thought in favour of that of the ruler or of the economically more powerful culture, a situation that obtains in the current Indian reality, and that requires the activation of the forces of retrieval and renewal to ensure the continuity of the valuable Hindu civilisation.

We hope the readers enjoy this first volume. We will welcome all comments, observations and responses. We also take this opportunity to invite contributions to the next volume in the series.

1

Some Philosophical Issues in Early Indian Grammar*

George Cardona

1

STATEMENTS and discussions about philosophical issues related to language in early Indian texts, and grammar in particular, have been objects of study for a considerable time, and an entire monograph has been devoted to logic in the *Mahābhāṣya*.[1] In this presentation, I will discuss briefly three issues in order to bring out one main point: Indian grammarians confronted certain logical issues that came to the fore because they were dealing with language in a particular way — describing it in terms of related rules. In at least one instance, the use of *iti* (section 5), the language itself lends itself to observing a logical distinction, but this does not necessarily imply automatic recognition of this distinction (see section 6).

2

The major principle recognized in Pāṇini's grammar and earlier

1. For bibliography on topics related to Pāṇinian grammar, see *Pāṇini, a Survey of Research*, pp. 256-59, 299-303 and *Recent Research in Pāṇinian Studies* (2nd edn., Delhi: Motilal Banarsidass, 2004), pp. 231, 265-69.

is that the language accounted for is described through a set of rules,[2] and that these rules are related to each other in particular ways that dictate how they apply. The most important way rules are related to each other is by virtue of their domains: a general rule (*utsarga*) concerning a given domain is blocked (*bādhyate*) by a related exception (*apavāda*), which concerns a domain included in that of the general rule, so that the exception applies first in its own domain, leaving the remaining domain for the general rule. Pāṇini himself simply assumes this principle,[3] but the *R̥gvedaprātiśākhya*, which is probably pre-Pāṇinian, explicitly states that exceptions are to be brought together with the general rules related to them, thus recognizing the principle in question.[4]

3

With this in mind, consider now two Pāṇinian *sūtra*s that assign the class name *sarvanāmasthāna* to particular nominal endings:

(1) *A* 1.1.42 — शि सर्वनामस्थानम्

(2) *A* 1.1.43 — सुडनपुंसकस्य ।

According to (1), the affix *śi*, which replaces *jas* and *śas* after a neuter nominal stem,[5] is given this class name; (2) provides that endings denoted by the abbrevation *suṭ* also have this name. The endings in question are: *su, au, jas, am, auṭ*. (2) also

---

2. *sūtra, śāstra, lakṣaṇa, yoga*; see *Pāṇini, his Work and its Traditions, volume I: Background and Introduction* (2nd edn., Delhi: Motilal Banarsidass, 1997), pp. 572-76.

3. As Patañjali remarks, the procedure in question is one known from ordinary life and does not need to be formulated explicitly: *Bh.* I.114.24-115.2: नैवेश्वर आज्ञापयति नापि धर्मसूत्रकाराः पठन्त्यपवादैरुत्सर्गा बाध्यन्तामिति किन्तर्हि लौकिकोऽयं दृष्टान्तः।

4. *RPr.* 1.53 — न्यायैर्मिश्रानपवादान् प्रतीयात्।

5. *A* 7.1.20 — जश्शसोः शिः (नपुंसकात् 19)

specifies *anapuṁsakasya*, which I discuss below. The derivation of the forms *sāmanī* and *sāmāni*, respectively nominative-accusative dual and nominative-accusative pl. of *sāman-*, illustrates how the rules interact: *sāman-au* (= *au*) → *sāman-ī*,[6] *sāman-au* (= *auṭ*) → *sāmanī*, *sāman-as* (=*jas*, *śas*) → *sāman-ī* (*A* 7.1.20 [note 5]) → *sāmāni*.[7]

As can be seen, *śī* should condition the replacement of penultimate *-a-* in the stem *sāman-* by *-ā-*, whether the ending replaces *jas* or *śas*. For this substitution to apply, moreover, the ending has to be a *sarvanāmasthāna*, since *A* (6.4.8 note 7) provides that it applies when a stem precedes a *sarvanāmasthāna* element.

Now, (2) contains the compound *anapuṁsakasya*, which can be understood in two ways, depending on whether the negative particle *a* (*nañ*) is constructed (a) directly with the second member of the compound or (b) with an understood verb *bhū* "be." Under (a), *anapuṁsakasya* is an instance of what is technically termed *paryudāsa* (exception) — that is, nominal negation — so that (2) provides for an ending of the set referred to by *suṭ* to be *sarvanāmasthāna* if it is linked to a stem other than a neuter. Accordingly, (2) now complements (1): the latter assigns to the *sarvanāmasthāna* class the ending *śi*, which replaces *jas* and *śas* after neuter stems, and the former adds to this class the endings denoted by *suṭ*, provided they are not used with a neuter base. Under (b), on the other hand, one has an instance of sentential negation (*prasajyapratiṣedha*),[8] and

6. *A* 7.1.19 — नपुंसकाच्च (औङः 18, शी 17). The use of the *anubandha ṅ* instead of *ṭ* does not concern the present discussion.

7. *A* 6.4.8 — सर्वनामस्थाने चासम्बुद्धौ (नोपधायाः 7, दीर्घः 6.3.111).

8. Although *nañ* in compounds usually involves nominal negation, instances of so-called *asamarthasamāsa*, where the negative particle is not construed with the nominal that follows in the compound, →

(2) is now an exception to (1): an ending referred to by *suṭ* is not *sarvanāmasthāna* if it occurs with a neuter base, so that (2) now denies *sarvanāmasthāna* classification to *śī* which would otherwise belong to this class by (1), that is, if it replaces *jas*. Clearly, interpretation (a) alone is acceptable, since (b) would not allow deriving nominative plural *sāmāni* (← *sāman-jas*) because *śī* replacing *jas* is now excluded from the *sarvanāmasthāna* set. Similarly, nominative plural neuter forms like *vanāni*[9] would also be disllowed.

4

Pāṇinīyas from earliest times are aware of this issue. Thus, the greater part of the *Mahābhāṣya*'s discussion of (1)-(2) concerns this, and Patañjali points out that (2) involves *paryudāsa*, not *prasajyapratiṣedha*, so that (2) does not concern neuters.[10] It is reasonable, I think, to consider that Pāṇini too was aware of the distinction between *paryudāsa* and *prasajyapratiṣedha* and, moreover, also saw the difference this could make to the way in which rules should apply, providing on the one hand that a given operation applies in a restricted domain that excludes certain elements or, on the other hand, that an operation does not apply in a given domain. Indeed, so far as early Indian technical matters are concerned, it is

---

→ are also possible. A standard example known from Pāṇini's own grammar is *asūryampaśya*, which involves the constituent *asūrya-* (*A* 3.2.36: असूर्यललाटयोर्दृशितपोः) but is equivalent to सूर्यं न पश्यति (does not see the sun) and not to असूर्यं पश्यति (sees something other than the sun).

9. *vana-as* → *vana-i* → *vanan-i* (*A* 7.1.72: नपुंसकस्य झलचः [सर्वनामस्थाने 70, नुम् 58]) → *vanāni* (*A* 6.4.8 [note 7]).

10. *Bh*. I.101.9-11: नायं प्रसज्यतिषेधो नपुंसकस्य नेति किन्तर्हि पर्युदासोऽयं यदन्यन्नपुंसकादिति। नपुंसकेऽव्यापारः। यदि केनचित्प्राप्नोति तेन भविष्यति। पूर्वेण च प्राप्नोति।

precisely in the context of grammatical rules as envisioned by Pāṇini and his predecessors that this important distinction comes to the fore most strikingly.[11]

5

Another well-known distinction to be observed in language is that between the use and mention of terms. Sanskrit differs from most other Indo-European languages in that it has a citation particle *iti*, used to show that a term is being cited.[12] This particle is also used in related ways in the earliest *padapāṭha*, the pre-Pāṇinian *Ṛgvedapadapāṭha* of Śākalya. In this work, *iti* is used after words with *pragṛhya* vowels to show that these are not subject to phonological changes before vowels. For example, in Śākalya's dialect a vocative singular form in *-o* such as *vāyo* is *pragṛhya*, so that, in contrast with the *saṁhitāpāṭha* to *ṚV* 1.2.1a (वायवा याहि°), which has *vāyāv* before *ā*, Śākalya's *padapāṭha* has *vāyō* followed by *itī* (वायो इति। आ। याहि।). In addition, Śākalya uses *iti* to indicate that the *visarjanīya* of a preceding word is rhoticizing (*rephin*). For example, the *saṁhitāpāṭha* of *ṚV* 7.41.1 (प्रातरग्निम्प्रातरिन्द्रं हवामहे प्रातर्मित्रावरुना प्रातरश्विना। प्रातर्भगंम्पूषणंम्ब्रह्मणस्पतिम्प्रातः सोमंमुत रुद्रं हुवेम॥) has *prātar* before vowels and voiced consonants, *prātaḥ* before *s-*. In the former instances, the *padapāṭha* simply has *prātaḥ* (प्रातः। अग्निम्। प्रातः। इन्द्रम्। हवामहे। प्रातः। मित्रावरुणा। प्रातः। अश्विना। प्रातः। भगम्। पूषणम्।°), since the contexts in the *saṁhitāpāṭha* clearly show that the *-ḥ* of *prātaḥ*, from which *prātar* derives, is rhotacizing. In the last instance, on the other hand, the context does not

11. I say this in this way in order not to deny the possibility that other thinkers, concerned with other issues, also had become aware of the distinction.

12. Cf., e.g., *Pr.* I.2 — अथेत्ययमिति। इतिशब्दोऽथसब्दस्य स्वरूपेऽवस्थापनाय प्रयुक्तः।

show this, so that Śākalya has प्रातरिति in his *padapāṭha*, with -*r* before the *i*- of *iti*.

6

In everyday Sanskrit, using *iti* serves to show that a preceding term or terms is being cited, while terms by themselves are used to signify their meanings. Since grammatical rules of a treatise such as the *Aṣṭādhyāyī* generally state operations with respect to linguistic units and not their meanings, Pāṇini astutely establishes a convention for his grammar that is the reverse of ordinary usage. According to

(3) *A* 1.1.68 — स्वं रूपं शब्दस्याशब्दसञ्ज्ञा ।

the form of a term (*svaṁ rūpam*) signifies that term (*śabdasya* [*sañjñā*]) itself, not its meaning, unless the item in question is a technical term of grammar. Thus, to cite a standard example, *agni* of *agneḥ* in

(4) *A* 4.2.33 — अग्नेर्ढक् ।

refers to the nominal *agni* and not to fire or the god Agni, so that the *sūtra* provides that a *pada* consisting of *agni* and a first triple ending is followed by the affix *ḍhak* to form a *taddhitānta* derivate meaning ". . . whose deity is Agni." That (3) *A* 1.1.68 reverses conventional usage is clear from another *sūtra*,

(5) *A* 1.1.44 — न वेति विभाषा ।

according to which a term signifying an option is understood to have the meaning of *na vā* (or not). Here *iti* is used with *na vā* not to refer to the terms themselves but to their meaning.

One might be tempted to consider that the availability of the citation particle *iti* in ordinary usage could suffice to make obvious the distinction between the use and mention of terms. This is not necessarily so. It is contextually obvious that an utterance like

(6) Say "cow"

involves the mention of *cow* and not the reference to a cow, in the same way that *gām* of

(7) गामुच्चारय ।

refers to the term *go* (cow, ox), though *iti* is not used. In both instances, the use of a term in construction with a word meaning "say, utter" requires that the term be understood as self-referring.[13] On the other hand, it does not follow necessarily that just any person would thereby be led to formulate a distinction between the use and mention of terms. Accordingly, we should be willing to accord to Pāṇini and his predecessor grammarians the acuity of recognizing this distinction, and to Pāṇini in particular the insight of seeing that the conventional usage should be reversed in grammar.[14]

---

13. Cf. *LM* 1153 — गामुच्चारयेत्यादेश्च गोशब्दमुच्चारयेत्यर्थः । उच्चारयेत्येतत्समभिव्याहाराच्छब्दपरता°

14. In the context of Indian thought, moreover, the view that all terms are first self-referential even without *iti* was generalized, so that it was considered that in ordinary usage any term was considered first to refer to itself. This point was elaborated upon extensively by Bhartṛhari (*VP* 1.56 [ग्राह्यत्वं ग्राहकत्वञ्च द्वे शक्ती तेजसो यथा। तथेव सर्वशब्दानामेते पृथगवस्थिते ॥] - 70 [सञ्ज्ञिनीं व्यक्तिमिच्छन्ति सूत्रे ग्राह्यामथापरे। जातिप्रत्यायिता व्यक्तिः प्रदेशेषूपतिष्ठते ॥] and the *Vṛtti* thereon), who also notes several interpretations by *Vṛtti* authors of (3) *A* 1.1.68 and the connection of these views with the positions taken concerning whether a nominal denotes an individual or a generic. The issue was broached earlier by Kātyāyana, who brings up (1.1.68 *vārttika* 2: न वा शब्दपूर्वको ह्यर्थे सम्प्रत्ययस्मादर्थनिवृत्तिः ॥) the possibility that *A* 1.1.68 might not be required for a purpose considered in a previous *vārttika*, since the understanding of a meaning is always preceded by perception of a given word, so that this is first understood and not a term's meaning. In the present brief discussion these points cannot be considered.

7

Authors of *padapāṭhas* such as Pāṇini's predecessor Śākalya (see section **5**) established a practice that was adopted by successors: positing a text from which a Vedic *saṁhitāpāṭha* could be derived by applying phonological rules. Pāṇini built upon this foundation by generalizing so as to account not merely for a given text but for a language, by positing utterances — called *alaukika vākya* by later Pāṇinīyas — from which actual utterances are derived. It is worth emphasizing that no Pāṇinīya considers such posited utterances anything more that means (*upāya*) to an end, namely, accounting for the actual utterances used in the language. Thus, these grammarians early on concretely operated with a contrast that permeates much of Indian philosophical thought: between a true reality — whatever that may be — and posited concepts that relate to this reality in ways that become objects of extended discussion.

8

In this necessarily brief discussion, I hope to have brought out how, in the context of accounting for actual language usage by means of rules of phonology and grammar, Pāṇini and his predecessors both recognized some important philosophical distinctions and operated intelligently with them.

Abbreviations

A: *Aṣṭādhyāyī*

Bh.: *Mahābhāṣya* (ed. Kielhorn, Abhyankar)

LM: Nāgeśa's *Vaiyākaraṇasiddhāntalaghumañjūṣā* (ed. Madhava Shastri Bhandari, *et al.*)

Pr.: Kaiyaṭa's *Pradīpa* (Rohatak edn.)

RPr.: *Ṛgvedaprātiśākhya* (ed. V.K. Varma)

VP: *Vākyapadīya* (ed. W. Rau)

2

Indian Logic (Nyāya) in Modern Information Technology

V.V.S. Sarma & Kalyani Gopal

NYĀYA in Indian philosophy denotes logic in its general sense of being a study of informal inference patterns, rules of debate and the acquisition of valid knowledge. This approach to logic is based on the underlying Indian philosophy of life and knowledge as a means to achieving liberation.[1,9] Logic grew in India as an independent discipline for over 3000 years from the tradition of *vādavidyā*, a discipline dealing with debate over various philosophical and moral issues. Logic was also used for identifying patterns of sound reasoning in the context of medical diagnosis as in the *Caraka Saṁhitā* (*c.* 100 CE), in matters of law and justice as in the *Arthaśāstra* and in philosophical and ethical issues as in the *Nyāya Darśana*. The *Nyāya-Sūtra* (Akṣapāda Gautama, *c.* 100 CE) proposes perception (*pratyakṣa*), inference (*anumāna*), verbal testimony (*śabda*) and analogy (*upamāna*) as the four *pramāṇas*, or the means of obtaining valid knowledge. The *Caraka Saṁhitā* includes causal inquiry (*yukti*) and tradition (*aitīhya*) also in this list. The study of the first four *pramāṇas* forms the core of the modern Indian logic (Navya-Nyāya) as in Gaṅgeśa's (*c.* 1325) *magnum opus, Pramāṇa-Tattva-Cintāmaṇi*. A brief historical account of Indian logic is shown in Appendix 1. Satish Chandra

Vidyabhushana's monumental work, *A History of Indian Logic* (1921), is the first systematic exposition of the subject-matter.[10]

Indian logic emphasizes the personal experiences of a knowledge-seeking individual in his acquisition of knowledge from various sources. The experience (which may also be mystical) alone can give a clearer and deeper understanding and meaning of life and nature, through intuitive perception. Indian systems are therefore extolled as *darśana*s due to this special feature. There are two streams of *darśana*s — one of which accepts the Vedas as authority (*āstika*) and the other which rejects this authority (*nāstika*). Of the *āstika darśana*s, six became famous as schools of thought: Nyāya-Vaiśeṣika, Sāṁkhya-Yoga and Mīmāṁsā-Vedānta. The acceptance of the Vedas means an implicit acceptance of the fact that the spiritual experiences of the seers recorded in the Vedas carry greater weight than purely intellectual arguments of speculative philosophers based on logical reasoning.[2,8] The *nāstika darśana*s include Bauddha, Jaina and Cārvāka.

Classical Indian philosophical texts in Sanskrit — Darśanas and Vedāṅgas — with their emphasis on logic, language and grammar provide a gold mine of ideas for work in modern information technology and knowlege systems. Cognitive science is working with a three-way analogy between the mind, the brain and computers. Knowledge representation is concerned with designing structures for storing knowledge — hypotheses, theories, facts and rules in a manner amenable to computer processing. A body of formally represented knowledge is based on a conceptualization — an abstract view of the world that we wish to represent. Logic and language studies in Nyāya, Mīmāṁsā, Śikṣā and Nirukta developed over millennia can provide a new conceptual basis for these studies.

Sanskrit has a well-structured, descriptive grammar. Pāṇini (*c.* 700 BCE) gave a comprehensive and scientific theory of language, phonology, morphology and syntax in his treatise on Sanskrit grammar, *Aṣṭādhyāyī*, which is formulated with a very concise and logically consistent set of rules (under 4000 rules) for the derivation of correct Sanskrit word forms and sentences. The World Wide Web and the IT world are moving into the semantic mode and the semantics (i.e., meaning and understanding) will come largely from knowledge systems. For the Artificial Intelligence (AI) community, this historic development affords an opportunity to design smart computer agents to help people navigate global information Webs, as they harvest knowledge over multi-lingual data sources. For Sanskrit scholars, this area provides a new opportunity for bringing ancient knowledge into the mainstream of present-day research.

Concepts from Indian Logic

THE WORLD-VIEW OF INDIAN LOGICIANS

A realistic view of Indian logic and its characteristics as observed by Matilal are[8]:

- Our perception permits a direct awareness of the physical reality that exists independently of our awareness of it.
- We see physical objects comprising wholes, parts and properties. We see and touch a flower, see its colour and shape, smell its fragrance but we do not hear anything of it. We may perceive the whole and our senses may cover only parts or properties. The whole is a distinct reality more than the sum of the parts.
- Perception leads to "knowing" in the most direct sense. This knowledge is not always verbalized but is amenable to verbalization.

- Perceptual illusions intervene between the perceiver and the physical world and can be analysed.
- Ordinary knowledge is neither self-revealing nor self-validating, for "*a* knows that *p*" does not entail "*a* knows that *a* knows that *p*." A cognitive event can occur and pass away unnoticed.

ONTOLOGY OF INDIAN LOGIC

We may look upon ontology as a general theory of entities, of "what there is." Vaiśeṣika starts with the characterization of real entities. The categories (*padārtha*) include substance, quality and action. Substances are the elements (earth, water, fire, air and ether), time, space, the soul and mind. The soul (*ātman*) has special qualities which make it different from substances made of elements. It can be apprehended by perception and inference. The concept of substance and attributes, the so-called paradox of "being and becoming," of permanence and change has captured the attention of early Indian philosophers. The concept of soul or self (*ātman*) and inference of existence of God (*Īśvara-anumāna*) are important topics in Indian logic studies.

PRAMĀṆAS — EPISTEMOLOGY

The common place belief of all of us is that there exists a physical, material world independently of our awareness of it. To prove it as either true or false is a difficult philosophical problem. This belief becomes knowledge only when such a proof is given. As Matilal defines "A *pramāṇa* is the means leading to a knowledge episode (*pramā*) as its end."[8] A *pramāṇa* (as an instrument) provides both the evidential base for a knowledge claim and a causal base for the generation of a knowledge episode. It is essential to understand the *prameya*s (or objects of study).

Sensory Perception (Pratyakṣa)

Gautama defines sense-perception (*pratyakṣa*) as "that knowledge which arises from the 'contact' of a sense-organ with its object, inexpressible by words, unerring and well-defined." Different factors involved in perception are: (1) the senses (*indris*); (2) their objects (*artha*); (3) the contact of the senses with their objects (*sannikarṣa*); and (4) cognition produced by this (*jñānam*). For example, the cognition of colour is not possible if there is no visual organ. This precludes an indefinite or hazy cognition producing a doubt of clearly perceiving a snake in a piece of rope in insufficient light, which is actually an illusion. There are five senses corresponding to the five characters of knowledge: visual, auditory, olfactory, gustatory and tactual. They vary in the nature of their processes (*gati*), forms (*ākr̥ti*) and constituents (*jāti*).

Mana or mind is another requisite instrument of perception, dealt at length in the *Nyāya Bhāṣya*s and *Vārttika*s (commentaries). What is internally experienced by the mind like emotions can also be classified under *pratyakṣa*. When we are deeply absorbed in some study, we do not hear the sound of wind, though the sound affects the organ of hearing and the self is in connection with it being all-pervading. Vātsyāyana in his *Nyāya Bhāṣya* (i.1.4) quotes "even when the contact of more than one sense-organ with their respective objects is present, there is no simultaneous perception of all these objects — which is due to the fact that while there is proximity or contact of the mind with one object, there is no such contact of it with the other objects, which shows that the participation of the mind is necessary in every act of perception." The mind mediates between the self and the senses. It accounts for the non-simultaneity of the acts of knowledge. Vātsyāyana includes the mind under the senses. He calls it the inner sense by which we apprehend the inner states of feelings, desires and cognitions. The self perceives the inner states through the instrumentality of the mind while the co-operation of the senses is necessary to apprehend the outer non-subjective states.

Perception provides a kind of awareness or *jñāna* that belongs to the self. Though the contact between the self and the mind is eternal in a certain sense, it may be said to be renewed with each fresh cognitive episode. Nyāya assumes a naturalistic relation between the self and the object. The definition of perception assumes the contact of the self and the mind which is present in all cognitions, and the contact of the mind and the senses, and specifies "sense-object contact" as its distinguishing feature. According to Gautama, inexpressible (*avyapadeśam*) is the first characteristic of the nature of perceptual knowledge. A thing is not perceived as bearing a name. While the name has value for social intercourse, it is not necessarily operative at the time when the object is perceived. If a man sees a fruit and experiences its nature, it is perception; but if he hears from somebody that its name is jackfruit, then it is not perception but verbal cognition. Vātsyāyana holds that an object may be perceived with or without the apprehension of its name. The former is the determinate perception and the latter is the indeterminate perception. The distinction between inexpressible (*avyapadeśya*) and the well defined (*vyavasāyātmika*) is equated with the indeterminate (*nirvikalpaka*) and the determinate (*savikalpaka*).

Savikalpaka or determinate perception implies knowledge of the genus to which the perceived object belongs, of the specific qualities which distinguish the individual object from the other members of the same class and of the union of the two. This distinct knowledge of the genus, the differentia and the union is absent in the indeterminate perception. The distinction between indeterminate and determinate perception answers roughly to that between acquaintance with and knowledge of an object, simple apprehension and perceptual judgement.[2]

According to the earlier Vaiśeṣikas, indeterminate perception is an immediate cognition of the generic and specific characters of its object without the knowledge of the difference between them. In determinate perception the distinction between the two sets of properties is apprehended and the object is perceived as belonging to a determinate class. The main tendency of the Nyāya is to regard indeterminate perception as the starting point of all knowledge, though it is not itself knowledge. Gautama's definition of perception includes the characteristic of freedom from error. All perceptions are not valid perceptions. Normal perception has: (1) the object of perception, (2) the external medium such as light in the case of the visual perception, (3) the sense-organ through which the object is perceived, (4) the mind or the central internal organ, without which the sense-organs cannot operate on their objects, and (5) the self. If any of these fail to function properly, erroneous perceptions arise.

Inference (Anumāna)

Anumāna in Sanskrit literally means measurement following something. It is the knowledge that follows other knowledge (already known). The knowledge of the sign (mark, *liṅga*) of the object gives the knowledge of the object (signified, *lingin*) possessing it. *Anumāna* is usually translated by the word "Inference" including both induction and deduction. This is tied to the theory of sound inference through an inference-warranting relation, based on a cause-effect relation, called *vyāpti*, translated variously as concomittance, invariable relation or pervasion. Diṅnāga and Dharmakīrti defined this concomittance of *B* with *A*, which legitimizes the inference of the signified *A* from the sign (*liṅga*) *B*. The invariable relation means: (1) an essential or necessary property of the class, e.g., this is a tree because it is a banyan tree or (2) a causally necessary relation between an effect and an invariable cause, e.g., there is fire here because there is smoke here.

In *anumāna*, the perceptual knowledge precedes the inferential knowledge. According to Vātsyāyana, there can be no inference in the absence of perception. Udyotakara mentions the following distinctions between perceptual and inferential knowledge: All perception is of one kind, if we exclude yogic intuition, while there are varieties of inference. Perception is confined to objects of the present time and within the reach of the senses, while the inference relates to the past, present and the future. Where perception is available, inference has no place. Inference operates "neither with regard to things unknown, nor with regard to those known definitely for certain; it functions only with regard to things that are doubtful" (*Nyāya Bhāṣya*, i.I.I). It is employed to know that part of the real which does not fall within the directly perceived and needs *vyāpti-jñāna* (knowledge of pervasion).

Gautama classifies inference into three kinds: *pūrvavat, śeṣavat* and *sāmānyato dṛṣṭam*. For example, when we see the clouds and expect rain, we have a case of predictive (*pūrvavat*) inference, where we perceive the antecedent and infer the consequent. It is, however, used to indicate not merely inference from a cause but also inference based on former experience. When we see a river in flood and infer that there was rain, we have a case of interpolating or smoothing (*śeṣavat*) inference, where we perceive the consequent and infer the antecedent. When we see a horned animal and infer that it has a tail, we have a case of *sāmānyato dṛṣṭa* (correlative) inference. It is based, not so much on causation, as on uniformity of experience.

Analogy or Comparison (Upamāna)

Upamāna is the means by which we gain the knowledge of the thing from its similarity to another thing previously well-known. An argument by comparison involves two factors, viz., (1) the knowledge of the known object, and (2) the perception of similarity. The ancient Naiyāyikas regarded the former as the principal cause of the new knowledge, while the modern Naiyāyikas attach more importance to the perception of similarity. Mere resemblance, whether it be complete, considerable or partial is not enough to justify an argument by comparison. Consider the example: The wild ox (*gavaya*) is like a cow. Hearing this we infer that the animal which we find to be like the cow is the *gavaya*. In the first case of complete resemblance or identity, there is not any new knowledge. We do not say the cow is like a cow. In the second case of considerable resemblance, the inference need not be valid, for a buffalo is not a cow, although there are many points of resemblance.

Verbal Testimony (Śabda)

The theory of language is very important in Indian philosophy. The relation between *śabda* (the linguistic element, a meaningful unit of speech for the grammarian) and *artha* (the meaning) has received wide attention. While considering Vyākaraṇa and Mīmāṁsā views and terminology, the Naiyāyikas have developed their own approach for using *śabda* as a *pramāṇa*. The Mīmāṁsakas consider the letter or permanent articulated sound unit (*akṣara*) or phoneme (*varṇa*) to be the unit of language and the meaning-bearer. The Mīmāṁsaka has to deal with apparent absurdities, inconsistencies, and contradictions besides ambiguities and evolved rules of interpretation that were accepted generally by all schools of thought. Mīmāṁsā, called vākyaśāstra, was concerned with interpretation and cogent explanation of scriptural texts. Mīmāṁsā gave a semantic definition of the sentence evolving the concepts of mutual expectancy (*ākāṅkṣā*), consistency (*yogyatā*) and contiguity (*āsatti*) as factors necessary for the existence of a sentence.[3]

Among grammarians, Patañjali defines *śabda* as that which, when articulated, conveys the idea of the referent. Maṇḍana Miśra in his *Sphoṭasiddhi* defines it as the cause that produces the idea of meaning. *Śabda* is thus the idea-bearer. Is it the articulated sound, or the phoneme (*varṇa*), or the word (*pada*) or the sentence (*vākya*) that is referred by the term *śabda*? According to the *sphoṭa* theory of Bhartṛhari it is the complete occurrence of the sentence that is the unit, and it is called *vākya-sphoṭa,* but at a lower analytical level the word can be considered as the unit, for which the word used by the grammarian is *pada-sphoṭa*. It is only those who do not have proper knowledge of the language, who hear words or phonemes or bits of sounds and struggle to get the meaning. The listener who understands the language comprehends the sentence as a whole in an instantaneous flash of insight (*pratibhā*). Yāska and Bhartṛhari have pointed out that a verb conveys a series of operations. Every verbal root (*dhātu*) involves two semantic factors: activity (*vyāpāra*) and goal or result (*phala*). The verb in *devadattaḥ pacati* (Devadatta cooks) means a series of activities in a temporal sequence such as preparing the fire, boiling water in a vessel on the fire, washing the rice, putting the rice in water and so on till the rice softens adequately.

Gaṅgeśa's *Tattva Cintāmaṇi* (Book 4: *Language as Instrument of Knowledge, Śabdaprāmāṇya-Vāda*) gives significant attention to *śabda*. Gaṅgeśa argues that knowledge does result from hearing a linguistic occurrence if the words constituting it have such properties as expectancy (*ākāṅkṣā*), and the hearer remembers what the linguistic elements mean. A word is said to bear the relation-expectancy to another word if it cannot, without the latter, produce awareness of interconnection in speech, e.g., *devadattaḥ grāmam gacchati* (Devadatta goes to the village). *Devadattaḥ* in the nominative bears expectancy to verb *gacchati*, which, in turn, bears expectancy for *grāmam*. Contiguity (*āsatti*) is another such property. The utterance *jalam ānaya* (bring water) will convey no meaning if the second word is uttered after a long time after the first word. If there are multiple meanings, the context will identify the intention (*tātparya*) of the speaker.

The notion of meaning (*artha*) itself has problems. Is it the universal that is intended, or the particular? The Mīmāṁsakas held that the primary meaning of a word is universal. The Naiyāyikas considered the meaning of the word as comprising the universal (*jāti*), the configuration (*ākṛti*) and the particular (*vyakti*). Later Naiyāyikas held that the primary meaning is the individual as qualified by the universal (*jāti-viśiṣṭa-vyakti*). The sentence-meaning is something more than some of the word-meanings. The *abhihitānvaya* theory (of Bhaṭṭa Mīmāṁsakas) says that in a sentence each word gives an isolated meaning (which is universal) and their *śakti* is exhausted with that. Then with the help of *lakṣaṇa* the syntactic relationship is obtained through which the sentence meaning is comprehended. In the *anvitābhidhāna* theory of the Prābhākara School, each word is assumed to convey both the isolated meaning and the syntactic relationship. The significative power of a word (*śakti*) is based on the relation existing between a word and its meaning.[3] The words of a language may develop more than one meaning in the course of usage. The secondary meaning is called *lakṣaṇa*.

Classical Methods of Indian Logic (Prācīna Nyāya)

The Prācīna Nyāya model of debate is illustrated by Akṣapāda

Gautama himself. The following steps are identified as the "prior" stage of a Nyāya model:

1. Doubt (whether *p* or not *p* is true) to be established by logical reasoning.
2. Proof of the thesis or counter-thesis.
3. Each side will use the following five-limbed syllogism to demonstrate one's reasoning.

Example: *Thesis*: (a) Soul is eternal. (b) For it is non-produced. (c) Whatever is non-produced is also eternal: witness, the space (*ākāśa*). (d) Similarly, the soul is also not produced. (e) Therefore, soul is eternal.

Counter-thesis: (a) Soul is non-eternal. (b) For it is amenable to perception. (c) What is perceived is non-eternal, witness, a pot. (d) The soul is also similarly amenable to perception. (e) Therefore, the soul is also non-eternal.

FIVE-LIMBED SYLLOGISM

There are five factors in Indian syllogism. They are shown with an example:

1. *Pratijñā* or the proposition (the hill is on fire).
2. *Hetu*, or the reason (because there is smoke).
3. *Udāharaṇa* or the explanatory example (whatever shows fire shows smoke, e.g., kitchen).
4. *Upanaya* or the application (so is this hill) and
5. *Nigamana* or the statement of the conclusion (therefore the hill is on fire).

- ***Proposition (pratijñā)*** : The proposition sets forth the thesis to be established at the very beginning. It fixes the problem and limits the inquiry. The suggestion to be established controls the process from the very start, and the act of inference tries to strengthen and reinforce the suggestion. The proposition is only a "suggestion" (*Nyāya Bhāṣya*, i.x.39). The proposition has two factors of subject and predicate. The subject is what is observed which is generally an individual or a class capable of being regarded as a single object. The predicate is that which is to be proved. In the above example "the hill is on fire," the hill is the subject or minor term or *pakṣa* or the *dharmin*. While "on fire" is the predicate or the major term, the *sādhya*, the *dharma* or the *anumeya* (that which is to be inferred). The syllogism is intended to prove that the subject presented in the perception possesses the feature indicated in the predicate. To find out whether the proposition is true the minor term is analysed into its elements and the presence of the middle term is discovered.

- ***Reason* (*Probans, Hetu*)** : This is the second part of the syllogism which is the means of proof, mark (*liṅga*) present in the minor term. It gives the possession of the character which entitles its possessor to be the subject of the conclusion or *pakṣa-dharmatā*. *Pakṣatā* is a necessary condition of inference. *Pakṣa*, according to Annām Bhaṭṭa, is defined as the subject in which the predicate is to be proved. Thus there are three terms necessary for a syllogistic inference, viz., the minor term (*pakṣa*) or that about which something is inferred, the major term (*sādhya*) or that which is inferred about the minor term, and the middle term by which the major is inferred to be true of the minor.
- ***Example* (*Udāharaṇa*)** : The example takes us to the basis of inference, the major premise. Gautama means by example a similar instance possessing the essential property of the major term. It may be that Nyāya

syllogism developed out of the argument by example. Though it is the way to reason, it is not logical inference where the conclusion is warranted by the premises. The argument will be invalid if the example is not indicative of a general rule. Inference cannot be drawn unless there is an invariable concomitance (*vyāpti*) between the mark and the character inferred. The mention of the example indicates that inference is both inductive and deductive. The generalization is based on instances and it helps in deducing new truths.

- ***Application* (*Upanaya*)** : This asserts the presence or absence of the ground suggested in the minor term. It is affirmative in the former case, as in the example "so is this hill," i.e., smoky and negative in the latter case as in the example "not so is this hill," i.e., not smoky (*Nyāya Sūtra,* i.I.38).
- ***Conclusion* (*Nigamana*)** : This restates the proposition as grounded. In the above example, it is concluded as "therefore, the hill is on fire." What is tentatively put forth initially is established or corroborated.

Vātsyāyana points out that some logicians regarded the syllogism as consisting of ten members. In addition to the above five, the following are included:

(a) *Jijñāsā* or the desire to know the exact truth of the proposition, whether the hill is on fire in all its parts or in only some.

(b) *Samasyā* or doubt about the reason, whether, after all, that which we regard as smoke is only vapour.

(c) *Śakyaprāpti* or the capacity of the example to warrant the conclusion whether the smoke is always a concomittant of the fire, since it is not present in the red hot iron ball.

(d) *Prayojana* or purpose of drawing the conclusion.

(e) *Samasyā-vyudeśa* or the removal of all doubts about the relation of the middle to the major term and its presence in the minor.

These five additional members, according to Vātsyāyana, are unnecessary for proof though they help to make our cognitions clear. A distinction was drawn between the five-membered syllogism, useful for convincing others (*parārthānumāna*) and the three-membered syllogism, sufficient for convincing oneself (*svārthānumāna*). The latter deals with inference as a process of movement of thought and so belongs to the science of discovery, while the former deals with the proof.

Liṅga-parāmarśa or the consideration of the sign is the essential element of the inferential process. The stock example of inference in Indian logic may be presented as in the following:

(A) Where there is smoke, there is fire.
There is smoke on the yonder hill.
Therefore there is fire there.
This looks like a classical deduction but the version in Indian texts is more like (B).

(B) Where there is smoke, there is fire, as in a kitchen hearth.
There is smoke on the yonder hill.
Therefore there is fire there.
The logical expression for (B) may be written as in (C).

(C) The hill is fire-possessing.
Because, it is smoke-possessing.
For example, the kitchen hearth.

The first premise in (A) above is universal often derived as an inductive generalization while (B) presents an experiential truth based on perception supported by an example, "as in kitchen hearth," which is always insisted upon by the Indian logician. The reasoning in (C) brings out the necessity of a pervasion (universal connection or *vyāpti*). Each *vyāpti* relates the two elements of a *vyāpaka* or the pervader and the *vyāpya* or the pervaded. *Anumāna* or inference derives a conclusion from the ascertained fact of the subject possessing a property, which is pervaded or constantly attended by another property. If the *pakṣa, hetu* and *sādhya* are denoted by the symbols *p, h* and *s* respectively, the *liṅga-parāmarśa* involved in inference can be characterized by a theorem of the form: "A cause of inferential awareness is awareness of pervasion of *h* by *s* qualified by the *p's* being an *h*."

CAUSAL REASONING

Causal reasoning has received considerable attention in Indian Logic:

(a) Causal reasoning is ubiquitous in daily life. *A* causes *B* is an often occurring observation. The relation is anti-symmetric and non-reflexive; if *A* causes *B, B* cannot cause *A. A* cannot cause itself. *A* and *B* fall naturally in a temporal ordering. After perception comes inferential cognition.

(b) Causation is not a material implication. It is complex. A distinction is to be made between necessary and sufficient causes. Even if we observe that *A* seems to cause *B* both might be effects of some hitherto unknown cause. But the practical utility of causal reasoning is unquestionable and is the obvious basis of plausible explanation.

(c) The positive benefit of causality is that it lends itself to powerful knowledge-representation-models such as influence diagrams and condition-event networks, (Example, the Petri Net).

REASONING WITH POSSIBILITIES (*SYĀDVĀDA*)

An extremely interesting contribution of the Jaina logicians (*Sāmantabhadra*, AD 600, in *Āptamīṁāmsā*) is Syādvāda or the seven-valued logic (*sapta-bhaṅgī-nyāya*). This can be called logic of possibilities and modern logic came to this point only in late twentieth century in the form of rough, fuzzy and multi-valued sets and logics. This includes seven forms such as: (a) may be it is, (b) may be it is not, (c) may be it is and it is not at different times, (d) may be it is and it is not at the same time and is indescribable, (e) may be it is and yet indescribable, (f) may be it is not and is indescribable, and (g) may be it is and it is not and also indescribable.

Some Methods of New Logic (Navya-Nyāya)

NOTATIONAL ISSUES

The proposition in Indian logic is a judgemental cognition. It is conveniently represented in terms of property and location (the *dharma-dharmin* concept introduced by *Diṅnāga*). The form is "x has p" or "p is in x." A simple predicate logic formulation such as "x is F" is to be represented as "x has F-ness," where F-ness is the abstract property derived from F by which F is cognized. We may have two sets of constants: property terms $\{r, s, t, u, v, w, h \ldots\}$ and location terms $\{l, m, n, o, p, \ldots\}$. In "$x$ is a blue pot," blueness is the property locatable in the pot, and *potness* is the property by which a pot is cognized and is distinguished from vessels such as a cup, a mug or a tumbler. Objects such as a cup, a pot, smoke, fire and water are treated as properties locatable in such loci as table, ground, mountain, kitchen hearth and pot. (Ground is a pot-possessor and pot is water-possessor identified by properties such as pot-possessorhood.) The suffixes *-ness* and *-hood* are used for representing abstract properties.

Negation is recognized in two ways: absence and difference. In the sentence, "pot is not blue," the representation is *m* has *-s*, where *m* is the locus "pot" and *s* is the property "blueness." This is an example of absence. "A table is different from a cup" is represented by "*t* is not equal to *s*" meaning "table has no cup-hood and cup has no table-hood." The difference from the cup in this way is equivalent to an absence of cup-hood.

RELATIONS

The edifice of Navya-Nyāya rests to a great extent on the concept of *sambandha* or relation.[3,4] This concept is an all-pervasive one on account of which Navya-Nyāya can be termed relational logic. It has potential benefits for realizing new and deep knowledge representation schemes superior to semantic nets and conceptual graphs used in AI. Relations also play a significant role in the process of cognition. The concept is also complex because it involves difficulties of various types, ontological, logical and epistemological. According to Dharmakīrti (*Sambandha Parīkṣā, c.* 600 CE), a relation will have any of the following characteristics:

1. Dependency is a relation.
2. Amalgamation or contact is a relation.
3. Expectancy is a relation.
4. Cause-Effect is a relation.
5. That which exists in two things is a relation.

What is a relation? An obvious answer is that a relation connects two entities. A relation that readily comes to mind between two objects is contact (*saṁyoga*). Navya-Nyāya regards all relations as dyadic relations between two terms; the first is called *anuyogin* or referend and the second, the *pratiyogin* or referent. The Navya Nyāya theory is that a relation is always a property resident in the referend. The relation *R* between two things *a* and *b* can be represented by *aRb*, where *a* is the referend, *b* is the referent and *R* is the relation. In the knowledge fire (is) on (the) mountain (*parvato vahnimān* — the mountain (is) fire-possessing), the mountain is called *anuyogin* and fire is called *pratiyogin*.

The Classification of Relations

Relations in Navya-Nyāya can be classified based on different criteria. According to one criterion, the relations are classified into *sākṣāt* (direct) and *paramaparā* (chain) relations. A relation not involving other relations is termed direct; while one which involves other relations is a chain relation. For example, *saṁyoga* (contact) is a direct relation while *samānādhikaraṇa* (co-locusness) is a chain relation. *Fig.* 1 shows the types of direct and chain relations.

The second criterion is based on whether the relation is occurrence-exacting or non-occurrence-exacting. In this "exacting" (*niyāmaka*) means "limiting" (*avacchedaka*). An occurrence-exacting (*vṛtti-niyāmaka*) relation is one wherein the occurrence is regulated/limited in an entity. The relation involves the notion of substratum-superstratum (*ādhāra-ādheya*), between two distinct objects otherwise unconnected. *Paryāpti* is a *vṛtti-niyāmaka* relation. Non-occurrence-exacting (*vṛtti-aniyāmaka*) is the opposite. Examples of non-occurrence-exacting relations are pervasion (*vyāpti*), essential identity (*abheda*), and describerness-describedness (*nirūpakatva-nirūpyatva*).

Relations

Direct	**Chain**
(*sākṣāt*)	(*paramaparā*)
saṁyoga	*saṁyukta-samavāya*
samavāya	*saṁyukta-samavāya-samaveta*
svarūpa	*samaveta-samavāya*
kālika	*svasamavāyī-samavetattva*

Fig. **1: Types of Relations**

The third category is for locus-pervading and non-locus-pervading relations. The relations are governed by pervasion (*vyāpti*). The former is generally known as complete occurrence (*vyāpya-vṛtti*) while the latter, incomplete occurrence (*avyāpya-vṛtti*). *Saṁyoga* between two material objects is usually an incomplete occurrence relation.

Some Essential Concepts for Understanding Relations

1. A sentence in Sanskrit is often a qualificative cognitive state (*viśiṣṭa jñāna*). An observer cognizes any object as qualified by a property or a qualifier.
2. According to some Navya-Naiyāyikas, knowledge having for its content a qualified object is called a relation (*viśiṣṭa-pratīti-niyāmaka-viśeṣasyaiva-sambandhatvāt*). The idea underlying this definition is that in a qualified knowledge entity three things become primarily the content of knowledge — the qualificand (*viśeṣya*), the qualifier (*viśeṣaṇa*) and the relation (*sambandha*) between the two. For Example, in the knowledge *daṇḍī-puruṣa* (a man with a stick) the qualificand is the man, and the qualifier is the stick. When a qualificand has two qualifiers one expressed in the subject and one in the predicate, that expressed in the predicate is distinguished as the *prakāra* or the cheif qualifier.

3. When two entities are related one may often conceive of one as superimposed on the other. The entity that is superimposed is called the superstratum or adjunct (*ādheya*) and the element on which it rests is called the substratum or subjunct (*ādhāra*). The *ādhāra* is also called locus (*adhikaraṇa*) or abode (*āśraya*). The term *avacchedaka* is used in two senses: limitor and resident limitor. It denotes that property which by itself being one of the primary meanings of a term differentiates that term from terms denoting other objects. In some cases, the substratum is considered as the *avacchedaka* of the property residing in the object. Yet in some other cases, the adjective of the substratum of a particular property is called the *avachchedaka* of that property. The term *avacchinna* means "limited."
4. When *jnāna* is analysed in Navya-Nyāya its contentness, i.e., *viṣayatā* becomes important. The *viṣayatā* is subdivided into three categories: *viśeṣyatā, prākāratā* and *saṁsargatā*. *Saṁsargatā* refers to the relation between the qualifier and the qualificand. The meaning of *saṁsarga* in this context is the point of intersection.

In several philosophical systems there is some ambiguity associated with words such as "is" and "exist." In normal usage the same word may be used in an existential sense as in "God is" in the sense of God exists and in the predicational sense as in "God is perfect." In Indian philosophy two words *sattā* and *bhāva* are the words for existence. The Naiyāyikas carefully distinguish between these two words. *Sattā* means existence or reality. It is traditionally defined as a generic character. Presence is denoted by *bhāva* and its opposite *abhāva* denotes absence.

Types of Relations in Navya-Nyāya

(a) *Saṁyoga* : Contact is one type of direct relation, e.g., *bhūtale ghaṭaḥ asti* (the pot is on the floor). This could have been said as *ghaṭasya saṁyogaḥ bhūtale asti* (the ground possesses the contact of the pot). In this example *ghaṭaḥ* is the *viśeṣaṇa*. In the language of the Naiyāyika this cognition is expressed as *bhūtalatvavacchinnaprakāraka saṁyogasaṁsargaka ghaṭatvāvacchinnaviśeṣya jñānam*. In English, the qualifierness is limited by the jarness and by the relation of contact determining the qualificandness, limited by groundness. *Saṁyoga* is also *vṛtti-niyāmaka* (occurrence-exacting) relation, from the notion of the *ādhāra-ādheya bhāva* (locus-locatee relationship). The Naiyāyika interprets this as *bhūtalatvavacchinnaniṣṭa ādhārata nirūpita saṁyogasambandhāvacchiṇa ghaṭaṭvāvacchiṇa ādheyaṭavān ghaṭaḥ*. That is, the pot is the superstratum, supported by the ground limited by groundness, through *saṁyoga* relation. So, there is *ādhāratā bhāva* in the ground and *ādheyatā bhāva* in the pot. This occurrence-exacting relation between the pot and the ground is generally known as a relation of incomplete occurrence (*avyāpya-vṛtti*) because when a contact takes place between two substances (*dravya*s) it has to occur only in a part of them (point of contact), provided the two substances have parts.

(b) *Samavāya* : *Samavāya* is considered as one of the seven fundamental categories (*padārtha*) of the classical Vaiśeṣika school, while *saṁyoga* (contact or conjunction) and *vibhāga* (disjunction) are considered as types of a second category *guṇa* (quality). *Samavāya* or inherence is an example of a direct relation and is also an occurrence-exacting relation. For example, in the knowledge of *ghaṭaḥ asti, ghaṭatva* is *viśeṣaṇa* existing in the *ghaṭa* by *samavāya* (inherence) relation. In *nīlaḥ ghataḥ asti* there is a blue jar, the blueness and the potness are inherent in the pot. *Samavāya* can be known by the sense-organs and hence through perception. This relation can also be easily seen as a *vyāpya vṛtti* relation. Navya-Nyāya distinguishes between two awarnesses such as a blue pot and a pot. To explain this difference Navya-Nyāya introduces the important concept of a limitor (*avacchedaka*). In a single word "pot" the potness (*ghaṭatva*) is the *avacchedaka*. In the relation *aRb*, *a* is the pot, *R* is inherence (*samavāya*) and *b* is the universal *ghaṭatva* which is cognized directly. Here *b* is the limitor of the property of being the qualificand and resident in *a*. A limitor is thus a qualifier in this case but all qualifiers are not limitors. In the phrase "blue jar" (*nīla ghaṭa*) there are two *avacchedaka*s residing in *nīlatva*, even though the objects *ghaṭaḥ* and *nīlaḥ ghaṭaḥ* are one and the same.

(c) *Svarūpa* : It is not always the case that *R* is either contact or inherence. For example, *R* may represent a cause and effect relationship. What is this cause and effect relationship? The standard answer of the Naiyāyika is that this relationship is not a distinct entity but merely the property of being either the cause or the effect. Under this category of relations a whole range of relationships exist from *pitṛ-putra bhāva* to *sambandhī-sambandha bhāva*. These relations are called *svarūpa* or self-linking relations.

Examples : In the knowledge "This is a man," the qualifier of "man" is the generic character "man-ness" by which every member of the class "man" is recognized. In the same situation, if one's knowledge is "This is Devadatta," the qualifier of Devadatta is the Devadatta-ness. Man-ness inheres in every man (*samavāya*). The Devadatta-ness resides in Devadatta not by relation *samavāya*, but a particular qualification relation, at which is a *viśeṣaṇatā-viśeṣa-sambandha*. The Devadatta-ness becomes an imposed property (*upādhi*) and the relation is a *svarūpa sambandha*. This relation is also a *vyāpya vṛtti* relation. So far as the *svarūpa sambandha* is concerned, it can be either a occurrence-exacting relation or a non-occurrence-exacting relation.

(d) *Tādātmya or abheda* : This is also one of the types of direct relations. This denotes essential identity or non-separateness. Navya-Nyāya recognizes this as a self-linking relation. The terms *abheda* and *tādātmya* have been used as synonymous terms in Navya-Nyāya. The term *abheda* would mean the constant absence (*atyantābhāva*) of *bheda*. *Tādātmya* is the uncommon property (*asādhāraṇa dharma*) existing in the self (*sva*). When defined in this way *tādātmya* exists in one and only one entity, being the essence of that entity.

(e) *Sādṛśya* : The Navya-Naiyāyikas use the term *pratiyogin* normally in the situation of similarity (*sādṛśya*), e.g., *candra iva mukham* (the face is like the moon). *Candra* is *pratiyogin* and *mukha* is *anuyogin* for the similarity relation. This is also a direct relation of the self-linking type.

(f) *Kālikā* : This denotes a temporal relation. This is of two sorts: direct (*sākṣāt*) and indirect (*paramparā*). Time is considered to be a single, formless, eternal substance. Everything resides directly in time through a temporal relation. Time is a substratum for all entities. For example, *asmin māse varṣā* and *vaṅgadeśe varṣā* have a similar syntactical relation. Direct temporal relation is of two sorts. In the first, all entities reside directly in universal time (*mahākāla*). The second is the more important relation to logic wherein all non-eternal entities reside directly in a portion of time. This is the relation between rain and a particular month. Now a portion of time is an imposed property (*upādhi*) on time. While time itself is eternal, its imposed properties are calibrations furnished by actions, contacts and disjunction. For example, these are set by the (apparent) motion of the Sun across a line.

(g) ***Avacchedakatva*** : An especially difficult and important relation is that of limitorness, i.e., *avacchedakatva* and its converse, limitedness (*avacchedyatva*). Raghunātha Śiromaṇi makes this relation an important tool in Navya-Nyāya analysis. When someone says *bhūtale ghaṭo nāsti* (there is no pot on the ground), the following questions arise in the listener's mind:

1. Whether the *pratiyogin* is any particular pot.
2. Whether it implies all pots.
3. Does the *pratiyogitā* exist only in pots and not in something else such as cloth.
4. Whether this absence of pot is with respect to the full pot or parts of it.
5. Or is it the denial of the relation of the pot with the ground.

The Navya-Naiyāyikas attempt to answer these questions with the concept of *avacchedaka*. The delimitor of the counter-positiveness can be stated as either *tadghaṭatva* or simply *ghaṭatva*. The former refers to a particular pot while the latter, to all pots. *Ghaṭatva* as delimitor also implies that there cannot be anything else other than pots. As regards issues (4) and (5), Navya-Naiyāyikas utilize the concept of a relational delimitorness (*pratiyogitā-avacchedaka-sambandha*). Navya-Nyāya literature gives a large number of examples where an *avacchedaka* may be used for the sake of avoiding ambiguity. We give some examples to illustrate different applications of *avacchedaka*.

1. *Pratiyogitā-avacchedaka*: In the case of the absence of the form *ghaṭo nāsti*, the *ghaṭa* is the *pratiyogī* (counter-positive) of the absence of *ghaṭa* and *ghaṭatva* is the *pratiyogitā-avacchedaka*.

2. *Viṣayatā-avacchedaka*: If the *ghaṭa* becomes the content (*viṣaya*) of knowledge, then the same *ghaṭatva* could be the *viṣayatā-avacchedaka* (limitor of contentness).
3. *Viṣayita-avacchedaka*: The corresponding knowledge which is the container (*viṣayī*) of the content (*viṣaya*) has got the generic charcater *jñānatva* (knowledgeness) which is *viṣayita-avacchedaka* in this case.
4. *Prakāratā-avacchedaka*: In the case of the knowledge of the form of *ghaṭavat bhūtalam* (the ground is jar-possessing), the *ghaṭa* is the *prakāra* of *bhūtala* and *ghaṭava* is the *prakāratā-avacchedaka.*
5. *Kāryatā-avacchedaka*: In the case of the *ghaṭa* being the effect of a stick (*daṇḍa*) *ghaṭatva* is the limitor of the effectness (*kāryatā-avacchedaka*), while *daṇḍatva* (stickness) is the *kāraṇatā-avacchedaka* (the limitor of the causeness).

(h) *Abhāva* : *Abhāva* is one of the seven categories under the Vaiśeṣika system. Where *R* is a self-linking connector (*svarūpa sambandha*) there are only two entities involved, although the situation is still triadic in form. The absence of a known entity denotes a case where there is no contact. For example, the relation between the place where something is absent (*abhāva*) and the absence in *bhūtale ghaṭo nāsti* or to be precise *bhūtale ghaṭābhāva asti* (there is absence of pot on the ground). The pot is said to be the *pratiyogin* or counter-positive of the absence of pot and the ground is said to be the *anuyogin*. This relation is called absential qualification (*abhāvīya viśeṣaṇatā*). This can be represented as "ground-(R-absence of pot)." The ground is characterized by (*svarūpa*) the absence of a pot. Here *R* does not designate a third thing beyond its relation; the ground is functioning as its own relation. Relational absences are denials of relations other than that of identity. These are said to be of three kinds:

1. Prior absence (*prāgabhāva*) denotes the absence of a thing somewhere before it is created. For example, prior to making a pot there is only clay and the pot is absent.
2. Posterior absence (*pradhvaṁsābhāva*) denotes the absence of an existing thing after it has been destroyed. For example, if the pot is broken it ceases to exist.
3. Constant absence (*atyantābhāva*) denotes the absence of a thing somewhere when this absence is not time-bound. For example, there is no fire in a lake. This may be expressed by "a lake is the locus of constant absence of fire."

In the knowledge of the constant absence of fire in a lake, the fire may be called *pratiyogin* and the lake, the *anuyogin* of an absence. Literally, the name for an adjunct in such a case is absential adjunct (*abhāvīya pratiyogin*). This is also frequently referred to as counter-positive. In every counter-positive there exists counter-positiveness (*pratiyogitā*).

(i) *Saṁyukta-samavāya* : This is an indirect relation which is formed by a combination of two relations, contact (*saṁyoga*) and inherence (*samavāya*). In producing the perception of a quality (*guṇa*) or any other object which inheres in a subject (*dravya*) this relation comes into operation. As the quality inheres in a substance and the substance comes in contact with the sense-organ the sense-organ is said to be associated with the quality through this relation. This is a compound relation between the sense-organ and the form (*rūpa*) of the object.

Example :

Eye —— Rel : *Saṁyoga* / in contact with (sees) ——▶ object —— Rel : *Saṁvāya* / has ——▶ Form

(j) *Saṁyukta-samaveta-samavāya* : This indirect relation comes into effect if the perception by contact of the generic character *jāti* which inheres in a *guṇa* which again in turn inheres in a substance *dravya*.

(k) *Samaveta-samavāya* : It is a compound of two *samavāyīs*. This relation is one where *a* is related to *c* through *b* in the form inherence of *c* in that which is inhered in, viz., *b*, by the subject *a*. Colour of the threads is related to the cloth by this relation. Here, *c* = cloth, *b* = threads and *a* = colour.

(l) *Svasamavāyī-samavetatva* : This is another type of indirect relation wherein *samavāya, saṁyoga* and *svarūpa* are involved. For example, *paṭe tanturūpam* — means thread-form in the cloth. Here, *tantu* = thread, is the co-locus for both *paṭa* = cloth and *rūpa* = form. In this relation there exists co-locus-ness.

Modern Information Technology Applications of Indian Logic

The concepts of Indian logic have never been used for modern applications as the IT and AI systems. Therefore, there is a need to familiarize these concepts to make them useful in today's application context.

Current Perspectives on Cognitive and Linguistic Sciences

The cognitive and linguistic sciences offer scope for a multidisciplinary study of the mind or what might be called "natural intelligence." Cognitive science seeks an understanding of such mental abilities as perception, recognition, categorization, memory, reasoning and problem-solving, motor control, speech, language, and communication. Linguistics focuses on the nature of human language — its theoretical, descriptive, behavioural, and evolutionary bases. It also serves as a window into human cognition. The approaches of a variety of disciplines, including cognitive psychology, linguistics, artificial intelligence, neuroscience, philosophy, and anthropology, are all brought to bear on common problems of mind, brain, and language. The future of the cognitive and linguistic sciences lies in crossing these traditional disciplinary boundaries. In linguistics and language processing, theories of phonology, syntax and semantics are increasingly enmeshed with the results of formal, computational, and experimental studies. It is in this context we believe that a serious exploration of Indian philosophical views on logic and language is helpful to integrate the classical ideas with the present-day thinking. Indian Logic may be used to develop IT tools and products for conducting administration, business and educational activities in Indian multilingual environment through contextualizing Indic knowledge.

KNOWLEDGE ENGINEERING

Some possible applications for Indian logic are the following:

- Development of methods for knowledge acquisition, representation and validation using the deeper notion of knowledge in Indian logic. (Example: Use of Petri Nets for Indian Logic.)
- Development of a Sanskrit Word-net that would lead to Sanskrit as an Indian Link Language (ILL) to support machine translation from one Indian language to the other.
- Formalization of the methodology of hierarchical semantic analysis of sentences of ordinary (*laukika*) language using several layers of knowledge such as lexicons (*koṣa*), grammar (*vyākaraṇa*), logic (*nyāya*), and exegesis (*mīmāṁsā*).

- Formalization of the methodology of semantic analysis of literary language (*alaṅkāra, vyañjanā, dhvani* aspects) that would facilitate machine translation and knowledge interpretation.
- Exploration of the methodology of *parārtha-anumāna* in *tarka* to train a researcher to defend a thesis, and to respond to the arguments of critics.

Knowledge Representation for Indian Logic

The perception through senses is the most important source of knowledge (*pramāṇa*) in Nyāya. The term *jñāna* or awareness is used in Navya-Nyāya only in the episodic sense and never in the dispositional sense. It is used in a very broad sense to include sensing, perception, memory, introspection, assumption, doubt and belief, etc. Sensory knowledge acquisition is a process initiated by a doubt (*saṁśaya*) and sustained by inquiry (*parāmarśa*). This involves a sequence of "mental episodes" or "events." They are equivalent to verbal thoughts or they are at least verbalizable according to Bhartṛhari.

Cognitions have three moments or phases: (a) a moment of origination, (b) a duration in which an act produces its own trace, and (c) a moment of cessation as a conscious state. Cognitions may be classified as: (1) informative (*anubhava*) and (2) recollective (*smṛti*). Perception can produce either a true cognition (*pramā*) or a false one leading to doubt (*saṁśaya*) and false belief episodes (*viparyaya*). Perception can be determinate or indeterminate and the former can either be ordinary (*laukika*) or special (*alaukika*). Determinate perception is qualificative cognition, the object of which is of the form *aRb*.

The cognition process can be explained as under. When an observer looks at a pot on the ground, the process is sequential in getting the knowledge of two parts of the object, pot and ground and the relation connecting them, confirming and concluding that as a true cognition, with the following steps:

1. The observer sees the object *ghaṭa* (pot).
2. Recalling from his memory, he decides that it has a *dharma*. Here *dharma* is pot-ness (*ghaṭatva*).
3. Then *buddhi* links the above two (pot and pot-ness) by a relation called *samavāya* (inherence).
4. So, it is then concluded by the *vyāpāra* implied by perception that the object *a* is *ghaṭa*.

   This process of cognition can be represented with the help of Petri Nets, which are bipartite graph representations consisting of place and transitions representing states and events (*fig*. 2).[6] This gives rise to the cognition "There is a pot."
5. The observer also recognizes that in addition to *dharma*, the pot has a *prakāra*, which covers its shape, size and other features (*ākṛti*). If he observes that in this case the feature seen is the blue colour related to the pot by inherence, here the resulting cognition is "There is a blue pot" (*fig*. 3).
6. Next, for the *ghaṭa* (pot) to be stable and intact it has to have some support. So, look/think about this supporting object *b*. He observes that the relation is contact (*saṁyoga*) and that location ground is the support for the superstratum pot.
7. Again from memory (because of previous knowledge as a result of learning), *bhūtala* has its own *dharma bhūtalatva*, related to *bhūtala* by *samavāya* relation.

8. This also brings in the concept of support-supported (*ādhāra-ādheya*) *bhāva*, wherein the earth is *ādhāra* (support) and the *ghaṭa* is *ādheya* (supported).
9. The link between the two — i.e., the pot and the floor — is established by understanding that the pot is supported by the earth by contact or *saṁyoga* relation.
10. So, the final conclusion is —

    The blue pot as qualified by pot-ness and blueness is related to the ground, qualified by ground-hood (through the relation of contact) and that the former, the super-stratum (*ādheya*) is supported by the latter as a substratum occurrent (*ādhāra*).

Example 1: The perception process of the four utterances:

ghaṭaḥ asti (There is a pot).

bhūtale ghaṭo asti (There is a pot on the ground).

bhūtale nīlo ghaṭo asti (There is a blue pot on the ground).

In the language of Nyāya-Vaiśeṣika the cognition process of an observer depends upon a determinate cognition regarding objects. This is propositional awareness and awarenesses of a complex whole containing a relation and its two terms. If *aRb* represents a proposition denoting a relation *R* between two entities *a* and *b*, what is cognized cannot be said to be a fact until its truth is established. The complex content of this awareness is represented by three technical expressions: qualificand (*viśeṣya*), qualifier (*viśeṣaṇa*), and qualification (*vaiśiṣṭya*).

In Navya-Nyāya the term "blue pot" and the sentence "pot is blue" produce the same type of qualified awareness. The qualificand is said to be cognized through the qualifier, which must have been already cognized. The cognition map of a Naiyāyika is a complete description of the cognized object, with the help of appropriate relations, that is necessary for its complete understanding, as compared to an ordinary observer. Navya-Nyāya specifies several types of relations defined by *bhāvas* such as: qualifier-qualified (*viśeṣaṇa-viśeṣya*) abstract properties (*dharma*), describer-described pairs (*nirūpaka-nirūpita*) and limitor-limited (*avacchedaka-avacchinna*).

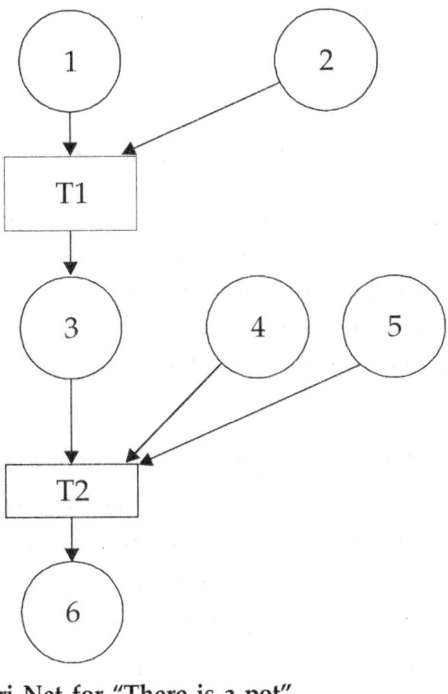

***Fig.* 2: Petri Net for "There is a pot"**

Legend for fig. 2: place 1: Desire to infer; Place 2: Contact of Eye with object of Interest; Transition 1: Perception of the object; place 3: Recognition of the object as "potness-possessor;" Place 4: Cognition of potness; Place 5: Cognition of the relation of inherence of "potness" in the object "pot." Transition T2: The perception process; Place 6: Cognition verbalizable as "There is a pot."

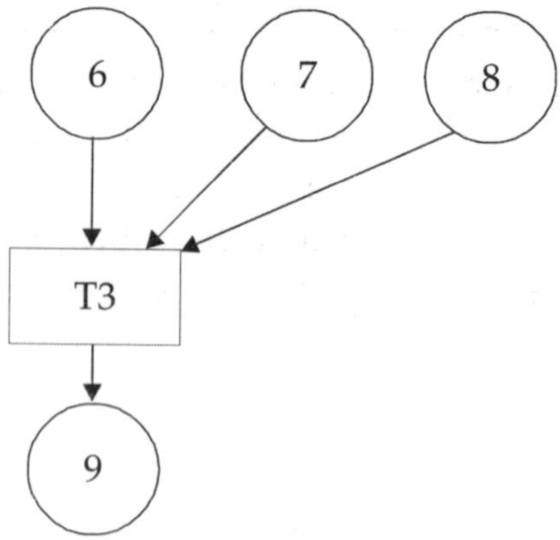

Fig. **3: Petri Net for "There is a blue pot"**

Legend for fig. 3: Place 6: Cognition "There is a pot;" Place 7: Recognition of the object as "colour-possessor;" Place 8: Cognition of blue colour; Place 9: Cognition of the relation of inherence of "blue colour" in the object "pot." Transition T3: The Cognition "There is a blue pot."

Example 2: *Inferential Cognition* — Inferential cognition arises from substantive reflection (*parāmarśa*) by a combination of the knowledge of pervasion (*vyāpti-jñāna*) and the presence of probans (*hetu*) in the subject locus (*pakṣa*) called (*pakṣa-dharmatā-jñāna*). What makes a thing a proper *pakṣa* or subject? In other words, what is *pakṣatā*? Arriving at a proper definition of *pakṣatā* is an important and difficult problem in Navya-Nyāya. There are several requisites for precisely defining this notion (Ramanuja Tatacharya, 1988):

(i) Certainty about *sādhya* (*sādhya-siddhi*).

(ii) Doubt about *sādhya* (*sādhya sandeha*), desire to infer (*siṣādhayiṣā*) and certainty.

(iii) Desire to infer but no certainty.

(iv) There is absence of both the desire to infer and certainty.

(v) Absence of causal aggregates leading to perceptual cognition and verbal cognition.

(vi) *Parāmarśa* leading to *anumiti*.

By considering the input states as: design to infer (*siṣadhaiṣa*), doubt regarding *sādhya* (*sādhya-sandeha*), certainty or otherwise of *sādhya*, perception of smoke in a locus (on the mountain), recollection of *vyāpti* between smoke and fire, knowledge of *pakṣadharmatā* (or *pakṣatā* or subjecthood), a Petri Net representation can easily be constructed (see *fig*. 4). Such an exercise will also be useful in checking the various definitions of concepts such as *pakṣatā*.

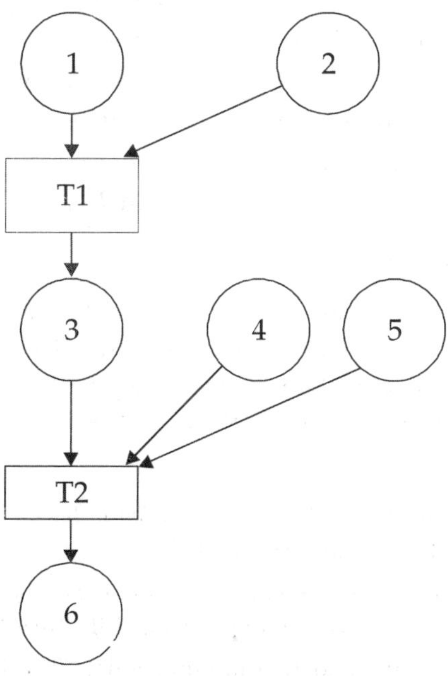

***Fig.* 4: Petri Net for Inferential Cognition**

Legend for fig. 3 : Place 1; Desire to infer; Place 2: Contact of eye with smoke in locus mountain; Transition 1: Perception process of smoke; Place 3: Perception of smoke being "smokeness-possessor;" Place 4: Recollection of *vyāpti* between smoke and fire; Place 5: Substantive reflection (*parāmarśa*); Transition T2: The inference process; Place 6: Inference verbalizable as "fiery mountain."

Concluding Remarks

Philosophers of the East and the West have long since recognized Indian contributions to logic. On the other hand, the Indian Technology and Science community is by and large unaware of these developments. This paper is an attempt to present the basic ideas of Nyāya in a form which appeals to those working in Information Technology and AI. The salient features of Indian logic and the issues of perception, inference and the concept of relation are discussed in some detail. We believe that present-day problems of intelligent search and retrieval of information from the world wide web (www) and Knowledge Engineering can considerably benefit from the application of these concepts from *Nyāya*.

Acknowledgements

The authors wish to thank Sri Srinivasa Varakhede and Sri Tirumala Kulkarni, both of Poorna Prajna Vidyapeetha, Bangalore, and Sri Ramanuja Tatacharya, formerly of Rashtriya Sanskrit Vidyapeeth, Tirupati for several useful discussions on concepts of Navya-Nyāya.

Notes

1. S.S. Barlingay, *A Modern Introduction to Indian Logic*, New Delhi: National Publishing House, 1976.
2. Sibajiban Bhattacharyya, *Gangesa's Theory of Indeterminate Perception*, Nirvikalpakavada, Pt I and II, New Delhi: ICPR, 1996.
3. H.G. Coward and K. Kunjunni Raja, "The Philosopy of the Grammarians" in *Encyclopedia of Indian Philosophies*, vol. V, New

Delhi: Motilal Banarsidass, 1990 (Indian Edition of Princeton University Press publication).

4. V.N. Jha, *Philosophy of Relations*, New Delhi: Sri Satguru Publications, 1990
5. Daniel H.H. Ingalls, 1951, *Materials for The Study of Navya Nyaya Logic*, Cambridge, Mass: Harvard University Press.
6. Y. Narhari, *Petri Nets, Resonance*, Bangalore: Indian Academy of Sciences, Aug 1999, 4, 8, p. 58.
7. B.K. Matilal, *Logic, Language and Reality*, New Delhi: Motilal Banarsidass, 1985.
8. B.K. Matilal, *Perception, An Essay on Classical Indian Theories of Knowledge* (Indian Edition), New Delhi: Oxford University Press, 2002.
9. B.K. Matilal, *The Character of Logic in India* (Indian Edition), Delhi: Oxford University Press 1998.
10. Satish Chandra Vidyabhushan, *History of Indian Logic*, Calcutta: Calcutta University, 1921.

References

Bhāṣā Pariccheda, Viswanatha "Nyaya Panchanana" Bhattacharya, Swami Madhavananda (ed.) (English tr.), Calcutta: Advaita Ashrama, 1996.

Nyāya-Bhāṣyas, Vātsyāyana and *Vārttika*, Uddyotakara incorporated along with *Nyāya-Sūtras* of Gautama, tr. Mahamahopadhyaya Ganganath Jha, New Delhi: Motilal Banarsidass, vol 1-4, 1999 reprints.

Nyāya-Sūtra, Akṣapāda Gautama, with tr. M.M. Satish Chandra Vidyabhushana, Nanda Lal Sinha (ed.), New Delhi: Motilal Banarsidass, 1981 reprint.

Pakṣatā, Ramanuja Tatacharya, Tirupati: Rashtriya Samskrita Vidyapeeth, 1988.

Pramāṇa-Tattva-Cintāmaṇi, Gaṅgeśa Upādhyāya, New Delhi: Chaukambha Sanskrit Pratisthan, 1990.

Appendix to Chapter 2

History of Indian Logic

Ancient Era (Prācīna Nyāya) (up to AD 500)

Contributions : Anvikṣikī, also known as Hetu Vidyā and Tarka Vidyā, was brought to light (Medhātithi Gautama) as the first stage of logic which came to be widely known in the second stage as Nyāya-Śāstra. The term *nyāya* as an equivalent for Logic came into use. *Nyāya-Sūtra* (Akṣapāda Gautama), the first systematic work on the Nyāya-Śāstra was written and this was succeeded by the first Bhāṣya on Sūtras (Vātsyāyana). *Padārthas* (tenets of Vaiśeṣika) as ontological basis of Nyāya (Kaṇāda) were accepted. Saptabhaṅgī Nyāya (the seven-valued logic treated as sevenfold paralogism (unreasonable or beyond reason by critics), Syādavāda and development of 10-limbed syllogism (all by Bhadrabāhu) were significant Jaina contributions in addition to the introduction of Nyāya (mood of statements), *Pratyakṣa Jñāna* and *Parokṣa Jñāna* (all by Umāsvāti). The Mādhyamika School of thought started to develop which discussed the nature of Truth (Nāgārjuna in *Mādhyamika Kārikā*). The period witnessed the evolution of 5-limbed syllogism, *jāti* and *nigrahasthāna* (Vasubandhu).

Contributors and Works : Medhātithi Gautama (*Anvikṣikī*), Kaṇāda (*Vaiśeṣika Darśana*), Kauṭilya (*Arthaśāstra*), Akṣapāda Gautama (*Nyāya-Sūtra*), Caraka (*Caraka-Saṁhitā*), Vātsyāyana

(*Nyāya-Bhāṣya*), Bhadrabāhu (*Daśavaikālika-Niryukti*, *Sūtrakṛtāṅga-Niryukti*), Umāsvāti (*Tattvārtha-Adhigama-Sūtra*), Nāgārjuna (*Mādhyamika Kārikā*, *Vigrahavyāvartanī-Kārikā*, *Pramāṇa-viheṭana*), Vasubandhu (*Tarka-Śāstra*).

Medieval Era (AD 500 - AD 1150)

Contributions : Systematization of logic by both Buddhists (Diṅnāga) and Jains (Siddhasena Divākara) was the significant contribution of this era. A further study of Syādavāda and 10-limbed syllogism of Bhadrabāhu was undertaken. The concept of Nyāya was elaborated further as a method of comprehend-ing things from particular viewpoints. Detailed theories of inference, characteristics of reason, theories of negation and momentariness, concepts of *svalakṣaṇa* and *svabhāva* are all major Buddhist contributions to logic based on Gautama *Nyāya-Sūtras*. Diṅnāga's description of *hetucakra* (wheel of reasons) was a novel contribution. The era gave rise to Prakaraṇa literature. Criticism of categories in the *Nyāya-Sūtra* with a detailed study of *pramāṇa* (Nāgārjuna), theory of *anyathā khyāti* (Bhāsarvajña), Mahāvidyā syllogism (free from fallacies of *asiddha*, *vyabhicārī*, *bādha*, and *upādhi*), which is a counter- syllogism refuting the established syllogisms (Śivāditya Miśra), were other significant contributions. Many *ṭīkā*s, *vārttika*s, *bhāṣya*s were brought out.

Contributors and works : Diṅnāga (*Pramāṇa Samuccaya*), Siddhasena Divākara (*Nyāyāvatāra*), Prasastapāda (*Padārtha-dharma-saṁgraha*), Udyotkara (*Nyāya Vārttika*), Dharmakīrti (*Nyāya Bindu*, *Hetu Bindu*, *Vāda Nyāya* and *Sambandha Parikṣā*), Jayanta Bhaṭṭa (*Nyāya Mañjarī*), Vācaspati Miśra (*Nyāya-Vārttika-Tātparya-Ṭīkā*), Bhāsarvajña (*Nyāya Sāra*), Śrīdhara (*Nyāya Kandalī*), Udayana (*Nyāya Kusumāñjali*), Śivāditya (*Sapta Padārthī*), Śrīvallabha (*Nyāya Līlāvatī*).

Modern Era (Navya-Nyāya) (AD 1150 onwards)

Contributions : *Tattva Cintāmaṇi* (Gaṅgeśa) laid the foundations of logic in this era. Rigorous reformulation of the theory of inference, clarity of the notions of *vyāpti* and *pakṣa* were the achievements. Some of the fallacies in the definitions of Nyāya schools were pointed out in *Khaṇḍana-Khaṇḍa-Khādya* (Śrīharṣa). Criticism of Śrīharṣa's *Khaṇḍana-Khaṇḍa-Khādya*, soundness of arguments, are also significant contributions during the period. New concepts such as *Buddhivāda*, *Viṣayatāvāda*, *Vyutpattivāda* and *Śaktivāda* (all by Gadādhara) were novel contributions.

Contributors and works : Śrīharṣa (*Khaṇḍana-Khaṇḍa-Khādya*), Gaṅgeśopādhyāya (*Pramāṇa-Tattva-Cintāmaṇi*), Vardhamāna (Commentaries), Pakṣadhara (*Tattva-Cintāmaṇi-Viveka*, *Tattva-Cintāmaṇi-Āloka*), Vidyāraṇya (*Sarva Darśana Saṁgraha*), Śaṅkara Miśra (*Nyāya Kusumāñjalī*), Vācaspati Miśra (*Nyāya Tattvāloka*), Vāsudeva Sārvabhauma (*Sārvabhauma Niryukti*), Raghunātha Śiromaṇi (*Tattva-Cintāmaṇi-Didhiti*), Annām Bhaṭṭa (*Tarka Saṁgraha*), Yaśovijaya (*Nyāya Khaṇḍa Khādya*), Viśvanātha Pañcānana (*Bhāṣā Pariccheda*), Gadādhara (*Tattva-Cintāmaṇi-Didhiti-Prakāśikā*), Bhīmācārya (*Nyāya Kośa*).

3

Buddhist Theory of Meaning

Rajnish Mishra

It is important to note that the Buddhist theory of meaning (*apohavāda*) has been expounded and discussed at length in the Buddhist epistemological treatises mainly by the logicians — philosophers of the Sautrāntika-Yogācāra Schools. This suggests that the theory deserves an epistemic status in the structure of Buddhist thought. This also supports the thesis that a theory of meaning is a theory of cognition too. Speaking from the epistemological point of view, verbal cognition has been included under inference (*anumāna*) in the Buddhist thought and its domain of operation is the phenomenal existence (*saṁvṛtti*) only. The Buddhist scholars maintain that perception (or sensation for *pratyakṣa*) and inference involve their specific domains of operation, i.e., transcendental and phenomenal truths respectively. The same cognition of the object cannot be obtained either by perception or inference or both. The cognition of fire by perception and by inference (where smoke is perceived) is not the same. That is why the Buddhist epistemology is known as *pramāṇa vyavasthā* as opposed to *pramāṇa samplava* in the other systems of thought. Perception and inference have their respective domains of operation and do not interfere with each other's areas.[1] In brief, we may present this taxonomy as follows:

Means of Knowledge (epistemology)	*Knowable/Domain of operation (ontology)*[2]
1. Perception (four types: sense, mental, intuitive and self)	Transcendental or the Thing-in-itself (*pāramārthika* or *svalakṣaṇa*)
2. Inference (two types: "for self" and "for others")	Phenomenal or Universal (*samvṛtti* or *sāmānya lakṣaṇa*)

The Buddhist theoreticians do not deny the other means of knowledge, i.e., verbal testimony (*śabda*), analogy (*upamāna*), postulation (*arthāpatti*) and non-presence (*anuplabdhi*). They argue that rest of these means could be included under inference as none of them involves direct cognition of the object. These all bring about the cognition of the "universal" of the object that bears the mental postulates (*kalpanā*) like name, class, quality, generic shape, etc. These scholars hold that the verbal cognition refers to the "universal" of that object and even this universal is posited by means of difference. The potentiality to exclude or diffentiate "the other objects" is inherent in words.[3] A word cannot even touch the "unique particular" (*svalakṣaṇa*) because this is in constant flux.[4] Perception or sensation is the only means to approach this "unique particular" which is the ultimate knowable ontological entity in the Buddhist system. This perception (indeterminate perception only) is free from all the mental postulates.[5]

1. Diṅnāga, *Pramāṇasamuccaya*, 2.1.
2. In the Buddhist epistemological texts *pāramārthika* and *saṁvṛtti* have also been referred as *svalakṣaṇa* (the thing-in-itself or unique particular) and *sāmānya lakṣaṇa* (universal) respectively.
3. *Pramāṇavārttika, Pratyakṣa Pariccheda*, 163-4.
4. *Tattvasaṁgraha*, 1966, 1075.
5. *Pramāṇasamuccaya* 1.3 (*Pratyakṣa*) *pratyakṣa kalpanāpoḍhaṁ nāmajātyādisaṁyutaṁ*.

However, in the system, there is no claim for the complete and absolute knowability of the Reality.[6]

Apoha is a carefully worked out theory of meaning and cognition in the contexts of Buddhist ontology and epistemology. This is a major thesis supported by all the four philosophical schools of Buddhism. It has been formulated and developed with complete conformity to the Master's exposition of *saddharma* as the opening *kārikā* of the *Pramāṇasamuccaya* reveals:

> Salute Him, who is the personification of the means of cognition, seeks the benefit of [all] living beings who is the teacher, *sugata*, the protector, I'll, for the purpose of establishing the means of cognition compose the [*Pramāṇa*] *samuccaya* uniting here under one head, my theories scattered [in many treatises].[7]

The *Kārikā* suggests that whatever is being discussed hereforth bears the authority from the original expounder, the Buddha, who was the source of all valid cognition (*pramāṇa bhūta*). For the first time in the Buddhist tradition, *apoha* was theorized in 52 *kārikā*s of the fifth chapter of this celebrated work of Indian Epistemology by Ācārya Diṅnāga — in the fifth century AD. We shall discuss the pertinent *Kārikā*s of this text in detail. But let us first posit the nature of linguistic sign as it emerges from the primary canonical texts of Buddhism:

1. A linguistic sign does not hold any direct and real relationship with the object it refers to.
2. It refers to a conceptual construct (*vikalpa*).
3. It is purely a subjective construction that varies from person to person.

---

6. See *Vigrahavyāvartanī* of Śrī Nāgārjuna.
7. *Dignāga, on Perception,* 1.1 (tr. Masaaki Hattori).

4. It is differential in nature (*atadvyāvṛtti rūpa*). It cannot express what a thing really is (because things are devoid of any "self-nature") but since a thing is mutually dependent on the other (dependent) things — it certainly refers to that relation by the means of its differential nature, i.e., it expresses what a thing is not, or that the object is different from those objects which are contextually incompatible with it.[8]

We may also draw a parallel of the notions of linguistic sign and meaning as elaborated by the four major schools in the tradition:

School	*Linguistic sign and Meaning*
1. Bauddha	Conceptual image, indirect, subjective, negative/differential, real and universal (which is only a mental postulate), by implication it refers to an individual also.
2. Nyāya-Vaiśeṣika	Ontological entity (not the conceptual image only), direct, objective, positive/identical, real and universal (which is a real category).
3. Mīmāṁsā	Ontological entity, direct, objective, positive, real and universal.
4. Vyākaraṇa	Conceptual image, indirect, subjective as well as objective, positive, real, individual as well as universal.

The schools of Buddhists and grammarians are known as the idealist schools and the schools of Naiyāyika-Vaiśeṣikas and Mīmāṁsakas as the realists in the taxonomy of Indian philosophical systems. These differences regarding the nature and meaning of linguistic sign are the outcome of their respective philosophical standpoints.

8. This idea is close to the Upaniṣadic conception of *neti* — that the absolute cannot be defined positively (see *Bṛhadāraṇyaka Upaniṣad*, 4.5.15).

According to the *Śabdakalpadruma*,[9] *apoha* is derived from the verb-root *uḥ* which means "to think" or "to differentiate." It has been classified under the set of *bhū*, etc., in the verb lexicon (*dhātu-pāṭha*). A negative prefix *apa* and a nominal suffix *ghañ* have been added to the verbal root *uh*.[10]

Apoha[11] literally means "to exclude by means of logical reasoning." It is an antique term and has been used by the Buddha as a method of inquiry into truth in his philosophical discourses. The term itself refers to inference (*anumāna*), a secondary means of knowledge in the Buddhist epistemology and supports the argument why the Buddhist logicians include verbal cognition (*śabda-jñāna*) under inference and deny any independent category to it. *Apoha* is a mode of reasoning in which we "exclude those which are not compatible or consistent with the context under discussion."[12]

Diṅnāga categorizes inference as (i) for the self (*svārthānumāna*) and (ii) "for others" (*parārthānumāna*).[13] He defines the first type as one that consists in discerning an object

---

9. The complete entry reads: *apoha pu.* (*apa+ uh + bhāve ghañ*), *apagata uḥ; vitarkābhāvaḥ; suśrudyāṣṭādhyāyī gaṇāntargata ssthaguṇaḥ; suśruṣā śravaṇaṁ caiva grahaṇam dhāraṇaṁ tathā; uhāpoho — arthavijñānaṁ tattva jñānaṁ ca dhīguṇaḥ* (Hemacandra). *Atadvyāvṛttiḥ; iti Kāvyaprakāśa ṭīkāyāṁ Māheśvaraḥ.*

10. One may derive the complete term *apoha* by the following pertinent rules of *Aṣṭādhyāyī* which take part in the derivational process by means of their own potential: 1.679; 775 (identifying the verb root form *Dhātupāṭha*) 1.3.3; 1.3.9; 1.1.60; 3.1.1; 1.3.3; 1.3.9; 1.3.8; 1.3.9; 6.1.87 and 1.2.46.

11. *Apoha* has been rendered in English as "discrimination" (John Brough). "Differentiation" (Dr. Dhirendra Sharma) "negation" (B.P. Bhattacharya) and "exclusion" (K. Kunjuni Raja).

12. *tadvāna apoha vā śabadārtha, atadvyāvṛtti tadbhinna vyāvṛtti.*

13. See *Pramāṇasamuccaya,* II.1.2 (Richard P. Hayes).

through a sign (that has three characteristics).[14] He also states that the object grasped by inference is otherwise (universal) and it is not named through its essential property. The object is described as "is seen" or as "is heard" or as "is desired" only. As in the case of cognition of "fire," only smoke becomes visible which leads to the cognition of fire. Diṅnāga has already established that the fields of operation of perception and inference are different and hence the resulting cognitions are also bound to differ. We may illustrate this as follows:

Means	*Knowable*	*Nature of Cognition*
Perception	thing-in-self (transcendental)	direct, unique particular, the knowable/the cognized object is present; inexpressible, vivid objective image.
Inference	Universal (phenomenal)	indirect, universal (*kalpanā*), the knowable (here "fire" or the main object)/the cognized object remains absent; expressible subjective, differential, conceptual image.

The other type of inference (*parārthānumāna*), as Diṅnāga defines, is a syllogism that consists in communicating the three aspects/marks of the logical sign to others.[15] A close and critical examination of these sources of knowledge (perception and

---

14. Quoted by Prof. Stcherbatsky in 13 L, vol. 1, p. 275 form *Nyāya Bindu* of Diṅnāga. Three aspects of the logical marks refer to major and minor premises and to its conclusion.

15. According to the Buddhist logic inference is rooted in the theory of co-origination and co-existence (*tadutpatti* and *tādātmya*) with a common substratum (*samānādhikaraṇa* as *śinśapā* and tree).

two types of inference) leads to the conclusion that a verbal or linguistic sign is very close to the notion of an inferential sign of the first type of inference. It means the cognition resulting from a linguistic sign is for one's self and the cognitive image triggered by this sign bears all the characteristics we have posited for the inference (*svārthānumāna*) above. The nature of cognition through the inferential sign (smoke) and verbal/linguistic sign is the same. Both are devoid of the unique particular (*svalakṣaṇa*) and result in the cognition of "universal" (*kalpanā*) only. The triangle below illustrates the same relationship between the sign, property and the object[16]:

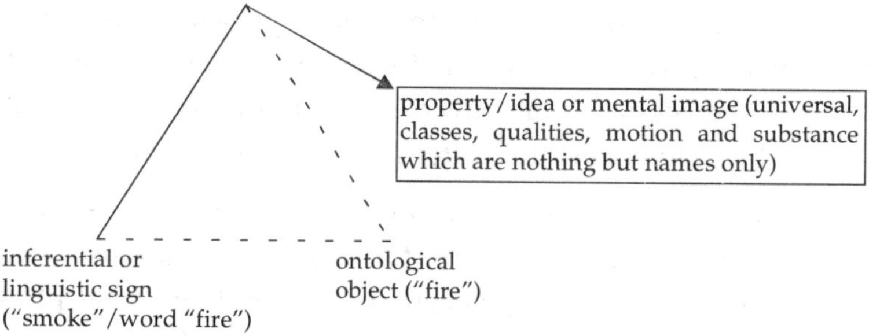

Diṅnāga suggests that through the inferential sign "smoke" — we may infer "fire" but we cannot infer its locus *also* because these two, the inferential sign and its locus, do not occur in relation. Moreover, an object may have many properties, all of which cannot be expressed through an inferential or linguistic sign.[17] By a process of eliminating others, the sign makes *known* those properties which are in some relation (*anubandha*). This relation is that of difference. For example, the cognition of fire is in accordance with things that are being

16. Cf. Patañjali's definition of *śabda* in the first *āhnika* of the *Mahābhāṣya* and the Ogden-Richards triangle.

17. See Kapil Kapoor's "The concept of *Padārtha* in Philosophy and Language" in *The 200 years William Jones Memorial Volume* (Pune, 1994-95).

related to it and can exclude only what is not fire. One does not observe them all in fire's absence, but one becomes aware of some of them in things other than fire.[18] Since the sign makes the inferred property known generally by exclusion of non-fire, we know "fire" by means of its general properties (universal). We get aware of its general form, but not that of the particular form. The Buddhist logicians hold that a universal cannot be confirmed because it is neither observed in the substratum nor outside of it. Moreover, a sign is non-interchangeable with the sign-bearer. For instance, "smoke"/ (word) and "fire" (an object) cannot be identical.

Diṅnāga expounds, herewith, that in principle there is no distinction between an inferential sign and linguistic sign. Both result in the cognition of universal which are not contextually compatible. However, the differences between these two are:

(i) They choose two different media for expression. In the case of an inferential sign, as "smoke," it is primarily a sense perception which in the second phase results in the cognition of "fire" through inference or mental function. In the case of a linguistic sign which is coventionally constructed (given or *nitya*) it is primarily a mental perception which constitutes the ideal image of the object.

(ii) An inferential sign is constituted of its three elements (*pakṣadharmatā, avinābhāva* and *hetu* or *liṅga*), whereas in a linguistic sign no such components are involved. The relationship between the sign and meaning/ cognition of the object is well established (*siddha*).[19]

---

18. Cf. Bhartṛhari's *Vākyapadīya*, 2.122.

19. The idea of an inferential sign and a linguistic sign comes very close to the concept of *index* and *symbol* as posited by the semiotician C.S. Pierce.

In this epistemological-ontological background, Diṅnāga expounds the theory of *apoha* in the 5th chapter of *Pramāṇasamuccaya*. He correlates the linguistic meaning with inference for one's self (*svārthānumāna*) which signifies that *apoha* is a valid means of acquiring knowledge for one's self. For cognition comes in the domain of mind (*mānasa vyāpāra*) which performs two functions simultaneously:

(i) to identify the object through pure sensation (*pratyakṣa*); and

(ii) as a next/subsequent phase to establish its distinction by means of differentiation.

When we know an object, we simply know how it is different from other entities in terms of general qualities, shapes, substances, etc. Language as a means of knowledge serves the same purpose. In the process of "languaging" the mind constructs a conceptual form of the object which posits universal only and even this universal is achieved through various hierarchies or levels of differentiation or exclusion. In this context the Buddhist philosophers maintain that language creates difference in the discrete reality. This characteristic of "differentiation" corresponds to both the limits and the potential of a verbal sign or language. This difference leaves out the "unique particular" (*svalakṣaṇa*) because it has no power to express it. This difference is our conceptual construct which we impose on the objects which ontologically exist. Now, the potentiality of difference lies in the fact that this suggests/indicates the "thing-in-itself" (*svalakṣaṇa* or *paramārtha satya*) which cannot be expressed in identical or in positive terms[20] (though incapable of expressing it as its primary denotation, *abhidhā*).

---

20. *Bṛhadāraṇyaka*, 4.5.15.

As stated above, *apoha* is a major thesis of the Buddhist philosophical system. Whatever is referred here in these epistemological treatises as "unique particular (*svalakṣaṇa*)" is known as *paramārtha* or *śūnya* in the Mādhyamika School of thought. Everything is devoid of its self-nature (*svabhāva śūnyatā*). In this case, a word like "cow" cannot refer to "cow-hood" (a universal, a real category in non-Buddhist systems). Similarly *svalakṣaṇa* or *śūnya* is inexpressible and does not pertain to the domain of verbal or inferential cognition. It could only be suggested through the differential nature of "universal," a conceptual construct, which is the import of the word.

Word does not refer to a void as things are devoid of any self-nature and since the unique particular is inexpressible, it cannot be referred directly and positively. So a word signifies only the universal which is established by its own potentiality of differentiation. This notion that a verbal import is exclusion of counter-correlates (*anyāpoha*) and that it suggests/indicates the unique particular, is important for the Buddhist theory of meaning. This will help us to understand the further development of the theory particularly with Śāntarakṣita and Ratnakīrti. This will also help to meet the counter-arguments of the *apoha* theory by the Naiyāyikas and the Mīmāṁsakas.

Hence, the *apoha* theory of meaning posits "an exclusion of counter-correlates" (*anyāpoha*). For example, the verbal import of the word "cow" is the exclusion of what is "not non-cow." In an algeberic expression we may put it like this:

Cow $\rightarrow$ not (non-cow), or

$\rightarrow$ - (non-cow).

Since there is no other way to refer to the "cow" (being) and positively, the meaning of this word comes by excluding the "non-cow." This phenomenon poses the problem of indeterminacy of meaning. Since the meaning of cow mutually depends on the "non-cow" and the domain of "non-cow" cannot be ascertained, there cannot be any ultimate meaning of the word "cow," too. *Apoha* does not claim to posit a determined object as the meaning; it refers to this relation of difference that holds between the signifier ("cow") and its signified, the counter-correlates (*anyāpoha*, "non-cow") and posits a universal (*vikalpa*, a mental postulate) as the meaning of the word "cow." Moreover, the theory seems to have been expounded from the hearer's/reader's point of view like the grammarian's *sphoṭa* theory of meaning.

Diṅnāga extends the domain of exclusion (*apoha*) from lexical meaning to the meaning of complex expressions like compound and sentence. In the stock example, "blue lotus" (*nīlotpala*) a word that names a property excludes those objects that lack that property, i.e., "blue" excludes all those objects which are "non-blue;" and so it divides the universe into the classes of things to which the word is applicable and the class of things to which the word is not applicbale. If the two words ("blue" and "lotus") are combined to form a larger unit of expression then each of them excludes some of the items from other's domains. Thus, the word "blue" in the compound "blue lotus" eliminates all those things to which the word "blue" is not applicable, while the word "lotus" eliminates from extensions of the word "blue" all those blue things to which the word "lotus" is not applicable. In theory, any two words remain in grammatical agreement (*samānādhikaraṇa*) unless their mutual exclusion form a null set. The same view can be extended up to the level of syntactic organization in which each word in a sentence mutually qualifies others by means of exclusion or difference. So in a linguistic expression (sentence) there are only differences. We may also apply the same notion and take the sentence as representing discourse (*mahāvākya*) or directly for a discourse analysis. Each discourse posits its own meaning or identity with its strength of exclusion/difference. However, there cannot be a well-defined domain of signification as the signifier and signified do not hold any direct and positive relationship.

Buddhist theory of meaning is associated with the Gestalt view (*akhaṇḍa pakṣa*, like the theory of *sphoṭa*). The notions established above clearly support this assumption. For more evidence we may quote this verse of Diṅnāga. "Since the thing expressed is a complex entity, neither 'blue' is in isolation, nor a 'lotus' in isolation is expressed. [The individual word] has no meaning, just as the individual phonetic components of a word have no meaning."[21] Diṅnāga's view on the relation of lexical and sentential meaning is of the moderate standpoint. He places his ideas in between ("the middle path") the controversy of *khaṇḍa pakṣa* and *akhaṇḍa pakṣa* and maintains that in a sentence, words do not give up their own individual meaning.

Explaining the logical implication of *apoha* theory of meaning, Diṅnāga states that a term does not exclude terms of wider extension, terms of narrow extension or co-existent terms, even if they differ from it.[22] Jinendrabuddhi elucidates that this is so because these terms are incompatible which is a prerequisite condition of exclusion. For example, a synonymous term which is the same with respect to what it excludes is excluded. Similarly the exclusion of the other objects that a wider term makes its own member is not overruled by a narrower term. For example, "tree" does not exclude *śinśapā* (the *aśoka* tree) or vice-versa. The expounder states that a wider term does not exclude its narrower terms because it creates

21. *Pramāṇasamuccaya*, 5.15.

22. *Ibid.*, 5.25.

an anticipation for them alone.[23] Similarly the term "cow" does not exclude "the red cow" or "the white cow," etc. which are only its narrower terms (elements or subjects).

One of the fundamental principles of Buddhism, i.e., cause-effect relationship is also implicit in the relation between the word and its meaning. Bhartṛhari while formulating his own theory of *sphoṭa*, provides a base of causal relationship to the signifier and the signified. Similarly, in the school of Diṅnāga it is maintained that as an efficient sign ("smoke") is the cause of the cognition of the object ("fire"). Similarly a word conventionally established, when properly articulated, triggers the meaning (cognition) of the object. We have already discussed in detail the nature of linguistic referentiality.

Thus, Diṅnāga expounds the theory of *apoha* in full confirmity with the Buddhist epistemology, ontology and logic.

Dharmakīrti (seventh century AD) elaborates upon *apoha* theory of meaning in the chapters on perception (*pratyakṣa*) and inference (*svārthānumāna*) of his widely acknowledged work *Pramāṇavārttika* — which is primarily a grand commentary on the *Pramāṇasamuccaya* of Diṅnāga. He extends the same view as stated by Diṅnāga that the meaning of linguistic sign is a purely subjective and conceptual construction. The speaker as well as the hearer, both deal with this conceptual image through the verbal expression which is devoid of ontological contents. So words have no direct access to the object (*vāstavārtha*) but only exclude the counter-correlates of the objects.

Dharmakīrti discusses the various aspects of counter-correlates.[24] He maintains that there is no need to posit an

23. *Pramāṇasamuccaya*, 5.26.

24. *Pramāṇavārttika* (*Pratyakṣa Pariccheda*), 163-73.

imaginary category like "class." By means of exclusion of the counter-correlates a word itself forms a class. Each word has this inherent potentiality to establish its own meaning by exclusion. There is no generic form as such inherent in the counter-correlates (non-cow) but certainly there is a form in the cognition (*vijñāna*) of the entity which is constituted by the previous experiences and impressions of the object in mind. Taking a firm theoretical position in Yogācāra-Vijñānavāda system, Dharmakīrti states that in the cognition of an object the meaning which appears to be existent in external reality is nothing but the form of our own self (*citta*) which the previous impressions and cognitions shape. The "universal mental image" appears as the object in our cognition.[25] Words refer to this counter-correlate (*anyāpoha*) which is inherent in all those entities which are not pertinent contextually. For example, the notion of "non-cow" is identifiable in all those animals which are non-cow. It is important to point out here that a word excludes its counter-correlates at the two levels:

(a) at the level of genus or class.

- as cow excludes non-cow (horse, ox, buffalo, etc.)

(b) at the level of individual

- as cow_1 excludes cow_2, cow_3 .... cow_4

So according to Dharmakīrti meaning is constituted by the exclusion of the counter-correlates. Here we should not be mistaken in believing that the meaning is a counter-correlate of the object. What Dharmakīrti is arguing for is the cognition of that positive entity which emerges from the exclusion of contextually incompatible objects. Meaning is nothing but experience or cognition. There are various ways of constituting cognition. Verbal import is also one of them.

25. *Ibid., anyāpoho vastubhūtaḥ.*

In the chapter on inference (*svārthānumāna*), Dharmakīrti concretises the theory of meaning. He states that by means of exclusion the word only indicates the difference between the two sets:

{Cow}	→	not {non-cow}
finite or single set		infinite set

Words have potentiality only to explicate this difference. They do not posit any essential nature of the entity (*vastu dharma*).[26] Words are included in inference but this does not amount to expounding that the word is equal to inference. In that case it will become an independent means of knowledge. In fact, words in the Buddhist thought are related to inference for one's self only. Hence, *apoha* (the differential signification of word) is not contradicted by any other means of knowledge.[27] *Apoha* refers to conceptual meaning (*baudhārtha*) in which the contextual elimination takes place in the mind.[28] Words do not establish any real and positive entity in themselves.[29]

Dharmakīrti states that differences among the object are posited on the basis of their respective substratum. The identity of an object has two aspects — positive as well as negative. When we know an object we know what it is in itself and also what it is not. For instance, a tree is a positive entity as well as a negative one in the form of non-tree. Both the aspects are expressed in the verbal comprehension. These two aspects are mutually exclusive and through difference they qualify each other and by this process the identity of an

26. *Ibid.*, (*Pratyakṣa Pariccheda*), 173.
27. *Ibid.* (*Svārthānumāna*), 46.
28. *Ibid.*, 88.
29. *Ibid.*, 91-92.

object is established.[30] But again, it is important to recall that this verbal import does not operate at the level of the transcendental truth (*pāramārthika*).

With this exposition of *apoha* theory by Dharmakīrti the phase of primary formulation comes to an end. The later two other great theoreticians Śāntarakṣita and Ratnakīrti responded to the sustained criticism of this theory mainly by the schools of Mīmāṁsā, Nyāya and Alaṁkāra (poeticians). In this tradition of one thousand years, debate on the theory has been re-interpreted and has undergone some modifications. But even this new interpretation/modification has been done in maintaining consistency with the major premises of Buddhism and with the authority of the original expounder, Diṅnāga.

Śāntarakṣita (eighth century AD), a Svatantra Mādhyamika philosopher, examines the import of words in the 16th chapter of his *Tattvasaṁgraha*. He sets forth the arguments in support of the view that truth is amenable to words and that what we designate as verbal cognition is nothing but only the superimposition of mental construction on the object. Kamalaśīla (author of *Pañjikā*, the renowned commentary on *Tattvasaṁgraha*) comments,

> There is nothing real that is expressed by words, all verbal cognition is expressed by words, all verbal cognition is deviant because it proceeds by imposing non-difference upon things that are really different. In a case where there is indirect connection with an entity, there is some sort of agreement with the object, even though the cognition is really deviant.[31]

---

30. *Pramāṇasamuccaya*, 113- 4.

31. Kamalaśīla's *Pañjikā* on 867-68 of *Tattvasaṁgraha* (henceforth *TS*).

The real essence (*svalakṣaṇa*) of the objects is not really cognized in the linguistic expressions. Śāntarakṣita critiques the illusory nature of verbal import and states that the "unique particular" cannot be determined by convention and usage which are prerequisites for verbal cognition.

Śāntarakṣita extensively records the criticism against the *apoha* theory of meaning by the Schools of Poetics (Bhāmaha), Mīmāṁsā (Kumārilabhaṭṭa) and Nyāya (Uddyotakara) in more than hundred verses and opines that these views of the opponents' school are wrong and based upon ignorance of what is meant by *apoha* — negation/exclusion of the other things.

From the verse 1003-4 he starts formulating and reinterpreting *apoha* theory mainly from the linguistic point of view. He establishes that *apoha* is of two kinds due to the difference between relative and absolute negation. Again the relative negation is of two kinds due to the difference of conception of idea and object. We may present them like this:

Negation (*apoha*)[32]

Relative/partial (*paryudāsa*) — Absolute (*prasajya pratiṣedha*)

Negation of ideal universal/conception (*budhyātman*) — Negation of
object (*arthātman*)

Absolute negation is complete denial or prohibition. In the relative or partial negation the negative suffix which bears this meaning (as in *anātman*, the negative suffix *ana*) posits

32. *TS*, 1003-4.

two facts — that there is a negation of some positive entity and simultaneously it also suggests that instead of that entity which has been negated something else is present. For example, consider a crucial term *anātman*. It denies the existence of *ātman* on the one hand, on the other it posits the existence of *dharma*.

We may summarize the three kinds of *apoha* as follows:

1. *Ideal*: no external reality (*budhyātman*) subjective, discrete and self-contained, negative, implication, functional at two levels — (i) at the level of class, and (ii) at the level of individual.
2. *Objective*: another name for the particular instance in question. That cognitive image which was of subjective nature now amounts to becoming objective (*arthātman*).
3. *Absolute*: attested by our own experience and introspection: this particular is "not non-cow" (= cow, and nothing else).

It seems these types of *apoha* constitute an integral hierarchy in verbal cognition. Only first of these *apoha* is directly expressed by words. Rest of these two function in complete integrity and harmony with it. Kamalaśīla, commenting on the verse 1011 of the *Tattvasaṁgraha* says (establishes), "what actually appears from the verbal cognition is only the reflection of the external object and this is the denotation of words."[33] The *absolute negation* is also (like the second type) apprehended by implication or suggestion as the nature of this thing is not the nature of other things.[34]

Śāntarakṣita explains why the name *apoha* has been postulated for the verbal cognition.[35]

33. *TS*, 1011 and *Pañjikjā* thereupon.

34. *TS*, 1013-15.

35. *TS*, 1007-9.

(a) because it appears excluded from other appearances;

(b) because it is the cause of the cognition of the thing as excluded from others (cause-effect relationship is always implicit as stated above);

(c) because it is cognized through an entity "excluded" (from others); and

(d) because it is apprehended in the form of the specific individuality (*svalakṣaṇa*) consisting in exclusion of unlike things.

Some critics have found this last argument inconsistent and contrary to the original expounder's view regarding the import of word. They try to establish that Śāntarakṣita has modified the theory under compulsion caused by the opponent theoreticians as he accepts the "specific individuality" (which is a positive, objective and only real entity in the Buddhist thought) as the import of word. Certainly, this criticism is superficial and baseless. We have already stated above that the Buddhist theoreticians have never given up the possibility of interpreting *apoha* with reference to "unique particular" or "specific individuality." This should be taken as the strength of the theory rather than a weakness. *Apoha* refers to specific individuality only indirectly or figuratively. The specific individuality is inexpressible so it does not come under the domain of verbal import. Moreover, in the verbal import it appears in the mind of the hearer confounded by its sameness with the exclusion of "unlike things." This standpoint does not amount to saying that *svalakṣaṇa* is the import of words. Responding to the counter-agrument put forth by Uddyotakara in *Nyāyavārttika* (2.2.63) against Diṅnāga, Śāntarakṣita very clearly establishes, "When the word brings about the exclusion of other things, it is said to *denote* its own meaning and there is no incongruity in this."[36] In fact, this is the *absolute apoha* (the third type) that *appears* in the hearer's mind as "unique particular" (*svalakṣaṇa*). This serves the substratum for the "exclusion of unlike." Śāntarakṣita states in the support of revered Diṅnāga declaration, "The word is said to 'denote' because it produces a reflection of the conception of the external thing; it does not touch the exclusive factor in the shape of the *specific individuality*; apart from the said production of the reflection, there is no other denotative function of the word."[37] *Svalakṣaṇa* as stated above comes close to the concept of *śūnya* (Śāntarakṣita is a Mādhyamika philosopher). An object is devoid of any self-nature (*svabhāva śūnya*). So the word cannot refers to this specific individuality. Again, if *svalakṣaṇa* or *śūnya* refer to any transcendental object (that is in constant flux or that is beyond the four categories of (i) it exists, (ii) it does not exist, (iii) it exists as well as it does not exist, and (iv) it neither exists nor it does not exist),[38] it is inexpressible and cannot be a part of the verbal import. *Apoha* may suggest/indicate figuratively this ultimate reality in terms of endless deferment or exclusion (*neti, neti*). *Svalakṣaṇa* is not a positive entity (only) as is mistaken by the realist schools of thought like the Nyāya and the Mīmāṁsā. Śāntarakṣita categorically states that words refer to the conceptual construct only and all cognitions brought about by words are *ultimately false*.[39] Verbal cognition is just like the meaning of an expression that a man whose eye has been attacked by a disorder says to another suffering from the same disorder: an expression such as "there are two moons."[40]

---

36. *TS*, 1016.
37. *TS*, 1017-18.
38. See *Mūlamadhyamaka Kārikā*, 1.7, 18.5, 18.9.
39. *TS* 1212.
40. *TS* 1211.

Only in one place Śāntarakṣita seems to hold a different position from that of Diṅnāga. Diṅnāga possibly does not indicate that exclusion of the counter-correlates is achieved secondarily/indirectly by means of implication. But this extension of the theory does not change the basic theoretical position. The contribution of Śāntarakṣita is that by introducing two more types of *apoha* — objective and absolute — he saved the theory from falling in the vicious circle of "cow" means the exclusion of "non-cow" and has made it competent for the analysing discourses constituted in language. He holds that externality attributed to these exclusions is only assumed (imaginary) and not real. In reality difference and non-difference subsists only in real things.[41]

Ratnakīrti (ninth century AD) in his *Apohasiddhiḥ* elaborates upon the *apoha* theory in view of the criticism by the Nyāya school. His reinterpretation of the theory is known as theory of qualified *apoha* (*viśiṣṭāpoha*). He criticizes the position taken by Śāntarakṣita that words posit their negative meanings secondarily. He asserts that no successive stage (like primary and secondary) is involved in the verbal comprehension. He defines *apoha* (with reference to Diṅnāga's position) as positive entity qualified by the exclusion of the other which is contextually incompatible. The meaning of a word is conceptually a distinctive concept which is actually an experiential content in terms of its distinction or negation of other terms. Ratnakīrti extends *apoha* at the level of sentential meaning and maintains that each word in a sentence excludes its counter-correlate. For example,

"This road leads to Mathurā."

Here "this" negates "non-this" (that, etc.), "road" excludes "non-roads" (not street, etc.) and so and so forth. A sentential

---

41. *TS* 1047.

meaning is also posited/conveyed by means of negation of the incompatible objects.

This long journey of *apoha* theory from Diṅnāga to Ratnakīrti evidences its own strength. It has never deviated from its original theoretical standpoint. Even the new interpretations of the theory by Śāntarakṣita and Ratnakīrti in order to meet the counter-arguments from the opponents' schools are not inconsistent with that of the original expounders. Śāntarakṣita, in response to the denial of positive connotation of a word in *Hetumukha* (of Diṅnāga) states that the Master denied the positive content of meaning from the logical standpoint. There is no objective reality in the verbal import but he does not mean the negative content of the direct import.[42] Dharmakīrti, in his auto-commentary of *Pramāṇa-vārttika* quotes the Master, "Differentiation is the meaning of the word. What is meant by this is not merely affirmation nor merely negation, but an affirmation qualified by negation of its counter-correlates."[43]

Critique of the Apoha Theory of Meaning

There has been a long debate in the tradition over this issue of verbal import. All of that cannot be reproduced here. Hence, only the potential critique of the theory (*apoha*) is being taken up.

Bhāmaha, a poetician of the middle of sixth century AD (*Kāvyālaṁkāra*, Chapter VI) lists three objections to the theory: (i) that if the term "cow" connotes only the negation of "non-cow" then how does it account for the positive concept of "cow;" (ii) that the same word cannot connote two opposite

42. *TS* 1097.

43. Quoted by D. Sharma in his translation of *Apohasiddhiḥ*, p. 52 — *śabdorthantara-vyāvṛtii-viśiṣṭaneva bhāvanāheti.*

meanings; (iii) that the word primarily expresses its positive meaning and only then we can exclude what are its counter-correlates.

There is some fundamental misconception in Bhāmaha's comprehension of this theory. The phrase *anyāpohana* (in the verse 6.16-19 of *Kāvyālaṁkāra*) actually means *atadvyāvṛtti* which simply signifies "negation of those elements which are opposed to the positive entity which a word actually refers to."[44] Again positive and negative are not contradictory but complementary to each other. Bhāmaha rightly thinks that *apoha*, like any other theory of meaning is a theory of cognition. But it deals not only with cognition but also how this cognition is constituted. This cognition is constituted by means of "differentiation" as explained above.

The critique of the theory by Kumārilabhaṭṭa (a great Mīmāṁsaka philosopher of seventh century AD) is more exhaustive and insightful. He examines the *apoha* theory in his celebrated work *Ślokavārttika* (section on *apoha*). It could be summarized with the Buddhist rejoinder as follows:

(i) "Those who admit universal 'negation of non-cow' as the verbal import, have by expression, admitted the universal 'cow' as an entity."[45]

In the Mīmāṁsā School of thought, as we have posited above, the positive and real universal is the import of words. Dharmakīrti expounds that universal (*sāmānya lakṣaṇa* as opposed to *svalakṣaṇa* in the Buddhist thought) is in its very essence exclusion of the other.[46] This universal is a differential conceptual construct

44. *TS*, 912-14.

45. *Ślokavārttika* (*SV*) *apohavāda* 1.

46. *Pramāṇavārttika* (*Pratyakṣa*), 30.

which has no direct access to the ontological reality. Moreover, it cannot be confirmed, Diṅnāga says, as it is neither in the substratum nor outside of it.

(ii) In response to Kumārila's argument that all inexistence has been held to be of the nature of some other "existence," the Buddhists hold that the positive entity in question is nothing but the real momentary and none other than the cow individual in-itself. This is intended to be the connotation of the word cow.

(iii) Kumārila consolidates his criticism, "If the import of the words be assumed to be of the nature of mere negation, then it would only be another kind of 'void' spoken by means of negative word. In that void, there would be no cognition and so it would be useless to posit *apoha* as the import of words."[47]

The Buddhists rejoin that the pure negative content of the word has been suggested from the logical point of view; . . . . that word has no reference to objective reality.[48] In *apoha* no question of mere negation emerges since the master has suggested himself that the positive entity is qualified by the exclusion of the others.

(iv) Every negation at last posits a positive entity.

Cow → not non-cow → cow (a positive entity)

Exponents' view: Every negation posits a positive entity in the form of ideas/image (*buddhyātman*) only. This subjective phenomenon is achieved through the differentiation or through excluding its counter-correlates.

---

47. *SV*, 919-20.
48. *TS*, 1097.

(v) Even in the case of individual cows (as white, red, black cows) this exclusive universal of the Buddhists functions well. Because all these individual cows are common in one way that they all exclude 'non-cow' and thus they form a class.

Kumārila's other main objections to the *apoha* theory are:

(a) The theory leads to absolute negativism and makes all linguistic activities utterly impossible.

(b) It fails to explain the negative particles, prepositions, verbal forms, number and gender.

(c) In the absence of the corresponding external object, *intuition* is expressed by the sentence and the same could be expressed by the word as well. So there is no need to postulate *apoha*.

Exponents' view:

(a) The concept of extreme or absolute itself goes against the major theoretical assumption of Buddhism (Philosophy of the Middle Path). Śāntarakṣita has already classified *apoha* as partial and complete which are twin concepts. Initially negation is partial but in the next stage this *appear*s to be complete in the form of "not non-cow." This ascertains the meaning of "cow" which is purely a conceptual construct (*baudhārtha* as opposed to *vāstavārtha* accepted in the Realist schools). This is the cognition of the object in the form of reflection which is posited by an imaginary "universal" (*sāmānya lakṣaṇa*). This, "universal" determines the meaning by the exclusion of "non-cow." Thus, the theory does not lead to any absolute negativism and it makes all linguistic activities possible at the level of phenomenal truth.

(b) The Buddhist theoreticians have argued for "nominalism" in the tradition. Form, substance, quality, gender, number, etc., are nothing but merely names "fabricated and postulated" and are devoid of any ontological content. These conceptual constructs are superimposed by the mind on the object. Śāntarakṣita has admirably established that the ideas of gender and number are not given but established conventionally. Here the will (*icchā*) of the speaker also plays a decisive role.[49]

(c) In regard to this view Śāntarakṣita agrees with Kumārila that *intuition* is expressed by the word and the sentence but maintains that even there *apoha* functions in the form of reflection.[50] Kamalaśīla elucidates, "We have described the meaning of the sentence as the form of Reflection, named 'Intuition;' so also is the meaning of word described in the same way. Because by the word also what is produced is the *apoha* in the form of *reflection*." Moreover, the intuition expressed by a particular word or sentence is bound to differ from other intuitions expressed by other words and sentences. This "other intuition" is negated in the context under discussion.

Thus, Kumārila's criticism has been answered. This debate helps to eliminate many doubts and speculations about the *apoha* theory. His criticism appears to be constructive rather than destructive. There is hardly any substance in the following remarks of the Naiyāyika, Jayantabhaṭṭa:

---

49. *TS*, 1122-34.

50. *TS*, 1028 and *Pañjikā* thereupon.

> Kumārilabhaṭṭa has brandished his sword of polemics with a view to demolishing the Buddhist position of negation of the opposite being the connotation of words.[51]

Uddyotakara (sixth century AD), a major thinker of Nyāya-Vaiśeṣika Shcool, in his *Nyāyavārttikam* has argued that in case of words such as "all" (*sarva*) the theory utterly fails, because there is possibly nothing that could be excluded.

Śāntarakṣita refutes this on the following grounds:

(a) The word "all" is used/presented in actual usage (in sentence or in certain utterance/context), hence something is excluded. In the sentence like, "All things are selfless," or "All men are gone" — what is apprehended is entirely by means of excluding the following counter-correlates:

"Only external things (jar, etc.) are selfless" or "Only some men can go." If the first set is an established fact then the second set (counter-correlates) would be false and this misconception is negated.[52]

(b) Neither "all" implies "the negation of one and the rest" which are mistaken for the parts of *all* and thus there is no "exclusion of its own meaning." "All" is not constituted of numerals like one, two, etc. This series may lead towards infinite; nevertheless, we would be able to posit "all." Here not even the question of the whole and its parts arises. The conceptual opposition of "all" is either with "some" or "none" (a category) which is, of course, negated.

---

51. Quoted by B.P, Bhattacharya in *A Study in Language and Meaning*, p. 97.

52. *TS*, 1185-88.

(c) What is the nature of "not non-cow"? If it is positive it is identical with the *cow* entity and if negative, it is "not-cow" which is not true.

Śāntarakṣita clearly states that in reality, it does not exist in the form it is apprehended. So it cannot be positive. But it cannot be negative also because it appears as an entity. Denotation of words is without any marked features because the features subsist in an actual object. So *apoha* has no markedness like — positive or negative, diverse or same, subsistent or non-subsistent, one or many, denoted or non-denoted.[53] This only leads to the "universal" of the object.

We have earlier suggested that the Buddhist logicians have tried to interpret *apoha* theory of meaning with reference to their meta-assumptions. Here, as Śāntarakṣita has stated above, we find an attempt to save *apoha* falling into a dichotomy and in this way the possibility of referring to the transcendental truth by implication has been maintained. Śāntarakṣita comments on the verbal expression, "What is expressed by words is only the reflection that appears, as created solely by impressions made by objectless (empty) conceptions."[54]

Vācaspati Miśra, an exemplary scholar and prolific writer of ninth century AD (in *Nyāyavārttika Tātparya Ṭīkā*) has quoted a verse of Diṅnāga which covers this whole discussion we have recorded so far. This is worth being quoted in full:

vikalpayonyaḥ śabdaḥ vikalpaḥ śabdoyonayaḥ ।
kārya kāraṇatā teṣāṁ nārthaṁ śabāḥ spṛśyantyapi ॥

The cause of words is the mental construct (*vikalpa*) and mental constructs are based on formation of words. Hence there is a cause-effect relationship between these two. Words do not even touch the ultimate reality.

53. *TS*, 1189-96.

54. *TS*, 1204.

Like *sphoṭa* theory of meaning, *apoha* has also an antique tradition in the Indian linguistic thought. Prof. Kunjuni Raja opines that the Buddhist theory of meaning has some similarity with the view of the great pre-Pāṇinian grammarian, Vyāḍi.[55] Vyāḍi also holds that the meaning of a sentence is not a conglomeration (*saṁgraha*) of word meanings but the mutual exclusion of these. But his view on word meaning as particular (*dravya*) seems close to the grammarian's theory of meaning. However, it is difficult to substantiate that Vyāḍi's concept of sentential meaning represents the early stages of Buddhist thought.

The strength and relevance of this theory could be deduced from the fact that it involves a very rich and live debate of around one thousand years. The schools of Grammarians, Mīmāṁsakas, Naiyāyikas and Jains, etc., have constantly commented upon this theory. In the first stage the theory seems to emerge from the classification of basic elements that constitute our world (i.e., *pañca skandha* — as name and form). The age of Diṅnāga and Dharmakīrti represents the second phase which provided a sound epistemological base. The third phase comes with Śāntarakṣita who not only classified the *apoha* but also attributed psychological-cognitive dimensions to it. The fourth phase involves the work of Ratnakīrti who gave a new orientation to this theory and reinterprets it as a "positive, qualified by negation."

In the linguistic philosophical debate of our century, some aspects of the Buddhist theory have been discussed in the West; though without due acknowledgement to these logicians — philosophers. This debate in fields of linguistics (late

55. See K.K. Raja, "The Theory of Meaning According to Buddhist Logicians," *Adyar Library Bulletin* (reprint), vol. XVIII, part 3-4 (undated) pp. 185-87.

nineteenth and early twentieth century), philosophy (around 1930) and lastly in literature (around 1960) started due to some subtle observation and powerful theory propounded by Ferdinand de Saussure who is known as the "Father of Structuralism." The competent linguistic theory advanced by him is very much close to the Buddhist's position on language and meaning. This deserves an independent study in the context of contemporary intellectual debates and any passing remark would not be much fruitful. The theory discussed by the great masters need not be reduced and misinterpreted just to establish its relevance in the contemporary debate. These issues and assumptions, whether addresed or un-addressed by the specific age have remained relevant all the time. Possibly no major theory of literature, language, aesthetics, philosophy, etc., in India has developed just to fit in a particular period. We have never perceived time in terms of synchrony and diachrony. There has always been a conscious effort to establish something beyond the co-ordinates of time and space. The exposition of Buddhist theory of meaning is such a noble advancement in this direction.

We conclude this discussion with this summing up from *Laṅkāvatārasūtra*:

> Words are neither different nor non-different form meaning and that meaning stands in the same relation to the words. If Mahāmati, meaning is different from words, it will not be made manifest by means of words; but meaning is entered into by (means of) words as things (are revealed) by a lamp.[56]

References

Bhāmaha, *Kāvyālaṁkāra* annotated by Acharya Devendranath Sharma, Patna: Bihar Rashtrabhasha Prakasana, 1962.

---

56. *Laṅkāvatārasūtra*, 3.33.

Bhartṛhari *Vākyapadīya (Brahma Kāṇḍa)*, ed. Pt. Suryanarayan Shukla, Varanasi: Chaukhamba Sanskrit Sansthana, 1990.

Bhattacharya, B.P., *A Study in Language and Meaning: A Critical Examination of Some Aspects of Indian Semantics*, Calcutta: Progressive Publishers, 1962.

Dharmakīrti, *Pramāṇavārttikaṁ of Ācārya Dharmakīrti* (ed. Ramchandra Pandey), Delhi: Motilal Banarsidass, 1989.

Hattori, M. *Diṅnāga, on the Interpretation of Sign*, London: Kluwer Academic Publisher, 1987.

Kapoor, Kapil, "The Concept of *Padārtha* in Philosophy and Language" *The 200 Years William Jones Memorial Volume*, Pune: Deccan College, 1994-95.

——— "Linguistic Meaning and Referential Reality" (mimeographed) 1991.

Kumārilabhaṭṭa, *Ślokavārttika* (tr. Ganganath Jha), Delhi: Satguru Publication, 1990.

Mookherjee, Satkari, *Buddhist Philosophy of Universal Flux*, Delhi: Motilal Banarsidass, 1935.

Nāgārjuna, *Mūlamādhyamika Kārikā* (tr./ed. David Kalupahana), Delhi: Motilal Banarsidass, 1986.

Podolony, R., *Something is Called Nothing* (tr. Nicholas Weinstein), Moscow: Mir Publication, 1986

Raja, K. Kunjuni, *Indian Theories of Meaning*, Madras: The Adyar Library and Research Centre, 1977.

Ratnakīrti, *Apohasiddhi* (tr. D. Sharma in *The Differentiation Theory of Meaning in Indian Logic*), The Hague: Mouton, 1969.

Śāntarakṣita, *Tattvasaṁgraha* (tr. Ganganath Jha), Delhi: Motilal Banarsidass, 1937.

de Saunssure F., *Course in General Linguistics* (ed. Charles Balley & Albert Sechehaye from French by Wade Baskim), London: Peter Owen, 1994.

Shastri, Swami Dwarikadas, *Apohavādaḥ*, Varanasi: Bauddha Bharati, 1992.

Stcherbatsky, Th., *Buddhist Logic* (2 vols.), Delhi: Motilal Banarsidass, 1993.

Suzuki, D.T. (tr.), *The Laṅkāvatārasūtra· A Mahāyāna Text*, London: Routledge & Kegan Paul, 1932.

4

A Critical Study of Ajita Keśakambali and his Philosophical Views

Upendra Rao

ACCORDING to the Buddhist records Ajita Keśakambali was believed to be the contemporary of Buddha. Buddha lived between 563 to 486 BC.

The sixth century BC, which was the period of both Ajit and Buddha, has given birth to many of the great figures in the world. Confucius and Lao Tzu in China; Thales, Xenophanes, Pythagoras, Heraclitus in greater Greece; Zarathustra in Persia; Jeremiah and the second Isaiah in Israel, all were spreading their views.[1] It seems probable that in the sixth century BC the mental life of India was in ferment and was permeated by a mass of mutually contradictory theories about the universe and man's place in it, some verging on the bizarre in their fancifulness, others more capable of logical justification. The chief mouthpieces of the new ideas were Buddha and Mahāvīra but many others, including the six heretics, have made some contribution to the thought of their time.

---

1. दीघनिकायट्ठकथा I.144; M.A II.233.

While unorthodox systems of Buddhism, Jainism and Ajivikism crystallized around the names of Buddha and Mahāvīra and Makkhali Gosāla respectively, the other finished doctrines are attributed to the six heretics in various parts of the Pāli canon, Makkhali Gosāla being one of them whose Ājivikism held sway contemporarily with Buddhism and Jainism. These heretics seem to be dissatisfied with the system of orthodox Brāhmaṇism which seems to have swept over the Ganges valley in the sixth and fifth centuries BC. The names of these six heretics are:

1. Pūrana Kassapa
2. Makkhali Gosāla
3. Ajita Keśakambali
4. Pakudha Kaccāyana
5. Sañjaya Belatthi Putta and
6. Niganta Nātaputtas (in fact, the actual word used for these heretics in the *Dīgha Nikāya* is *titthakara* (अयं देव, अजितो केसकम्बलो . . . यसस्सी . . . तित्थकरो) which means the propounder of the doctrines: तीर्थं शास्त्रं करोति इति तीर्थकरः। This word is also used in the *Viṣṇusahasranāma* as मनोजवस्तीर्थकरो; in *Vācaspatya* it is mentioned that चतुर्दशविद्यानां बाह्यसमस्यानाञ्च प्रणेता प्रयक्ता चेति तीर्थकरो, etc.)

In *Dīgha-Nikāya* each one of these is depicted in the same terms as each is referred to as the leader of an order (*gaṇacariya*) well-known, famous, the founder of a sect (*titthakara*), respected as a saint (*sādhu-sammato*), revered by many people, a homeless wanderer of long standing (*cirapabbajito*) and advanced in years.

Ajita Keśakambali was one of the six heretics mentioned in the *Dīgha-Nikāya*. When we check the texts of Pāli literature to locate Ajita, we find 11 other wanderers, brāhmaṇas and *arhants* with the name Ajita. But they are different from Ajita Keśakambali. Let us now see what Ajita Keśakambali means.

This heretic's personal name was Ajita and the title of Keśakambali was attributed to him because of his garb. Ajita used to wear a blanket of hair (Kesakambala). This blanket, as per the commentary of the *Dīgha-Nikāya*, contained human hair. In the Pāli canons this blanket was described as the meanest of all garments. It was cold in winter, hot in summer, ill-coloured, foul-smelling and unpleasant to touch.

There are references in the Pāli texts that during this period a blanket was a type of dress adopted by ascetics.[2] Ajita is always grouped with the other five leaders of the heretical sects and his name comes third in order.

Ajita's philosophical views are preserved in the *Sāmānna-phalasutta* of the *Dīgha-Nikāya*. Let us, therefore, have a look at it from the hisṭorical perspective. While the Buddha accompanied by the 1250 *bhikṣus* was staying at Rājagṛha, the then capital of the Magadha dynasty, King Ajātaśatru wanted to know about the appreciable benefits to be derived from asceticism *sandiṭṭhakaṁ sāmaññaphalam* (सन्दिट्ठकं सामञ्ञफलम्) just like the benefits of various worldly trades and professions. He put this question to many ascetics and brāhmaṇas but had received no satisfactory answer from them.

On hearing the question from the King, Pūrana Kassapa answered that "when we act or cause others to act, it is not the soul that acts or causes others to act. The soul is in fact a passive one (*niṣkriya*)." King Ajātaśatru being dissatisfied with this answer puts the same question to the other four. Makkhali Gosāla says,

---

2. दीघनिकायपालि I.167 and मज्झिमनिकायपालि I.78, and अङ्गुत्तरनिकायपालि I.240.

"There is neither cause nor a basis for the sins of living beings." Gosāla maintains that in the world as a whole all come about by necessity, and fate regulates them all. Pakudha Kaccāyana tells that the seven elementary categories are neither made nor ordered, neither caused nor constructed. They are barren, as firm as mountains and as stable as pillars. These seven are the bodies of the earth, of water, of fire, of air, of joy and of sorrow with life as the seventh one. Individual beings may come and go without affecting in the least either the nature or the existence of the substrata of change.

Niganta Nātaputta says that one should practise restraint with regard to water, and then he avoids all sins, and thus surrounded by the barrier of a fourfold restraint one's mind is perfected, controlled and firm. Sañjaya Belatthiputta says, "If you ask me if there is another world and if I believe that there was, I should tell you so. But that is not what I say. I don't say that it is so; I don't say that it is otherwise; I don't say that it is not so, nor do I say that it is not not so." Thus the same formula is followed after various hypothetical questions. We can synthesize their theories in the following manner:

1. Pūrana Kassapa's theory was Antinomianism (though the word antinomianism is used by some authors for *akriyāvāda* it does not seem to be the correct word for it. Actually it denotes the doctrine that the Christians are released by grace from the obligation of observing moral law. This view was attributed to St. Paul by his opponents and was held by many of the Gnostic sects). *akriyāvādaḥ* (अक्रियावादः)।
2. Makkhali Gosāla's theory was Determinism. *sansāraśuddhivādaḥ athavā akarmaṇyatāvādaḥ athavā daivavādaḥ* (संसारशुद्धिवादः अथवा अकर्मण्यतावादः अथवा दैववादः)।

3. Pakudha Kaccāyana's theory was the postulation of seven elements or substances. *saptakāyavādaḥ athavā nityapadārthavādaḥ* (सप्तकायवादः अथवा नित्यपदार्थवादः)।
4. Niganta Nātaputta's theory was the doctrine of the fourfold restraint. *cāturyāmaṁsavaravādaḥ athavā sarvajñatā-vādaḥ* (चातुर्यामसंवरवादः अथवा सर्वज्ञतावादः)।
5. Sañjaya Belatthiputta's theory was of prevaricating scepticism. *amarāvikṣepavādaḥ athavā anekāntavādaḥ* (अमराविक्षेपवादः अथवा अनेकान्तवादः)।
6. Ajita Keśakambali, while replying to the King's question, unveils his own theory of Materialism.

What Ajita says is that there is no merit in almsgiving, sacrifice or offering, no result of good or evil deeds, and one cannot pass from this world to the next.[3] (Here Buddhaghoṣa says that Ajita admitted the existence of the world beyond but mortals cannot enter that.)

There is no afterlife, there are no ascetics or brāhmaṇas who have reached perfection on the right path and who, having known and experienced this world and the world beyond, publish their knowledge. Man is formed of four elements; when he dies, the earth returns to the earth, the water returns to the water, the fire returns to the fire and the air returns to the air and his senses vanish into the space. Four persons with the *bier* take the corpse; they gossip about the dead man as far as the burning ground where his bones turn the colour of a dove's wing and his sacrifices end in ashes. They are fools

3. Here Buddhaghoṣa the commentator of *Tripiṭaka*s says नत्थि अयं लोकोति परलोके ठितस्सपि अयं लोको नत्थि। नत्थि परलोकोति इधलोके ठितस्सपि परलोको नत्थि। सब्बे तत्थ तत्थेव उच्छिज्जन्तीति दस्सेति (सं. नास्ति अयं लोकः इति परलोके स्थितस्यापि अयं लोकः नास्ति, नास्ति परलोकः इति इहलोके स्थितस्यापि परलोको नास्ति। सर्वे तत्र तत्रैव उच्छेद्यन्ते इति दर्शयति) सुमङ्गलविलासिनी दीघनिकायट्ठकथा। I.P 165).

who preach almsgiving and those who maintain the existence of immaterial categories speak nonsense. When the body dies, both fool and wise alike are cut off and perish. They do not survive after death.[4] But according to the Pāli canon (*Dīgha-Nikāya*) King Ajātaśatru does not appreciate Ajita's words just as those of the other five ascetics. He tells Buddha that their answers to his question were very different.[5]

A similar passage about Ajita Keśakambali's doctrine is found in the *Sūtrakṛtāṅga*, a text of Jaina Ardhamāgadhī canon.[6]

---

4. नत्थि दिन्नं नत्थि यिट्ठिं नत्थि हुतं नत्थि सुकतदुक्कतानं कम्मानं फलं विपाको, नत्थि अयं लोको नत्थि परो लोको, नत्थि पिता, नत्थि सत्ता ओपपातिका, नत्थि लोके समणब्राह्मणा सम्मग्गता सम्मापतिपन्ना सत्ता ओपपातिका, नत्थि लोके समणब्राह्मणा सम्मग्गता सम्मापटिपन्ना ये इमं च लोकं परं च लोकं सयं अभिञ्ञा सच्छिकतत्वा पवेदेन्ति। चातुमहाभूतिको अयं पुरिसो यदा कालं करोति, पठवी पठविकायं अनुपेति, अनुपगच्छति, वायो वायोकायं अनुपेति अनुपगच्छति, आकासं इन्द्रियानि सङ्कमन्ति। आसन्दिपञ्चमा पुरिसा मतं आदाय गच्छन्ति। यावाकाहना पदानि पञ्ञायन्ति। कपोतकानि अट्ठीनि भवन्ति। भस्सन्ता आहुतियो। दत्तुपञ्ञत्तं यदिदं दानं। तेसं तुच्छं मुसा विलापो ये केचि अत्थिकवादं वदन्ति, बाले च पण्डिते च कायस्स भेदा उच्छिज्जन्ति, विनस्सन्ति, न होन्ति परंमरणा ति।

   — *Dīgha-Nikāya*, Pali Publication Board, Bihar Govt., General Editor, Bhikshu Jagadish Kasyap, 1958, 48, 49.

5. इत्थं खो मे भन्ते अजितो केसकम्बलो सन्दिट्ठिकं सामञ्ञफलं पुट्ठो समानो उच्छेदं व्याकासि। सेय्यथापि भन्ते अम्बं वा पुट्ठो लबुजं व्याकरेय्य, लबुजं वा पुट्ठो अम्बं व्याकरेय्य ...... सो खो अहं भन्ते अजितस्स केसकम्बलस्स भाखोतं नेव अभिनन्दिं, नप्पटिक्कोसिं।

   — *Dīgha-Nikāya*, Pali Publication Board, Bihar Govt., General Editor, Bhikshu J. Kasyap, 1958, 49).

6. 1. पत्तेयं कसिणे आया जे बाला जे य पंडिता।
   संति पेच्चा ण ते संति णत्थि सत्तावववाइया॥
   2. णत्थि पुण्णे व पावे वा णत्थि लोए इतो परे।
   सरीरस्स विणासेणं विणासो होति देहिणो॥

   — सूत्रकृताङ्ग : प्रथमःउद्देशकः गाथा 11, 12, p. 25, श्री आगम प्रकाशन समिति, ब्यावर, राजस्थान।

In the *Sūtrakṛtāṅga* we find an interesting passage: upwards from the soles of the feet, downwards from the tips of the hair on the head, within the skin's surface is what is called soul (*jīva*) or what is known as *ātman*. The whole soul lives. When this body is dead it does not live. It lasts as long as the body lasts. Other men carry it (viz., the corpse) away to burn it and when it has been consumed by fire only dove-coloured bones remain and the four bearers return with the hearse to their village. Therefore, there is no soul that exists apart from the body. Those who belive that there is no soul speak the truth. But on the contrary those who maintain that the soul is something different from the body cannot tell whether the soul can be separated from the body. Is it long or small? Is it globular or circular or tringular or square of sexagonal or octagonal? Is it black or blue or red or yellow or white or of good smell or of bad smell, is it bitter or pungent or astringent or sour or sweet or hard or soft, heavy or light, cold or hot, smooth or rough? Those, therefore, who believe that there is, and exists no soul speak the truth. Those who maintain that the soul is something different from the body don't see the following objections.

As a man draws a sword from the scabbard and shows it to you saying, friend, this is the sword and that is the scabbard; as a man draws a fibre from a stalk of *mūñja* grass and shows it you saying, friend, this is the stalk and that is the fibre, or takes a bone out of the flesh or the seed of *āmalaka* from the palm of his hand or a particle of fresh butter out of coagulated milk and shows you both things separately or as he presses oil from the seed of *atasi* and shows the oil and oil cake separately or as he presses the juice from the sugarcane and shows the juice and the molasses separately, so nobody can show you the soul and the body separately.

Those who believe that there is and exists no soul, speak the truth and those who speak differently are wrong. In the *Sūtrakṛtāṅga* these ascetics are censured harshly and labelled as murderers. As per the *Sūtrakṛtāṅga* these murderers say kill, dig, slay, burn, cut, or break into pieces, destroy, for life ends here and there is no world beyond. These *śramaṇa*s cannot inform us about whether the action is good or bad, meritorious or not. They shamelessly propagate their own law. Others believe and adopt it saying: well, you speak the truth O! *śramaṇa*! and they present food, drink, sweet, robe, bowl, etc.[7] (*śramaṇa* means a *yati* or ascetic). *Śrāmyati tapasyati iti śramaṇaḥ* "श्राम्यति तपस्यति इति श्रमणः" In the *Rāmāyaṇa* also this word has been used (1.14.12) *tāpasī bhuñjate cāpi śramaṇaścaiva bhuñjate* "तापसी भुञ्जते चापि श्रमणश्चैव भुञ्जते."

Thus in the records of the Buddhist and Jaina canons Ajita has denied a past and future life, virtue and vice, heaven and hell, the fruits of good or evil deeds. He has denounced the Brāhmaṇic ritualism upholding the theory that man is composed of four elements which disperse at death; he rejected the Upaniṣadic theory of *ātman*. His views come very close to those of Cārvāka, the materialists who followed the Lokāyata system propounded by Bṛhaspati, a legendary figure.

Cārvāka denied a future life and said that the individual was formed of four elements — earth, water, fire and air — and that consciousness (*caitanyam*) was a product of the combination of these four elements which destruct with the body at death. They have preached that if one enters heaven by killing many animals in a *Jyotiṣṭoma* sacrifice, why does he not replace the animal with his own father? *Paśūñcennihataḥ svargaṁ jyotiṣṭhome gamiṣyati । svapitā yajamānena tatra kasmānna*

---

7. Sacred Books of the East, vol. XLV, *Jaina Sūtras*, Part II, Motilal Banarsidass, and tr. from Prākṛt, Herman Jacobi, pp. 339 to 346.

hinsyate? (पशूश्चेन्निहतः स्वर्गं ज्योतिष्ठोमे गमिष्यति। स्वपिता यजमानेन तत्र कस्मान्न हिंस्यते?) ॥ see the *Sarvadarśana Saṁgraha* of Madhvācārya — verses 3-11; as cited in *A Short History of Indian Materialism*. Ajita too was a materialist and preached the doctrine of annihilation (*Ucchedavāda*) and hence B.M. Barua described him as the historical founder of Indian Materialism.[8]

In the book *A History of Indian Materialism, Sensationalism and Hedonism* the author says that Indian materialism has passed through four logical stages of development such as Bārhaspatya, Svabhāvavāda, Cārvāka and Buddhism. Ajita has two aspects to his doctrine: one is negative and the other is positive. In the negative aspect his doctrine has a resemblance to that of Epicurus, a Greek philosopher who rejected purpose in nature and denied the moral government of the world. Epicurus was the exponent of ancient materialism and lived between 314 and 270 BC. He defined philosophy as a daily business of speech and thought to ensure a happy life. In his opinion the soul is a corporeal substance, a compound of atoms of four different species. There is a close similarity between these Epicurean doctrines and those of Ajita's. On the positive side, however, he seems to be a Stoic. According to the early Stoic philosopher's doctrine, knowledge and its pursuit are no longer held to be ends in themselves. Reason alone could reveal the constancy of cosmic order and the originative source of unyielding value; thus reason becomes the true model for human existence. To him the world is composed of material things with some few exceptions.

In the later periods these teachings of Ajita exercised multi-dimensional effects on Cārvākas. Bṛhaspati was a materialist

8. *A History of Pre-Buddhistic Indian Philosophy*, by Benimadhab Barua, Motilal Banarsidass, 1970, p. 228.

and Parameṣṭhin was a sceptic but both had similarities with the doctrines of Ajita.

Buddha seems to have simply rejected Ajita's doctrines whereas Mahāvīra terms him as ignorant and a speaker of unrealistic theories.

The Pāli canon talks about only the four elements and is silent about Ajita's view of the soul. But the parallel Jaina *Sūtrakṛtāṅga*'s passage gives his theory of the soul which is similar to Cārvāka's view that the soul is not different from the body.

No original work of the Cārvāka School is available at present. The *Sarvadarśana* account of Cārvāka's philosophy is a curious combination of Ajita and Payasi. Payasi, the chieftain of Setavya in Kośala who appears on the scene a few years after the Buddha's *nirvāṇa*, professed views very close to those of Ajita. He says that "there is no other world, there are no beings reborn other than from parents, there is no fruit or result of deeds well-done or ill-done." He gives various arguments in support of his theory of Annihilation, each of which is however refuted by Kumārakaśyapa the disciple of Buddha and who finally wins him over to the teachings of Buddha. (Payasi Rajanna Suttam of *Dīgha-Nikāya* 316ff.). The work of Jayasuri called *Tattvopaplava Siṁha* is an important new chapter in the history of Indian philosophy. *Tattvopaplava* means "upsetting of all principles."

Jayasūri Bhaṭṭa, who probably belonged to the first half of the seventh century AD, rejected *anumāna-pramāṇa* and accepted Bṛhaspati as his *guru* with whose permission he demolished the doctrines of the other schools. Though no original *sūtra* of Bṛhaspati is available, in the later periods some of the genuine *Lokāyata-Sūtras* were rescued from the obscurity[9] and gleaned from various commentaries. Out of these eight, the seventh aphorism quoted by Śrīdhara (in his commentary on the *Bhagavad-Gītā*) which says *tathāca bārhaspatyaṁ sūtram* (तथाच बार्हस्पत्यं सूत्रम्) or that which belongs to Bṛhaspati of the Lokāyata School is an important one, for its close relation with the doctrine of Ajita.

In sāmaññaphalasutta of *Dīgha-Nikāya* it is not clear that Ajita like Cārvāka advocated hedonism. Ajita Keśakambali was identified with some Kambalasvatāra, a Cārvāka mentioned in *Tattvasaṁgraha*. His theory of consciousness proceeds from the body itself which is equipped with the five life breaths: *prāṇa, apāna, samāna, udāna,* and *vyāna*.[10]

What Ajita meant by his doctrine is not clear but his views have certainly stimulated the thinking of Indian philosophers of that age. It seems that the Pāli and Ardhmāgadhī accounts have not rightly projected his views. Therefore, they always wanted to see them through their own angle and refuted without proper investigation which can be inferred from their interpretation of views of Ajita. But Ajita's views were accepted by the people of those times. His revolutionary thoughts proved to be great hindrances for the spread of the ideologies of Buddha and Mahāvīra.

The Buddhists claimed that they had defeated Ajita. Hieun-Tsang speaks of a monastery in Śrāvastī where the Buddha is said to have held a discussion with the six heretics including Ajita. He also refers to a *stūpa* erected on the spot where Sāriputra silenced the six heretics. In a book named *Buddhist*

---

9. 1. पृथिव्यप्तेजोवायुरिति तत्त्वानि 2. तत्समुदाये शरीरेन्द्रियविषयसंज्ञा 3. तेभ्यश्चैतन्यम् 4. किण्वादिभ्योमदशक्तिवत् 5. काम एवैकः पुरुषार्थः 6. अनुमानमप्रमाणम् 7. चैतन्यविशिष्टः कायः पुरुषः 8. मरणमेवापवर्गः

10. *Tattvasaṁgraha*, 1864.

Records of the Western World (book XI p. 10) a reference is also made to a monastery and a *stūpa*, built where the Buddha defeated them.

All the information we can glean about Ajita Keśakambali is from the works of other systems where he is treated as a heretic of hedonism. One can obviously understand that these accounts of other systems may not be free from prejudice. Mahāvīra in *Sūtrakṛtāṅga* censured the doctrines of Ajita who teaches men to kill, burn and destroy and to be engaged in pleasures as there is no world beyond. But if we carefully study these accounts we experience that the reality was something different. In fact, Ajita has fully understood the momentariness of human life and taught others about the same. Contemplating on death, he experiences the transitoriness of worldly pleasures developing a dispassion towards them. In reality it appears that he was the actual examiner of the soul, more than any soul-accepter (*ātmavādin*). When, during his investigation, he could not find a concrete proof of the soul he started disbelieving in the theory of the soul. He was also extremely troubled and disgusted when he heard a number of theories of soul emanating from various heretics and brāhmaṇas who described the soul from various angles without probing into the problem perfectly. Hence, Ajita asked the people not to follow these stereotyped utterances but to believe in life and to think about the problems related to life.

In fact, Ajita's assertions were not baseless. An Upaniṣadic passage formed the background to his views said that one should follow life more than think about the soul.[11] The *Chāndogyopaniṣad* says

---

11. प्राणो वा आशया भूयान्यथा वा अरा नाभौ समर्पिता, एवमस्मिन्प्राणे सर्वं समर्पितम्। .... स यदि पितरं वा मातरं वा भ्रातरं वा स्वसारं वा आचार्यं वा ब्राह्मणं वा किञ्चिद्भृशमिव प्रत्याह—

→

> *Prāṇa* surely is greater than aspiration. Just as the spokes of the wheel are fastened to the naïve so is all this fastened to this *prāṇa*. *Prāṇa* moves by *prāṇa*. *Prāṇa* gives *prāṇa*, *prāṇa* is the daughter, *prāṇa* is the mother, *prāṇa* is the brother, *prāṇa* is the sister, *prāṇa* is the preceptor, *prāṇa* is the brāhmaṇa. If one answers harshly to his father, mother, brother, sister, preceptor or a brāhmaṇa, people say thus to him, Fie on you, you are indeed a slayer of your father, you are indeed a slayer of your mother, etc. On the other hand, when the *prāṇa* has departed from them even if one piles them together, dismembers them with a fork and burns them up surely people would not say anything to him, because *prāṇa* indeed becomes all these.

Observing these Upaniṣadic lines one can understand how *prāṇa*, i.e., soul is associated alongwith the body of beings. From Śaṅkara's commentary we know that *prāṇa* means *ātman*.[12] Through his body-soul theory (*dehātmavāda*) what Ajita wanted to say was that one should show proper regard to parents and teachers and other relatives and friends while they were living rather than showing honour to them after death. In fact, it was the eternalist theory of unchangeable being which appeared to inspire men to take lives and also live happily at the same time because they could wash away their sins in the next birth as their souls would be a permanent element though their bodies perish.

→ "धिक्त्वास्त्वित्येवैनमाहुः पितृहा वै त्वमसि मातृहा वै त्वमसि, भ्रातृहा वै त्वमसि ...."

अथ यद्यप्ये नानुत्क्रान्तप्राणान् शूलेन समासं व्यतिषंदहेन्नैवैनं ब्रूयुः पितृहासीति .... न मातृहासीति ...... प्राणो ह्येवैतानि सर्वाणि भवति स वा एष एवं पश्यन्नेवं मत्वान........

— छान्दोग्योपनिषद्, अध्याय 7, खण्ड 15 1 to 4, pp. 767-73.

12. In the commentary of Śaṅkara प्राण आत्माहमिति ब्रुवाणं यदि ब्रूयुरतिवाद्यसीति *Ibid.*, p. 773.

While Mahāvīra criticizes Ajita Keśakambali, Buddha only distinguished between the Annihilationists and the Eternalists stating that the Annihilationists were wise or as much in error as the Eternalists themselves. The fault which he found was that both were extremists and dogmatists, but that Ajita formulated his views with the base of philosophical propositions of the Mahidāsa of *Aitareya Āraṇyaka,* his fundamental thesis being the materialistic "from the five-fold hymn, called otherwise the embodiment of *prāṇa,* the living soul, springs and to it returns all that is."[13]

But a further study of the views of Śīlāṅka (the *Vṛttikakāra* or the writer of *Vṛtti* to *Sūtrakṛtāṅga*) and Sāyaṇa-Mādhava compel us to think that the actual foundation of Ajita's doctrines was laid in the statement of Yājñavalkya of the *Bṛhadāraṇyaka Upaniṣad* which is that the intelligence (*vijñanaghana* = soul) of a living body emerging from the five elements vanishes into them at death.[14]

---

13. B.M. Barua in *A History of Pre-Buddhistic Indian Philosophy,* Motilal Banarsidass, 1970 p. 55.
14. इदं महद् अभूतं अनन्तं अपारं विज्ञानघन एवैतेभ्यो भूतेभ्यो समुत्थाय तान्येवानु विनश्यन्ति, न प्रत्यसंज्ञा अस्तीति — बृहदाण्यकोपनिषद्, II.4.12; IV.6.15.

5

The Paraśurāma Narrative

Randhir Singh

In the stories or *kathā*s available in the narrative and intellectual texts, the character of Paraśurāma has been presented in different forms. In one form it represents the knowledge of astronomy, in the other, it explains the secrets of mathematics, yoga and genetics. In the present article, I will show that the story of Paraśurāma, as described in *Śrīmad Bhāgavata,* in irreverant words, has actually represented the value of *Pi* which is the ratio between the circumference of a circle and its diameter up to six decimal places. It details a few methods for solving recurring numbers also. The statement, which is full of knowledge in itself, is supported by the narration of the *Vālmīkīya Rāmāyaṇa* in the chapters entitled "Triśirā Vadha" and "Ghora Yuddha" between Śrī Rāma and Khara. In addition to providing the knowledge of mathematics the present example provides us with an art full of wisdom of the higher sciences in the form of stories. Such descriptions, hundreds in number, which involve mathematics, are available in the epics the *Vālmīkīya Rāmāyaṇa, The Mahābhārata* and *Śrīmad Bhāgavata.* Surely, it may appear sensational but it is a fact that it may change our outlook towards history, archaeology, science, mathematics and about the stories (*kathā*s). One may remember that these texts were compiled centuries before the birth of Christ.

Ancient Sanskrit books such as the *Vālmīkīya Rāmāyaṇa,*[1] *Mahābhārata*[2] and *Śrīmad-Bhāgavata*[3] give an account that the brāhmaṇa Paraśurāma had wiped the kṣatriya race of the face of the earth twenty-one times. The original verses from these texts and translations by scholars are given in the Appendix [A-1].

According to *Mahābhārata,*

sa sarvaṁ kṣatramutsādya svavīryeṇānaladyutiḥ ।
samantapañcake pañca cakāra raudhirān hṛrān ॥
— *Mbh.*, Ādi Parva, 2.4

Paraśurāma, who was fearsome like a fire had killed the whole kṣatriya race and made *five pools full of blood* in the area of the Samantapañcaka.

But, contrary to the above statements, the *Śrīmad Bhāgavata* has emphasized that "forgiveness was the foremost duty of a *brāhmaṇa*" [A-2].

Paraśurāma was a brāhmaṇa; he had taken a vow for forgiveness. The killing of a ruling king was considered worse than the killing of a brāhmaṇa; therefore the killing of one kṣatriya king, not to say of the whole race and that too twenty-one times, is doubtful. *Vālmīkīya Rāmāyaṇa* [*Bāl. K.S. 75*] also supports this view [A-3].

Such statements as given above make the whole narration doubtful. In order to get to the truth, we must re-examine the original *śloka,* about clearing the earth of the *kṣatriya* race by Paraśurāma more carefully. The relevant *śloka* is :

---

1. *Śrīmad Vālmīkīya Rāmāyana Maharṣi Vālmikī Praṇīta,* Gorakhpur: Gita Press.
2. *Mahābhārata — Veda Vyāsa Praṇīta,* Gorakhpur: Gita Press.
3. *Śrīmad Bhāgavata Mahāpurāṇa* — Veda Vyāsa, Gorakhpur: Gita Press.

> *triḥ sapta kr̥tvaḥ pḥthivīṁ kr̥tvā niṇ kṣatriyām prabhuḥ* ।
> *samantapañcake cakre śoṇitodān hr̥dān ṇr̥pa* ॥
> — *Bhāg.*, 9.16.19

The *śloka* has been translated as,

> Making the murder of his father an issue, Paraśurāma had wiped the earth off the warrior race twenty-one times in the region named Samanta-pañcaka where he had created (five) pools full of the blood of kṣatriyas.

There existed a word *ekaviṁśati* for twenty-one. Therefore, there was no need to use the words *triḥ sapta* (3 x 7 = 21) in it in the above *śloka* [A-4].

The use of the word *sarva* in the above *śloka* (*Mbh.*, Ādi Parva 2.4) refers to a complete destruction. This word also creates a doubt as to how could the kṣatriya race have survived after a complete destruction. King Yudhiṣṭhira also had doubts about it [A-5].

Later on it is stated that a few warrior men had always survived after the killing [A-6].

The words of the *śloka* appear to have deeper meanings, which when correctly interpreted appear as follows:

Having a particular arrangment of the numbers 3 and 7 (*triḥ sapta kr̥tvaḥ*); making (*kr̥tva*) the earth (*pḥthivīṁ*) devoid of (*niḥ*) the zero (*kṣa*) 3, 6 and 9 (*triyām*). Putting the number 5 (*pañcaka*) after the even (*sama*) numbers 2, 4, 8 (*samantapañcaka*) and then making the sum of the pairs of numbers in the cycle (*cakre*) as 9 (*prabhuḥ*), the pools full of blood (*śoṇitodān hr̥dān*) of kṣatriyas (*nr̥pa*, recurring number).

We have a parallel example in mathematics: dividing 21 by 7 we are left with a zero, which refers to a complete destruction since the process of division ends up at the very first step. The higher number next to 21 is 22. Dividing 22 by

7 we get 3.142857. Here the group of numbers (142857) keeps on repeating itself continuously. Actually we can never exactly divide 22 by 7.

We have only nine digits, viz.; 1, 2, 3, 4, 5, 6, 7, 8, 9 excluding zero. 9 is the highest digit and it is said to represent the supreme power (*prabhu*).

Following the procedure step by step as given in the above *śloka*, we note:

1. *kr̥tvaḥ niḥ kṣatriyām* — *kr̥tvaḥ* (after making) ; *niḥ* (devoid of, removing) *kṣa* (zero, 0); *triyam* (the threes 3, 6, 9)

   which means that by removing 0, 3, 6, 9 from the nine numbers.

   we are left with 1, 2, 4, 5, 7, 8............... (1)

2. *samantapañcaka* — *sama* (the even numbers 2, 4, 6, or 8); *anta* (in the end) *pañcaka* (5). *samantapañcaka* means that 5 succeeds an even number and then 1, 2, 4, 8, 5, 7.

3. *cakre, prabhu* [9] — Use the cyclic process so that the sum of the first three digits with the respective last three, in pairs, should be equal to 9. In other words (1 + 8 = 9, 4 + 5 = 9, 2 + 7 = 9). Therefore, the order of the above numbers (1, 2, 4, 8, 5, 7) should be

   1 4 2 / 8 5 7............. (2)

   triḥ sapta — The first number is 3 and the last one is 7 [A-7].

   So we get 3.142857........ (3)

   We note that the above numbers 3.142857 represent the value of ***Pi.***

In this way following the dicutm of the *śloka,* step by step, we arrive at a group of numbers which represents the value of ***Pi***, the ratio of the circumference to the diameter of a circle.

Since this might have occurred, only by chance, it still remains to be seen what sense the words *samantapañcaka* and *pañca cakra raudhirān hṛdan* (*Mbh.*, Ādi Parva, 2.4) or five pools full of blood could convey!

Dividing a natural number, excluding zero, by 7 we are left with one of the six fractions: 1/7, 2/7, 3/7, 4/7, 5/7, 6/7. The value of which may be one of the following:

1/7 = 0.142857	142857
2/7 = 0.285714	285714
3/7 = 0.428571	428571
4/7 = 0.571428	571428
5/7 = 0.714285	714285
6/7 = 0.857142	857142

We note that in the above six cases:

- There is no *triyām* (threes such as 3, 6, or 9).
- There is no *kṣa* (zero).
- 4/7 is not a Samantpañcaka since in its decimal equivalent 5 is not after an even number.
- Only in five cases out of the six [1/7, 2/7, 3/7, 5/7, 6/7] 5 always follows an even number meaning that there is a situation of *samantapañcaka* in five cases only.
- In the form of the decimal equivalents of these five numbers — 1/7, 2/7, 3/7, 5/7, and 6/7 — we have the five pools full of the blood of the kṣtariyas.
- Kurukṣetra represents the mathematical process of division.

Therefore, we may conclude that the story of Paraśurāma contains the value of ***Pi*** and the related recurring numbers. In this story of Paraśurāma we find enshrined a deep curiosity for the knowledge and value of ***Pi*** in ancient times [cf. B].

We note that the existence of the process of mathematical division (Kūrukṣetra), five pools filled with blood (*śoṇita sarovaras*) and five groups of numbers having 5 at the end of even numbers (Samantapañcaka) is as real as the existence of religious places having the same names.

The above analysis brings up a few very serious questions related to history, archaeology and religious beliefs. In science or mathematics we do not make guesses. Before coming to any conclusion it is necessary to see if stories available in other scriptures also support our assertion. We must also be sure that there existed such a tradition of describing mathematical knowledge in the form of myths (*kathā*s).

We have an answer to the above query in the affirmative. *Vālmīkīya Rāmāyaṇa* which has presented itself like a textbook of Vedic sciences provides us with such examples. In the following discourse we quote only two examples from the Araṇya Kāṇḍa of the *Vālmīkīya Rāmāyaṇa.*

Example 1 : The death of Triśirā (Vālmīkīya Rāmāyaṇa Araṇya Kāṇḍa, Sarga 27)

At first sight the word *khara* looks like the word *kharam,* which gives a sense of the recurring nature of numbers. The word *khara* (*kha* = 2, *ra* = 2) has its numerical value as 22.

Khara's *senāpati* appears as the first digit of a group of decimal numbers. Therefore in the related story Khara's *senāpati,* Triśirā might represent some form 3 of the number 22. In the language of science the word *yuddha* (war) has a special meaning; in mathematics it refers to a process of division or multiplication. Rāma was a Sūryavaṁśī or the Sun himself. The Vedic Sun is called a *sapta saptī* or *sapta raśmi* meaning that the Sun had 7 horses or 7 bonds. In this way the Sun or the Rāma of *Rāmāyaṇa* represents the number 7. A duel between Khara (22) and Rāma (7) may thus represent the number 22/7. The use of Triśirā, 22 and 7 in the story of *Vālmīkīya Rāmāyaṇa*, (Araṇya Kāṇḍa, *Sarga* 27) attracts our attention. According to the story [~*kathā*]:

Looking at the pleasure of being killed by Śrī Rāmacandra, Triśirā availed a permission from his master Khara to have a duel with Rāma. Triśirā, riding in a chariot yoked with horses, entered the battlefield. At that time Triśirā appeared like a mountain having three peaks. The text says

tatastriśirasā bāṇairlalāṭe tāḍitastribhiḥ ||11 ||

Which means that he pierced the forehead of Rāma with three arrows.

triśirovakṣasi kruddho nijadhān caturdaśa |
caturbhisturagānasya śaraiḥ saṁnataparvabhiḥ ||14 ||
nyapātayata tejasvī caturastasya vājinaḥ |
aṣṭabhiḥ sāyakaiḥ sutaṁ rathopasthe nyapātayat ||15 ||

This means that Śrī Rāma was very angry and he pierced Triśirā with 14 arrows. Those arrows were formidable like poisonous snakes. After that Raghunātha killed the four horses with four arrows of lower knots and killed his driver with 8 arrows and made him lie in the seat of the chariot. We note that in the recurring number 3.142857, which is the value of ***Pi***, the 3 arrows of Triśirā is the first digit 3.

The 14 arrows pierced in the chest is the number 14 after the decimal.

4 arrows having *nataparva* — the lower multiple of the number 4 which is "2." Again 8 arrows represent the number 8, in the figures 3.1428.

The seat of the chariot represents the first number "8" of the right hand half (857) of the cyclic process. Again,

rāmaściccheda bāṇena dhvajaṁ cāsya samucchritam |
tato hatarathāt tasmādutpatantam niśācaram ||16 ||

It means, that Rāma used an arrow (= 5) and cut down the flag of the chariot. After that Triśirā jumped out of the chariot which had been ruined.

"5" represents an arrow (*bāṇa*). In this way the arrow becomes 3.14285. Jumping out of the chariot represents a completion of the cyclic process. And again,

> *ciccheda rāmastaṁ bāṇairhṛdaye so'abhavajjaḍh* ।
> *sāyakaiścāprameyātmā sāmarṣastasya rākṣasaḥ* ॥17 ॥
> *śirāṁsyapātayat trīṇi vegavad bhi stribhiḥ* ।
> *sa dhumaśoṇitodgāri rāmabāṇabhipiḍitaḥ* ॥18 ॥
> *nyapatat patitaiḥ pūrva samarastha niśācaraḥ* ।
> *hata śaisāstato bhagṇa rākṣasāḥ khara saṁśrayāḥ* ॥19 ॥

It means that Rāma (7) pierced the chest of that demon with arrows. Then the demon could not move forward and died. It is clear that this group of arrows represents the number 0.142/857. In the end Rāma the *aprameyasvarūpa* getting angry used 3 fast moving and crushing arrows and cut down all the three heads of the demon. The above number, with the addition of head digit (3) thus becomes 3.142/857.

The body of the demon fell down on the ground. Then all the demons in the service of Khara ran away. The number of arrows used in this battle was the same as the numbers which represent the value of ***Pi***. In this way the story of Triśirā is in conformity with the tradition and form of the story of Paraśurāma as narrated earlier.

Nobody was counting the number of arrows in the battlefield, therefore it must have been a purposeful statement of the author for the numerical value of ***Pi***.

***Example* 2 : A fierce battle between Rāma and Khara (Vālmīkīya Rāmāyaṇa; Araṇya Kāṇḍa, Sarga 28)**

In our previous discussion, we noticed a recurring decimal number (3.142857) elaborated in the form of a duel (*Sarga 27*).

We now look at a duel between Rāma and Khara. The word Khara represents the number 22. The Sun or Rāma of *Rāmāyaṇa* represents the number 7. Therefore a duel between Khara (22) and Rāma (7) may represent the number 22/7. The story which describes a combat between Khara and Rāma is found to have solutions for the recurring numbers 1/7 and 1/3. The procedure is similar to the one which has been given by the Jagadguru Śaṅkarācārya Bhāratī Kṛṣṇa Tīrtha in his book *Vedic Mathematics*.[4] According to the story:

During his combat with Rāma, Khara started moving in the battlefield in various forms — *cacāra samare mārgānśarai rathagataḥ kharaḥ*. Meaning that during the fight more than one method was adopted to solve the problem.

> *sa punastvaparān sapta śarānādāya marmaṇi* ।
> *nijadhāna raṇe kruddha śakrāśanisamaprabhāṇ* ॥16 ॥

Which means that taking 7 arrows the angry Khara pierced the sensitive points on the body of Rāma. This clearly refers to a division by 7.

> *tataḥ kanaka puṁkhaistu śaraiḥ saṁnataparvabhiḥ* ।
> *ciccheda rāmaḥ saṁkruddhaḥ kharasya samare dhvajaṁ* ॥22 ॥

It means that Rāma cut down Khara's flag with arrows made of the golden feathers of lower knots (factors). The *dhanuṣa* or the *cāpa* (an arc's flag) represents the cyclic process of recurring decimals in which one half cycle of the equivalent decimal number is a complement to the other half cycle.

The first method is as follows :

---

4. *Vedic Mathematics* by Jagadguru Swāmī Śrī Bhāratī Kṛṣṇa Tīrtha Śaṅkarācārya of Govardhan Maṭha, Puri. Gen. Editor Dr. V.S. Agrawala, Delhi: Motilal Banarsidass.

taṁ caturbhiḥ kharaḥ kruddho rāmaṁ gātreṣu mārgaṇaiḥ ।
vivyādha hṛdi marmajño mātaṁgamiva tomaraiḥ ॥24 ॥

The *śloka* means that Khara who knew the sensitive points of the body pierced 4 arrows in Rāma's chest in a way an elephant driver attacks his elephant with the club.

According to the Vedic formula *ekādhikena pūravena,* in order to solve 1/7, we write it in the form 7/49. The left digit of the denominator is 4 therefore the guiding number becomes (4+1=) 5. Doing this we perform the process of division from left to the right or multiplication from right to the left. We get,

1/7 = 7/59 = 0.142/857 - equivalent decimal numbers

214/230 - remainder numbers

The story gose on,

mumoca parameśvasaḥ ṣat śarānabhilakṣitān ॥26 ॥

Meaning that, Rāma shot 6 arrows towards Khara using the aforementioned bow. This means that using the above method one can get the decimal equivalent of the six recurring numbers, viz., 1/7, 2/7, 3/7, 4/7, 5/7, and 6/7.

It goes on :

śirasyekena bānena dvābhyāṁbahvorathārpayat ।
tribhiścandrārdhavaktraiśca vakṣasyābhijadhāna ha ॥27 ॥

Rāma pierced 1 arrow in Khara's forehead, 2 in the arms and hurt deep with 3 semi-circular arrows in the chest.

If we represent the decimal equivalents of 1/7 by the forehead, of 2/7 by the arms and of 3/7 by the chest and make the sum up with the decimal equivalents of 4/7, 5/7 and 6/7 respectively the sum of the complementary pair in each case should be 9. The sum of the respective pairs of the remainders should be 7. We have,

Decimal equivalent	*Place*	*Remainder*	*Dividend/Remainder*
1/7 = 142/857	forehead	326/451	[1:3]
2/7 = 285/714	arms	645/132	[2:6]
3/7 = 428/571	chest	264/513	[3:9, 2]
4/7 = 571/428	chest	513/264	[4:12, 5]
5/7 = 714/285	arms	132/645	[5:15, 1]
6/7 = 857/142	forehead	451/326	[6:18, 4]

Another method

We note that the ratio between the first dividend and the remainder in all the above cases is 1 : 3. Maintaining the same ratio we may get the remainder for all the above fractions. Again multiplying the remainders by 7 and ignoring totally any number other than the one at the place of unity, we get the decimal equivalent for all the above fractions.

In the case of 1/7 the ratio between the first dividend and the first remainder is 1 : 3. We many write all the remainders 3, 2, 6, 4, 5, 1 by maintaining the same ratio. Multiplying the remainders 7 and taking the right hand digits only, totally ignoring any other number, we get the decimal equivalent as 142857. According to the *Rāmāyaṇa,*

tataḥ paścānmahāteja nārācān . . . . kruddhastrayodaśa śilāśitān ||28 ||

This means that getting very angry Rāma pierced Khara with 13 arrows. The decimal equivalent of 1/7 is 0.142/857 and the respective dividends are 132/645.

We note that 1 and 3 are the first two digits of the dividends of 1/7.

Again it says,

rathasya yugamekena caturbhiḥ śabalān hayān |
ṣaṣṭhena ca śiraḥ saṁkhye ciccheda kharasāratheḥ ||29 ||

Meaning that Rāma slashed the yoke of the chariot with an arrow (5), killed the 4 spotted horses of the chariot by 4 arrows, by the 6th arrow he cut down the head of the driver of the chariot in the battlefield.

The number and the order of the arrows (6, 4, 5) given above represent the right half of the dividends [132/645]. Multiplying the remainders 3, 2, 6, 4, 5 and 1 by 7 and considering the numbers at the place of unity only, we get 142857 as the decimal equivalent. Following the same procedure, the values of 2/7, 3/7, 4/7, 5/7 and 6/7 may be obtained easily.

Solution of 1/13

In the following description a solution for 1/13 is available.

To have a solution of 1/13 it should be written in the form 3/39. Its guiding number is (3+1=)4.

The last digit of the decimal equivalent is 3 [9=3x3].

In the procedure from the left to the right : dividing the numerator 3, by the guiding number 4, continuously we get 0.076/923 as the decimal equivalent of 1/13, the respective remainder numbers being (323/010).

The sum of the pairs (0+9, 7+2, 6+3) of the numbers of the components of the decimal equivalent being 9 and for the remainders being 3.

We get the same result by multiplying 3, the last number of the decimal equivalent by 4, continuously from the right to the left. According to the *Rāmāyaṇa*:

tribhistriveṇūn balavān dvābhyāmakṣṁ mahābalaḥ ।
dvādaśena tu bāṇena kharasya saśaraṁ dhanuḥ ॥30 ॥
chitvā bajranikāśena rāghavaḥ prahasanniva ।
trayodaśenendrasamo bheda samare kharaṁ ॥31 ॥

The *śloka*s mean that after destroying the *triveṇu* of the *yoka* with 3 arrows and the axis of the chariot with 2 arrows, powerful Rāma broke both the bow and the arrow of Khara with 12 arrows in two pieces. Rāma who looked like the glittering Indra wounded Khara in the battlefield with the 13th arrow with much ease.

In the light of the meanings of the above *śloka*s (30 and 31) we note :

The destruction of the *triveṇu* with 3 arrows represents the last digit of the decimal equivalent. 3 is the basis of the multiplication or division by the guiding number 4. In multiplying 3 by 4 we get 12 the right hand digit being 2. The left hand digit 1 is at the tenth place which is to be taken as a remainder number. Again, multiplying 2 by 4 and adding 1 to it we get 9 which is the third digit from the right. 9 is the sum of the numbers represented by the bows (4) and arrows (5). After getting the digits of the right half [923] we can get the digits of the other half [076] with help of the complementary formula easily. Again,

> *prabhagnadhanvā viratho hatāśvo hatasārathiḥ* ।
> *gadāpāṇiravaplutya tasthau bhūmau kharastadā* ॥32 ॥

Which means that the bow having been broken, the chariot having been crushed, the horses killed, the driver wiped off, Khara jumped out of the chariot and stood on the ground with the club in his hands. This simply means that the process thus got completed.

Conclusions and Possibilities

From our present discourse we have concluded that the ancient Hindu scriptures compiled centuries before Christ can be related with mathematical processes such as the decimal system, recurring numbers, ***Pi*** and its value. The study further suggests that we should not undermine these *kathā*s by taking them as simple myths.

In Haryana we have places like Kurukṣetra, Samantapañcaka and Soṇitasarovaras. The history of these places is associated with the story of the killing of the warrior race by Paraśurāma. Our interpretation of the *kathā* of Paraśurāma has revealed that the importance of these nouns in mathematics too, is without question. One asks which Samantapañcaka, the one related with mathematics or the other associated with the place for pilgrimage, came into prominence first. One possibility is that in the distant past the area had been a centre of learning. Following the knowledge of mathematics the place was named Samantapañcaka. In order to maintain the secrecy of the knowledge it was narrated in the guise of a *kathā*. As time passed the tradition of learning got lost in the fanfare of religious ceremonies. It might be that the goddess of learning was named Sarasvatī because in the past the river Sarasvatī flowed through that region.

In ancient times, history, science and spiritual knowledge blew together and were narrated in the form of stories. However, the narration varied from one epic to the other in the use of names and forms. Hence, there are the same narrations in *Rāmāyaṇa, Mahābhārata* and *Śrīmad-Bhāgavat*.

The association of the names of places like Kurukṣetra, Samantapañcaka and Soṇitasarovaras and of persons Triśirā, Khara, Paraśurāma and Rāmacandra — with mathematics is really interesting. The parallelism between the *kathā*s and mathematics or science evokes questions connected with archaeology, history and theology. We are further tempted to investigate if similar *kathā*s associated with other places and persons also contain secrets related with science and mathematics.

Glossary to Chapter 5

aprameyātma — which cannot be proved or constructed; not a *prameya* or *nirnaya.*

cakra — A cyclic process; a process which repeats itself after a regular interval.

cāpa — A chord of an arc of a circle.

dhanuṣa — An arc ; a bow.

kathā — A description in which facts are personified and the meanings of the words used for nouns convey the sense of the subject-matter. *A kathā* is not the same as a story. In the Vedic literature, particularly in the epics, specialized knowledge had been found described in the form of *kathā*s in subtle fashion.

Khara — A recurring number [*kha* = 2 and *ra* = 2, *khara* = 22]; a demon who was the half-brother of Rāvaṇa.

kṣa — Zero; *śūnya.*

kṣatriya — A group of digits which constitute a recurring number.

Kurukṣetra — A country where the battle was fought; a process of division or multiplication.

nata parva — A lower factor or a lower multiple of certain number, e.g., 2 is a ***nata parva*** of 4 and 3 is a ***nata parva*** of 9.

prabhu — The highest digit, 9.

sama — An even number [2, 4, 6, 8].

Samantapañcaka — A situation of number 5 being after an even number.

tri sapta — A combination of numbers 3 and 7 under reference.

Triśirā — being before the decimal in a number such as 3 in 3.142857; chief warrior of demon Khara.

triyam — the threes; 3 or its integral multiples ; 3, 6 or 9.

Aknowledgements

The author expresses his thanks to Dr. A.K. Bag [INSA, Delhi] for his constructive suggestions.

Appendix to Chapter 5

A-1 : The *Vālmīkīya Rāmāyaṇa* spoke of Paraśurāma as *rājā rājavimardanam* meaning one who had crushed the self-respect of the kṣatriya kings [*Bāl. Kā.* 74.17] and the *kṣatramutsādayaṁ rosajjātaṁ jātamanekaṣaḥ* meaning one who out of anger crushed the kṣatriya kings as they were born time and again [*Bāl. Kā.* 75.24].

According to the *Śrīmad-Bhāgvata*:

. . . triḥ saptakṛtvo ya imāṁ cakre niḥ kṣatriyām mahīm.
— *Bhāg.*, p. 9.15.14.

Meaning that "He had wiped off this earth the kṣatriyas 21 times," It again stated,

mārge vrajan bhṛgupatervyanayat prarūḍhaṁ ।
darpaṁ mahimakṛta yastrirarājabijām ॥
— *Bhāg.*, p. 9.10.7

Meaning that while returning back [from Ayodhyā, Rāma-candra] had an encounter with Bhṛgupati Paraśurāma, who had wiped the kṣatriya race off the earth 21 times.

A-2 : According to the *Śrīmad-Bhāgavata* (9.15.39-41). Jamadagni, the father of Paraśurāma, spoke to him:

vayaṁ hi brāhmaṇastāt kṣamayārhaṇatāṁ gatāḥ ।
yayā lokagururdevaḥ pārameṣṭhayamagāt padaṁ ॥39 ॥

kṣamayā rocate lakṣmīrbrāhmī sourī yathā prabhā ।
kṣamiṇamāśu bhagavāṁstuṣyate harirīśvaraḥ ॥40 ॥

rajño mūrdhābhisiktasya vadho brahmabadhād guruḥ I
tīrthasaṁsevayā cāṁho jahyaṅgācyutacetanaḥ II41 II

The above *ślokas* means : "We are brāhmaṇas, forgiveness is our foremost duty. The great grandfather of all the beings, Brahmā, had risen to the status of Brahmapada due to the observance of forgiveness. The grandeur of the brāhmaṇas shines like the glitter of the Sun, because of the forgiveness. God gets pleased easily with those who observe forgiveness. Killing of a ruling king is worse than the killing of a brāhmaṇa, so wash away your sins by going on pilgrimage." It further stated:

pitropaśikṣito rāmastatheti kurunandana......[*Bhā.* 9.16.1]

Which means, "O, Kurunandana, Paraśurāma has accepted the above advice of his father saying — it will be so observed."

A-3 : The *Vālmīkīyā Rāmāyaṇa* [*Bāl. Kā. Ś.* 75] says :

kṣatrarosāt praśantastvaṁ brāhmaṇaśca mahātapāḥ II6 II

Which means, having shown his anger for the kṣatriyas, he [Paraśurāma] had become silent. Also:

sahasrākṣe pratijñāya śastraṁ prakṣiptavānasi II7 II

Which means, having taken an oath before Indra, Paraśurāma had shunned the weapons.

A-4 : In the *Mahābhārata* [*Ādi. Anu. Ad.* 1.33], the word *ekaviṁśati* has been used for 21 *prajāpatis*. It said, *prajānām patayaḥ prabhavanneka viṁśatiḥ.*

Again the word *ekaviṁśati* has been used for 21 as,

ekaviṁśatimedhānte rāmaṁ vagaśariríṇī II
— *Mbh. Āśva. Anu.*, 29.18

The respecitve *parvas* or chapters in *Mahābhārata* and *Vālmīkīya Rāmāyaṇa* had been designated by the word *ekaviṁśati.*

A-5 : The use of the word *sarva* in the *śloka,* 2.4 (*Mbh.,* Ādi Parva) refers to a complete destruction. This also costs doubt as to how could the kṣatriya race have survived after a complete destruction. In this context is mentioned. [*Mbh.,* San. Rāj. *Anu.* A 48].

King Yudhiṣṭhira spoke to Vaiśmpāyana,

triḥ sapta kr̥tvāḥ pr̥thvī kr̥tā niḥ kṣatriyām purā I
rāmeṇeti tathā attha tvamatra me saṁśayo mahān II10 II

Which means, "In the past Paraśurāma had wiped off the kṣatriyas from the face of earth 21 times. I have developed doubts about that statement. Yudhiṣṭhira again asked!

kṣatrabījāṁ yathā dagdhaṁ rāmeṇa yadupuṅgava I
kathaṁ bhūyaḥ samutapattiḥ kṣatrasyāmitavikrama II11 II

Which means, O Yadunāth full of unlimited valour, Paraśurāma had destroyed even the seed of the kṣatriyas then how could the kaṣatriya race survive after a complete destruction

A-6 : *Mahābhārata* [Śānti Parva, Anuśāsana Parva, *Ad 49. ślokas* 62-84] details that after each killing a few kṣatriyas were left. Accordingly:

arakṣṁśca sutān kāṁścit tadā kṣatriyayositaḥ [49.63]

Which means that the kṣatriya women could save only a very few sons.

The *Māhābhārata* [Āśvamedhic Parva, *Ad.* 29] states :

tataśca hatavīrāsu kṣatriyāsu punaḥ punaḥ I
dvijarut pāditaṁ kṣatraṁ jāmadagnyo nyakr̥ntata II17 II

Which means, "After the kṣatriyas had been killed, the kṣatriya women gave birth to sons from the brāhmaṇas according to the sysem of *niyoga,* but they too were killed by Paraśurāma."

It goes on to state,

gobhīḥ samudreṇa tathā golaṇgularkṣavānaraiḥ ।
gupta rāmabhayodvignāḥ kṣatriyāṇamkulodvhaḥ ॥
— *Mbh., San. Raj. Anu.*, 50.3

Which means that, "The kṣatriyas, who had been hiding due to the fear of Paraśurāma were protected by the cows, oceans, apes, bears and monkeys.

The cows are known for their milk, motion, groupings and calves; the monkeys for their restlessness, greed and forward jumps; the apes for their capability to change the direction of their motion during flight and the *ṛṣi*s as the most reverent among men. The Sanskrit word *samudra* means both an ocean and the heavens.

A-7 : The very first line of the *Atharvaveda*[5] runs :

ye tri saptāḥ pariyanti viśvā rūpāṇi vibhrataḥ ॥ — *AV* 1.1.1.

It means that, "All the forms [*rūpa*s] of the bodies of the Solar system are moving, getting filled in three-sevens." The words *rūpa, pariyanti* and *vibhrata,* can only be used for a physical body.

In an article on BLT, we have shown that the word *tri sapta* does not mean 3x7 = 21.

Tri sapta actually represented the relative distances of the planets Mercury and Venus from the Sun.[6]

B-1 : In the value of ***Pi***, the group of numbers [142857] following 3, is repeated continuously. In the *kathā* of

---

5. *Sanskrit-English Dictionary* by Vamana Shivram Apte, Delhi: Motilal Banarsidass.
6. *Sanskrit-English Dictionary* by Sir Monier-Williams, Delhi: Munshiram Manoharlal, 1995 (rpt.).

Paraśurāma these groups represent the heaps of corpses of the kṣatriyas erected by Paraśurāma in Mahiṣmati Purī. The circumference of the circle represents mother Reṇukā. The four quadrants of a circle represent her four sons who refused to kill Reṇukā. A diameter which divides a circle [mother] into two halves represents Paraśurāma who killed her. The chord [*cāp, dhanuṣa*] represents Arjuna, the radius an arm or a *bāhu.* In this way, 1000 arrows [*bāṇa*] shot by Sahasrabāhu Arjuna using 500 bows represents 1000 radii and 500 semi-circles or 500 bows subtended on 500 diameters.

B-2 : The presence of the ***Pi,*** is one of the essential conditions for any existence. In the *kathā* an interest for ***Pi*** shows that the ancients had a curiosity about the creation of a line [*diś*] out of a point [*vāmana*]; of an area [*kṣetra,* surface] out of a *diś,* and of a body [*bhūta,* volume] out of an area. The idea propounded here appears to represent the three steps advanced by Vāmana-Viṣṇu for fathoming the entire creation.

6

Some Thoughts on Vipratiṣedha

Rama Nath Sharma

PĀṆINI presents the following two rules:

ā kaḍārād ekā saṁjñā ॥1.4.1 ॥
vipratiṣedhe paraṁ kāryam ॥1.4.2 ॥

Rule 1.4.1 *ā kaḍārād ekā saṁjñā*, is formulated so that more than one name (*saṁjñā*) could not be assigned to a single nominatum (saṁjñin). The phrase *ā kaḍārād* or "up to *kaḍā*" is used to clearly indicate the extent of this domain up to rule 2.3.38 *kaḍārāḥ karmadhāraye*. This domain of rules is aptly called *ākaḍārīya*. Rule 1.4.2 *vipratiṣedhe paraṁ kāryam* states that in matters of conflict in the application of the two rules, one should apply the rule which is subsequent in order of enumeration. A situation of conflict, namely *vipratiṣedha*, is explained as *tulyabala-virodha*, that is the "conflict among two rules of equal strength," as follows: *dvau prasaṅgāv anyārthāv ekasmin yugat prāpnutaḥ*, "where two rules with independent application, elsewhere, find application in a single context, at the same time." Kāśikā, in its interpretation of 1.4.1 *ā kaḍārād ekā saṁjñā*, reads *param* of *paraṁ kāryam* (1.4.2) as *parā* "that which is subsequent in order of enumeration," obviously, as a qualifier to *ekā saṁjñā* "one name." Answering the question "what one name should be assigned," Kāśikā states: *yā parā anavakāśā ca*, "that which is subsequent in order of enumeration, and also that which, if not assigned, would be rendered without any scope of application." We thus get twin conditions of *parā* "subsequent" and *anavakāśā* "with no scope of application" in so far as assigning one term under the provision of 1.4.1 *ā kaḍārād ekā saṁjñā* is concerned. It is interesting to note that, in view of the explanation offered for *vipratiṣedha*, i.e., *tulyabala-virodha*, we also find twin conditions for application under the provision of 1.4.2 *vipratiṣedhe paraṁ kāryam*, namely (*anyatra*) *sāvakāśatva* "independently valid scope of application, elsewhere" and *paratva* "subsequent order of enumeration." The condition of *anavakāśatva* "no valid scope of application, elsewhere," under the provision of 1.4.1 *ā kaḍārād ekā saṁjñā*, is exactly the opposite of the condition of (*anyatra*) *sāvakāśatva* "independently valid scope of application, elsewhere" under the provision of 1.4.2 *vipratiṣedhe paraṁ kāryam*. The condition of *paratva* "subsequent order of application" is common to provisions of both rules. This clearly sets apart the domain of application of these two rules. Accepting the common condition of *paratva*, and thereby *vipratiṣedha* "conflict in application of two rules of equal strength," we can establish two types of *vipratiṣedha*, namely (i) *saṁjñā-vipratiṣedha* "conflict among two rules which both assign different names" with the twin-conditions of *anavakāśatva* and *paratva*, and (ii) *saṁjñetara-vipratiṣedha* "conflict among two rules of equal strength" with the twin conditions of (*anyatra*) *sāvakāśatva* and *paratva*.

Now consider the following two rules:

> *hrasvaṁ laghu* ॥1.4.10 ॥
> *saṁyoge guru* ॥1.4.11 ॥

Where the first rule assigns the name *laghu* "light" to a short (*hrasva*) vowel. Rule 1.4.11 assigns the name *guru* "heavy" to a short vowel which occurs before a cluster of consonants (*saṁyoga*). The name *hrasva* is defined as a vowel used with the duration of half a *mora* (*ekamātrika*; 1.2.27 *ūkālo jj hrasva-*

dīrgha-plutaḥ). The same *hrasva* vowel of 1.4.10 here qualifies for assignment of the name *guru* under the provision of rule 1.4.11, of course under the following condition of a *consonant* cluster. These two names will both become applicable to the *hrasva* vowel *i* of *śikṣ* "to instruct" and *bhikṣ* "to beg" as in *śikṣā* "instruction" and *bhikṣā* "begging." If the term *guru* is not uniquely assigned to a *hrasva* vowel when followed by a consonant cluster (*saṁyoga*), as in the context of *śikṣ* and *bhikṣ* under the following condition of a consonant cluster (*saṁyoga*), rule 3.4.103 *guroś ca halaḥ* could not introduce the affix *a*, and hence, 4.1.4 *aj ādyataṣ ṭāp*, could not introduce the affix *ṭāp*. more importantly, with no application in *śikṣā* and *bhikṣā*, rule 1.4.11 *saṁyoge guru*, and thereby the name *guru* will be rendered without any scope of application, elsewhere. It is in this sense that the *saṁjñā* named *guru* which is also assigned subsequently in the order of enumeration will become *anavakāśa*. Let us now consider the following rules:

> *ato dīrgo yañi*
>
> an *aṅgā*- final -*a* is replaced with its long counterpart when a *sārvadhātuka* affix beginning with a sound denoted by the abbreviatory term *yañ* follows. — 7.3.101
>
> an *aṅga*- final -*a* is replaced with its long counterpart, also when an affix termed *sup* beginning with a sound denoted by the abbreviatory term *yañ* follows. — 7.3.102
>
> *bahuvacane jhaly et*
>
> the final -*a* of *aṅga* is replaced with -*e*, instead, when an affix termed *sUP* beginning with a sound denoted by the abbreviatory term *jhal* follows with the signification of plural. — 7.3.103

The *Mahābhāṣya* finds a situation of conflict (*vipratiṣedha*) in the application of rules 7.3.102 *supi ca* and 7.3.103 *bahuvacane jhaly et*. These two rules both have their independent scope of application in the derivation of *vṛkṣābhyām/plakṣābhyām* and *vṛkṣeṣu/plakṣeṣu*, respectively. They both become concurrently (*yugapat*) applicable in the context of *vṛkṣebhyaḥ/plakṣebhyaḥ*. Patañjali rules in favour of the aplication of replacement in *-e* based on *vipratiṣedha* (*etvaṁ bhavat vipratiṣedhena*). This happens to be one of the clearest statements in the *Mahābhāṣya*, relative to the resolution of a conflict among two rules of equal strength, based on *paratva*. There is no additional discussion about it either by Kaiyaṭa or by Nāgeśa. The condition of *bahuvacane* "when the denotation is plural" not only brings *bahuvacane jhaly et* (7.3.103) on a par with *supi ca* (7.3.102) in terms of equality of strength (*tulyabalatā*) but also enables it not to be treated as an exception (*apavāda*).

Now consider the following three rules:

> *ata iñ* — 4.1.95
> *ṛṣyandhakavṛṣṇikurubhyaś ca* — 4.1.114
> *itaś cāniñaḥ* — 4.1.122

Rule 4.1.95 introduces the affix *iñ* after a syntactically related nominal stem which ends in *-a* and is used with the genitive denoting an offspring (*apatya*). Rule 4.1.114 introduces the affix *aṇ* (*ṛṣy-aṇ*) after a syntactically related nominal stem used with the signification of a sage (*ṛṣi*), *andhaka*, *vṛṣṇi* and *kuru*. Rule 4.1.122 *itaś cāniñaḥ* introduces the affix *ḍhak* after a syntactically related nominal stem which ends in *-i*, though not of *iñ*, and is formed with two vowels. Rule 4.1.122 *itaś cāniñaḥ* blocks the application of *aṇ* of 4.1.114 *ṛṣyandhaka-vṛṣṇikurubhyaś ca* in favour of affix *ḍhak* on the basis of *paratva*. The examples are *ātteryaḥ* and *naidheyaḥ* where *atri* and *nidhi* both denote a sage. A similar blocking can also be witnessed in the application of 4.1.53 *udīcām iñ* and 4.1.157 *udīcām vṛddhād agotrāt*, where *kāriṣeṇiḥ* "son of Kariṣeṇa" and *nāpitāyaniḥ* "son of Nāpita" are offered as respective examples. But affixes *iñ* and *phiñ* of these two rules may also become applicable in the derivation of *nāpitāyaniḥ* "son of a barber" when the nominal stem denotes an artisan (*śilpin*). The affix *iñ* can be viewed as having its independent scope of application in the derivation of *tantuvāyiḥ* "son of a weaver," where as *phiñ* could have its independent scope of application in deriving *āmraguptāyaniḥ* "a descendant of Āmragupta." Commentators explain that rule 1.4.1 *ā kaḍārād ekā saṁjñā* is formulated as a restrictive provision (*niyama*) so that, elsewhere, i.e., in the outside world of usage (*loka*), and in the inside world of grammar (*vyākaraṇa*), class inclusion of names (*saṁjñā-samāveśa*) could be accepted as norm. However, to ensure the class-inclusion of names, elsewhere, *parā* "subsequent in order of enumeration" is read here, from 1.4.2 *vipratiṣedhe paraṁ kāryam*, as a qualifier to *ekā saṁjñā* "one name." This then becomes the domain of *eka saṁjñā*, and thereby of *saṁjñā-vipratiṣedha*, with the twin conditions of *anavakāśatva* and *paratva*. I shall not discuss here any further details of *eka saṁjñā*, nor of *saṁjñā-samāveśa* for lack of space. It should be noted, however, that there is hardly much to establish *vipratiṣedha* in the domain of *eka-saṁjñā*, and thereby in *saṁjñā-vipratiṣedha*. For, the operational function of 1.4.1 *ā kaḍārād kā saṁjñā* is best at its bare minimum. It is the domain of assignment of terms (*saṁkhyā*) and not of operations guided by the names *per se*. There is hardly any *virodha* "conflict," let alone conflict of equal strength (*tulyabalatā*) among names, especially since elsewhere in grammar, *saṁjñāsamāveśa* is the norm. To facilitate the assignment of one name in the domain of *eka saṁjñā*, Pāṇini arranges his rules in this domain in such a way that a name which may be rendered without any scope of application, elsewhere, is placed subsequently in the order of enumeration. The idea of *virodha* in the assignment of names (*saṁjñā*), and thereby *saṁjñā-vipratiṣedha*, is, therefore, imagined (*kalpanā*) mostly due to the qualification of *parā* "subsequent in order of enumeration" brought to this rule from the *paraṁ* of rule 1.4.2 *vipratiṣedhe paraṁ kāryam.*

Now consider the following two rules:

> *dhruvam apāye 'pādānam* — 1.4.24
> *sādhakatamaṁ karaṇam* — 1.4.42

The first rule assigns the name *apādāna* to a participant in action which serves as a fixed point with reference to the action denoted by *apāya* "movement away from." Our next rule assigns the name *karaṇa* to a participant in action which serves as most instrumental in accomplishing the action. Given the sentence *dhanuṣā śarair vidhyati mṛgam* "he pierces the deer by means of arrows shot with the bow," the names *apādāna* and *karaṇa* both become applicable to *dhanuṣa* "bow" at the same time. The name *apādāna* becomes applicable to *dhanuṣa* since it serves as the fixed point from whence movement away (*apāya*) of *śara* "arrow" occurs. The name *karaṇa* becomes equally applicable to *dhanuṣa* since it also serves as the most instrumental participant in the shooting of arrows. There is clearly a conflict among the two rules of equal strength (*vipratiṣedha*). This conflict is resolved by 1.4.2 *vipratiṣedhe paraṁ kāryam* in favour of assignment of the name *karaṇa* to *śara* "arrow," on the basis of *paratva* "subsequent in order of enumeration." Notice that *dhanuṣā śarair vidhyati mṛgam* is an example which straddles between the separately identified scopes of *saṁjñā-vipratiṣedha* and *saṁjñetara-vipratiṣedha* in the sense that it relates to the assignment of names (*saṁjñā*) but it subscribes to conditions of (*anyatra*) *sāvakāśatva* "scope of application, elsewhere," and of course of *paratva*, subsequent in order of enumeration. Such instances of *saṁjñā-vipratiṣedha* where the condition of *anavakāśatva* is not met are very few, indeed. Rule 1.4.2 *vipratiṣedhe paraṁ kāryam* is also explained as a restrictive provision (*niyama*), though not as a kind of *parisaṁkhyā* "exclusive restriction." A rule which is subsequent in the order of enumeration, in the *parisaṁkhyā* view, could win its application on the basis of *paratva* by blocking the application of a prior rule only when a situation of conflict (*vipratiṣedha*) arises. That is, *eva* has to be construed with the subject (*uddeśya*), i.e., *vipratiṣedhe* in the context of 1.4.2 *vipratiṣedhe paraṁ kāryam*. A non-*parisaṁkhyā* view of *niyama* would construe *eva* with *param kāryam* to yield the interpretation: *vipratiṣedhe paraṁ eva kāryam* "apply only that which is subsequent in the order of enumeration, when a situation of conflict arises." This clearly establishes a comparatively wider domain of application of 1.4.2 *vipratiṣedhe paraṁ kāryam*, particularly outside the domain of *eka saṁjñā* headed by 1.4.1 *ā kaḍārād ekā saṁjñā*. It applies throughout the *sapāda-saptādhyāyī*, of course with the exclusion of the domains of *eka saṁjñā*, and of the *tripādī* "the last three quarter" of rules governed by 8.2.1 *pūrvatrāsiddham*. Kāśikā's statement about the condition of *anavakāśatva* in connection with the scope of *eka saṁjñā* is an important evidence for this. The most telling evidence in favour of a much wider scope of application of 1.4.2 *vipratiṣedhe paraṁ kāryam*, as against limiting its scope to the domain of *eka saṁjñā* (1.4.1 *ā kaḍārād ekā saṁjñā*), is offered by this very statement (*vacana-prāmāṇya*) of Pāṇini. It is generally accepted in the Pāṇinian parlance that a particular rule blocks the application of its general counterpart (*sāmānyasya bādhako viśeṣaḥ*). That is, an exception (*apavāda*) always blocks the application of its corresponding general (*utsarga*).

Now consider the following rules:

halantyam — 1.3.1
na vibhaktau tusmāḥ — 1.3.4

The first rule assigns the term *it* to a final consonant in *upadeśa* "initial citation." The second rule denies the assignment of this term *it* to a final consonant when this same happens to be a consonant of the *ṭ*-series, or is *-s*, or else, is *-m* contained within a *vibhakti*, i.e., *sup* and *tiṅ*. The scope of application of rule one is delimited by the general property of final consonantness. This property of final consonantness is also present within the scope of application of our second rule. However, this general scope of application is delimited with some particular property of final consonantness, i.e., consonants of the *ṭ*-series, *-s*, and *-m*. If we follow the maxim of pervasion (*vyāpti-nyāya*), we can say that the general scope of application of our first rule 1.4.3 *halantyam* is shrunk from within by the scope of a particular property of final consonantness common to the general property. It is in this sense that a scope of application delimited by a particular property common to the general properties is called *vyāpya* "pervaded." A scope of application delimited by the general properties is likewise called *vyāpaka* "pervader." A rule which is delimited by the particular properties of *vyāpya* is called particular (*viśeṣa*) in relation to its corresponding general (*utsarga*). Our first rule is thus a general rule and the next rule is its related particular (*viśeṣa*). It is in this sense that a particular rule blocks the application of its corresponding general. Commentators here invoke the maxim of *takra-kauṇḍinya*, i.e., *dadhi brāhmaṇebhyo dīyatām takraṁ kauṇḍinyāya* "let curds be given to the brāhmaṇas, butter-milk to Kauṇḍinya." The general gifting of curds (*dadhidāna*) must here be blocked by the particular gifting of butter-milk (*takra-dāna*). Note that this blocking of the gifting of curds by the gifting of butter-milk is possible only when the gifting of curds to Kauṇḍinya is possible (*sati sambhave bādhaḥ*), and only when it would be impossible (*asambhava*) to make these two gifts both at the same time (*yugapat*).

The assignment of a name (*eka saṁjñā*) which would otherwise be rendered without any scope of application, elsewhere, would block the assignment of another which enjoys its independent scope of application, elsewhere. This is likened to the blocking of a general by its corresponding particular. What we find generally in the context of 1.4.2 *vipratiṣedhe paraṁ kāryam* is not a conflict between the assignment of two terms. For, there always is a possibility of the assignment of two names concurrently (*yugapat pravṛttisambhavāt*). There is no blocker-blocked relationship (*bādhya-bādhaka-bhāva*), either. For, the results are different (*bhinnaphalakatvāt*). It is interesting to note here that the result of the *dadhi-dāna* to the brāhmaṇas, and of *takra-dāna* to Kauṇḍinya, is the same, i.e., soaking of rice (*odana-seka*). This discussion clearly shows that instances of *vipratiṣedha* of either kind could not be handled under the rule-interaction provisions characterized with *utsarga* and *apavāda* "general and its related exception."

Let us now turn to the following interpretive conventions:

ṣaṣṭhī sthāneyogā, whereby a genitive (*ṣaṣṭhī*) ।

not interpretable otherwise, is to be interpreted as meaning "in place of"; — 1.1.49

alo'ntyasya ।

whereby a provision is made for an operation to obtain on the final sound-segment of that which is specified with the genitive; — 1.1.52

ṅic ca ।

whereby that which is marked with *ṅ* as in *it* also comes in place of the final sound-segment; — 1.1.53

ādeḥ parasya ।

whereby an operation in place of that which follows applies to its initial sound segment; — 1.1.54

anekālśit sarvasya ।

> whereby that which consists of more than one sound segment, and which is marked with *ś* as an *it* comes in place of the final sound; — 1.1.55
>
> *tasmād ity uttarasya* ।
>
> whereby a specification made with the ablative *(pañcamī)* requires an operation to obtain on that which immediately follows. — 1.1.67

These interpretive conventions all regulate the loci of replacement operations. 1.1.52 *alo'ntyasaya* is a general rule to which rule 1.1.54 *ādeḥ parasya* is an exception. It is for this reason that the application of rule 1.1.52 *alo'ntyasya* does not find any scope of application relative to provisions of rule 8.4.61 *udaḥ sthāsthambhoḥ pūrvasya* and 7.1.29 *śaso na*. Rule 1.1.53 *ṅic ca* is similarly an exception to 1.1.55 *anekālśīt sarvasya*. Rule 1.1.55 *anekālśit sarvasya* is an exception to not only 1.1.52 *alo'ntyasya* but also to 1.1.54, *ādeḥ parasya*, of course, read with 1.1.67 *tasmād ity uttarasya*. A separate formulation of 1.1.54 *ādeḥ parasya* as against a formulation such as *tasmād ity uttarasyādeḥ* was made to facilitate its interpretation as follows:

> an operation which is specified with the ablative (*pañcamī*) is to be peformed in place of the initial of that which immediately follows.

Now consider 2.4.52 *aster bhūḥ* whereby *-as* is replaced with *bhū* in view of 1.1.55 *anekālśit sarvasya* as an exception. But now consider 7.1.29 *aṣṭābhya auś* whereby *auś* comes as a total replacement (*sarvādeśa*) of 1.1.67 *anekālśit sarvasya*, against the initial replacement proposal of 1.1.54 *ādeḥ parasya*. Commentators recognize that in application of rules such as 7.1.9 *ato bhis ais* we find a situation of conflict between these two exceptions. Rule 1.1.54 *ādeḥ parasya* would require *-ais* to replace only the initial sound of *-bhis*. Rule 1.1.55 *anekālśit sarvasya* would require *-ais* to replace *-bhis* in toto. Rule 1.4.2 *vipratiṣedhe paraṁ kāryam* resolves the conflict in favour of total replacement with the application of the subsequent rule 1.1.55 *anekālśit sarvasya*. Here one need not doubt that a non-application of 1.1.55 *anekālśit sarvasya* will render its condition of *anekāltva* "more than one sound segmentness" vacuous (*vyartha*). A formulation of 1.1.53 *ṅic ca* is evidence enough to justify the condition of *anekāltva*. In fact, *anekāltva* should be considered most conducive towards establishing the equal strength (*tulyabalatā*) status of 1.1.55 *anekālśit sarvasya*, against 1.1.54 *ādeḥ parasya*.

Note that wherever 1.1.53 *ṅic ca* finds its scope of application, rule 1.1.55 *anekālśit sarvasya* also finds its scope of application. Rule 1.1.53 *ṅic ca* blocks the application of 1.1.55 *anekālśit sarvasya* at the strength of being an exception. Thus, under the provision of *avaṅ spoṭāyanasya*, etc., *ṅ* as an *it* accomplishes replacement in place of the final sound (*alo 'ntya*), as against a total replacement. Now consider the derivation of *jīvatāt* "may you live long" of *jīvatād bhavān* and *jīvatāt tvam* where given *jīv + a + ti*, rule 3.4.86 *eruḥ* replaces the *-i* of *-it* with *-u* to yield *jīv + a + u*. Rule 7.1.35 *tuhyos tātaṅ* (read with 1.1.53 *ṅic ca*) now applies to replace the final *-u* of *-tu* with-*tātaṅ*. But this replacement will yield the wrong form **jīvattāt*. The correct form *jīvatāt* can be derived by applying 1.1.55 *anekālśit sarvasya* whereby *-tu* of *jīv + tu* is to be replaced by *tātaṅ* to yield: *jīv + a + (tu->tātaṅ)* ⟶ *jīvatāt*. Recall that 1.1.53 *ṅic ca* is an exception to 1.1.55 *anekālśit sarvasya*. A context of *vipratiṣedha* appears within this interactional context of a relatively general (*utsarga*) rule against its corresponding exception (*apavāda*). This situation of conflict is resolved in favour of the subsequent rule 1.1.55 *anekālśit sarvasya* on the basis of *paratva (*1.4.2 *vipratiṣedhe paraṁ kāryam*).

This preceding part has been a discussion of *vipratiṣedha* with its two types of *saṁjñā-vipratiṣedha* and *saṁjñetara-vipratiṣedha*. Each of these two types fall within the scope of

1.4.1 *ā kaḍārād ekā saṁjñā* and 1.4.2 *vipratiṣedhe paraṁ kāryam*, respectivley. They both share one common condition, namely of *paratva*. An additional condition of *anavakāśatva* "no scope of application, elsewhere," joins *paratva* in the application of *saṁjñā vipratiṣedha* of 1.4.1 *ā kaḍārād ekā saṁjñā*. A similar additional condition of (*anyatra*) *sāvakāśatva* "scope of valid application, elsewhere" joins *paratva* in the application of *saṁjñā-vipratiṣedha* is limited to the domain of *saṁjñā-vipratiṣedha* (1.4.1 *ā kaḍārād ekā saṁjñā*). The scope of application of the domain of *saṁjñetara-vipratiṣedha* is generally outside the domain of *ekā saṁjñā* though throughout the *sapāda-saptādhyāyī* (the first seven *adhyāya*s plus one quarter of rules).

It has been shown here that the nature of interaction which obtains between an exception and its related general counterpart is different, particularly in the sense that a general rule finds its scope of application by leaving aside the scope of application of its related particular (*prakalpya cāpavādaviṣayam utsargo'bhiniviśate*). That is, instances of *vipratiṣedha* cannot be resolved by taking recourse to *apavādatva*, the notion of exception. I have not shown some interactional contexts of *ekā saṁjñā* and *saṁjñā-samāveśa* "class-inclusion of terms." I have also not shown instances of *vipratiṣedha* interacting with *nitya* "obligatory" and *anataraṅga* "internally conditioned" proposals. Finally, I have not mentioned any instances of *pūrvavipratiṣedha* "conflict among two rules of equal strength where a prior rule wins application." These and some other issues remain to be discussed elsewhere.

---

* This summary paper was written when I was in residence at the Special Center for Sanskrit Studies, Jawaharlal Nehru University, under a Fulbright Lecture Grant (February, 2005). I thank Professor Shashiprabha Kumar, the Chairperson of the Center for inviting me for lectures on Pāṇini (RNS).

7

The Concept of Brahman in the Three Schools of Vedānta

K.T. Pandurangi

Introduction

THE Indian mind has been in search of the source of the universe, the manner in which it evolved and its purpose right from Ṛgvedic times. The Nāsadīyasūkta (नासदीयसूक्त) describes the position before the universe was created when there were neither beings nor non-beings, no space or matter, no day or night. There was one unique entity that functioned by its own free will without being moved by anything else. There was none superior to it.

(i) नासदासीत् नोसदासीत् तदानीं नासीद्रजो न व्योमा परोयत्।

nāsadāsīt nosadāsīt tadānīṁ nāsīdrajo na vyomā paroyat ।

(ii) आनीदवातं स्वधया तदाकं तस्माद्धान्यन्न परः किमासीत्।

ānīdavātaṁ svadhayā tadākaṁ tasmāddhānyanna paraḥ kimāsīt ।

The concept of an uncaused cause, an unmoved mover, and an independent Supreme Being is present here.

In the Viśvakarma sūkta (विश्वकर्म सूक्त) the question as to how this universe was created is raised. What is the place on which the creator stood? What were the instruments with which he created the universe? What was the manner in which he created it?

> किं स्विदासीदधिष्ठानं किमारम्भणं कतमत् स्वित् कथासीत्।
> *kiṁ svidāsīdadhiṣṭhānaṁ kimārambhaṇaṁ katamat svit kathāsīt* ।

These questions are not answered directly. The creator is described in such a way that these questions are irrelevant for him.

> विश्वतः चक्षुः विश्वतो मुखः
> विश्वतो बाहुः विश्वतस्पात्
> संबाहुभ्यां धमति सं पतत्रै
> द्यावाभूमी जनयन् देव एकः
>
> *viśvataḥ cakṣuḥ viśvato mukhaḥ*
> *viśvato bāhuḥ viśvataspāt*
> *saṁbāhubhyāṁ dhamati saṁ patatrai*
> *dyāvābhūmī janayan deva ekaḥ*

The creator is figuratively described as one whose arms and feet are spread all over the universe; his eyes look at the entire universe. He creates heaven and earth spreading wide his arms. These statements convey that he is omniscient and omnipotent and the concept of the cause is brought out.

Such a cause is not given any name in the *Ṛgveda*. The Nāsadīyasūkta (नासदीयसूक्त) does not contain any name. Viśvakarma (विश्वकर्म) is not a name but a designation indicating his role. Elsewhere the names Hiraṇyagarbha and Prajāpati occur in the context of creation. The word *Brahman* occurs in the *Ṛgveda* but not for a creator or cause. In the Upaniṣads the concept of *Brahman* is developed as a cause as well as a creator of the universe.

Along with Vedic thought, the Sāṁkhya and Nyāya-Vaiśeṣika thoughts were also developing. Both these do not subscribe to the concept of *Brahman.* The theories of causation for these are quite different. Sāṁkhya adopts the theory of evolution while Nyāya-Vaiśeṣika adopts the theory of creation. *Prakṛti* is the primary cause for Sāṁkhya and the *paramāṇus* are the primary cause for Nyāya-Vaiśeṣika. Sāṁkhya totally rules out *Īśvara* while Nyāya-Vaiśeṣika nominally accepts him.

Apart from these two major theories of causation, the *Śvetāśvatāra* mentions some ancient theories of causation.

> कालः स्वभावो नियतिः यदृच्छा
> भूतानि योनिः पुरुष इति चिन्त्याः।
> संयोग एषां न तु आत्मभावा-
> दात्माप्यनीशः सुखदुःखभावात्।

> *kālaḥ svabhāvo niyatiḥ yadṛcchā*
> *bhūtāni yoniḥ puruṣa iti cintyāḥ* ।
> *saṁyoga eṣāṁ na tu ātma bhāvā-*
> *dātmāpyanīśaḥ sukhaduḥkhabhāvāt* ।

Time, intrinsic nature, the regularity of Nature, the element of chance, elements, a combination of these or man himself have the claim to be the cause. But in the presence of man, these non-sentient things cannot be considered as the cause. Man also cannot be considered the cause as he suffers from the pain and pleasure caused by these. Stating these views *Śvetāśvatāra* concludes that (*devātmaśakti*) देवात्मशक्ति is the cause. The views stated here have not survived in later discussion.

In the Upaniṣads, *Brahman* occupies the central position both as the cause and the creator. The expression *ātman* is also used to convey *Brahman.* In the majority of passages it conveys *Brahman.* However, in a few passages it refers to *jīva.* Whether it refers to *Brahman* or *jīva* has to be understood from the context.

The concept of *Brahman* is fully developed in the *Vedānta-Sūtras* of Bādarāyaṇa utilizing the Upaniṣadic sources and reconciling different statements. In the Upaniṣads *sat, akṣara prāṇa, ākāśa, ap,* (सत्, अक्षर, प्राण, आकाश, अप्), etc., are also stated as the first cause in different places. In the *taittirīya* (तैत्तिरीय) and the *Bṛhadāraṇyaka* (बृहदारण्यक), *Brahman* is prominently stated as the cause. In *Vedānta-Sūtras* all these passages are reconciled and *Brahman* emerges as the first cause.

The task of the *Vedānta-Sūtras* was two-fold: (i) to reconcile the claims of those other than *Brahman* as the cause within the Upaniṣads, and (ii) to reject the claim of the *prakṛti, paramāṇu,* and other entities stated by systems outside the Upaniṣads.

With respect to causation, important questions which are not expressly raised in the Upaniṣads but which have to be taken into account while rejecting the Sāṁkhya view, are whether the non-sentient alone can be the cause of the universe, whether a sentient can be the cause of the non-sentient and whether the sentient and the non-sentient are two separate categories but function in co-operation with each other. This may be put in modern terminology as under:

(i) Whether matter is the source of the mind or whether the mind is the source of matter?

(ii) Whether mind and matter are separate but co-operate with each other?

In the second alternative the holistic concept of the universe has to be protected by suitable means.

Keeping these questions in mind the three schools of Vedānta have formulated the ontological position on *Brahman* and its status as the cause. Upaniṣadic statements are utilized for this purpose. With this background I propose to give an exposition on the concept of *Brahman* in these three schools.

Brahman is the central doctrine of Vedānta Philosophy. I will not go into the details of the historical aspect of the development of this concept and term, tracing it through the Vedas and the Upaniṣads.

My purpose is to present this concept as understood in the three schools of Vedānta, viz., Advaita, Viśiṣṭādvaita and Dvaita as propounded by Śaṅkara, Rāmānuja and Madhva.

This concept has three dimensions — the metaphysical, the epistemological, and the theological. In the Indian tradition, philosophy and theology are not totally separate. Within philosophy, the issues of ontology and cosmology are also brought in. All these have a bearing on the central doctrine of Vedānta, viz., *Brahman*. Therefore, to give an exposition of the concept of *Brahman,* one has to touch upon these aspects to some extent.

In philosophy, certain nomenclatures like realism, idealism, empiricism, rationalism, monism, dualism and pluralism are current. Terms like absolutistic and theistic are also used. However, it is difficult to bring these Vedānta schools under one or the other of these nomenclatures. Therefore, it is better not to use these nomenclatures with reference to these schools. These terms may be occasionally used to indicate the nature of approach to some of the problems and concepts.

I

Let me first take up the question of the very nature and definition of *Brahman.* The three schools are agreed on its nature as being that of *sat, cit* and *ānanda*. However, Advaita does not consider these as three different aspects or different attributes. *Brahman* is *Nirviśeṣa, cinmātra,* i.e., he is pure consciousness without any features or characteristics that introduce any difference, internal or external. He is free from the three kinds of differences, viz., *svagatabheda, sajātīyabheda, vijātīyabheda* (स्वगतभेद, सजातीयभेद, विजातीयभेद)।

> वृक्षस्य स्वगतो भेदो पत्रपुष्पफलादिभिः।
> वृक्षान्तरात् सजातीयो विजातीयः शिलादितः।
> तथा सद्वस्तुनो भेदत्रयं प्राप्तं निवार्यते। — *PD*
>
> *vṛkṣasya svagato bhedo patrapuṣpaphalādibhiḥ* ।
> *bṛkṣāntarāt sajātīyo vijātīyaḥ śilāditaḥ* ।
> *tathā sadvastuno bhedatrayaṁ prāptaṁ nivāryate* ।

Brahman is *kūṭastha, nirguṇa, nirākāra,* i.e., he does not undergo any modification, has no attributes, has no forms and he is *śuddhabuddhanityamuktasvabhāva* (शुद्धबुद्धनित्यमुक्तस्वभाव).

Though this is the ultimate nature of *Brahman,* he plays a very important role in assoation with *avidyā* in the evolution and functioning of the world and its souls. In that capacity, he is called Īśvara and is omniscient, omnipotent, a creator, a regulator, a destroyer and so on. He has all the attributes and roles of a theological God.

As creator, he has to play the role of an agent and also provide the basis or *adhiṣṭhāna* for the creation. He plays both the roles — *nimittakāraṇa*, i.e., the agent, and *upādānakāraṇa* the basis, i.e., *adhiṣṭhāna.*

To bring out these two aspects of *Brahman,* viz., the pure and the functional aspect, Advaita offers two definitions of *Brahman.*

(i) *Svarūpalakṣaṇa* or intrinsic definition.

(ii) *Taṭasthalakṣaṇa* or contingent definition.

His being *nirviśeṣacinmātra* (निर्विशेषचिन्मात्र) is his intrinsic definition, and his being creator, sustainer, destroyer, etc., is the contingent definition. The intrinsic definition is not a feature or characteristic of *Brahman* but it is *Brahman* itself.

II

In Viśiṣṭādvaita the metaphysical and theological aspects of *Brahman* are not two different levels as in Advaita. Nor are the world and the souls projections of *avidyā*. *Brahman,* the world and the souls are one complex unit. This complex is metaphysically called *Brahman* and theologically, Nārāyaṇa. The metaphor of the soul and the body, i.e., *śarīra-śarīrī bhāva* is utilized to explain the relative status of *Brahman* and the other two. The world and the souls are distinct from, subordinate to, and inseparable from, *Brahman.*

> श्रीमन्नारायण एव चिदाचिद्विशिष्टं तत्त्वम्।
> *śrīmannārāyaṇa eva cidācidviśiṣṭaṁ tattvam* ।

He is the principal to all, he is the ruler of all, he is the source of all, he has to be worshipped by all and bestows good for all. All constitute his body.

> सर्वेश्वरत्वं सर्वशेषित्वं सर्वकर्माराध्यत्वं सर्वफलप्रदत्वं सर्वकार्योत्पादकत्वं स्वस्वज्ञानेतर समस्तद्रव्यशरीरत्वं इत्यादीनि ईश्वरलक्षणानि

> *sarveśvaratvaṁ sarvaśeṣitvaṁ sarvakarmārādhyatvaṁ sarvaphalapradatvaṁ sarvakāryotpādakatvaṁ svasvajñānetara samasta-dravyaśarīratvaṁ ityādīni īśvaralakṣaṇāni*

Here we find that the *Brahman's* metaphysical and theological roles are brought to the fore. The theological role is spelt out more clearly. The concepts of worship and God's grace are introduced. The fact that the *Brahman* is the cause of the world is mentioned.

No distinction between intrinsic definition and contingent definition is made. According to Viśiṣṭādvaita as well, the *Brahman* is both the *nimittakāraṇa*, i.e., agent, and the *upādānakāraṇa* the basic cause.

> अयमीश्वरः सूक्ष्मचिदचिद्विशिष्टवेषेण जगदुपादानम्, संकल्पविशिष्टवेषेण निमित्तकारणम्, कालाद्यन्तर्यामिवेषेण सहकारिकारणम्।

ayamīśvaraḥ sūkṣmacidacidviśiṣṭaveṣeṇa jagadupādānaṁ, saṁkalpaviśiṣṭaveṣeṇa nimittakāraṇam, kālādyantaryāmiveṣeṇa sahakārikāraṇam ।

III

The concept of *Brahman* in Dvaita agrees with that of Viśiṣṭādvaita in-so-far as the identities of *Brahman* and Nārāyaṇa are concerned. The metaphysical and theological God are one and the same. The two levels of *nirguṇa* and *saguṇa* conceived in Advaita are not present here. *Brahman* is not *nirguṇa*. He is *guṇapūrṇa*. He is omniscient, omnipotent. He is not only creator, sustainer and destroyer, he causes knowledge, ignorance, bondage and release. He regulates in all respects.

उत्पत्ति स्थितिसंहाराः नियतिः ज्ञानमावृत्तिः ।
बन्धमोक्षौ च पुरुषात् यस्मात् स हरिरेकराट् ॥

utpatti sthitisaṁhārāḥ niyatiḥ jñānamāvṛttiḥ ।
bandhamokṣau ca puruṣāt yasmāt sa harirekrāṭ ॥

The world and the souls are different from him but at the same time entirely dependent upon him.

Brahman is *svatantra*, i.e., independent, though the world and the souls are dependent on him. *Brahman* is independent in his very essential nature, functions and cognition. The metaphor of *bimba-pratibimba* is utilized to explain the relation between *Brahman* and the souls. *Brahman* is only *nimittakāraṇa*, i.e., agent. He is not *upādānakāraṇa*, i.e., material cause. It is *prakṛti* that is *upādānakāraṇa*.

परमात्मा अनन्तगुणपरिपूर्णः सृष्ट्याद्यष्टकर्ता जीवजडेभ्यः अत्यन्तविलक्षणः सर्वस्वतन्त्रः एक एव नानारूपः सर्वाण्यपि रूपाणि पूर्णानि ।

paramātmā anantaguṇparipūrṇaḥ sṛṣṭyādyaṣṭakartā jīvajaḍebhyaḥ atyantavilakṣaṇaḥ sarvasvatantraḥ eka eva nānārūpaḥ sarvāṇyapi rūpāṇi pūrṇāni ।

IV

From the above brief introduction of the concept of *Brahman* in the three schools of Vedānta it is clear that Advaita conceived of *Brahman* at two levels — a pure level and a functional level — while in Viśiṣṭādvaita and Dvaita no such difference is made. However, *Brahman* is transcendental and not empirical according to the three schools. Though he is not empirical in the ordinary sense of the term, his knowledge could be obtained and has to be obtained. He is the basis of the empirical set-up. It is the nature of this basis and his relation with this empirical set-up that gives the correct picture of the ontological and the metaphysical position of both *Brahman* and the rest of the empirical set-up.

This can be understood from the nature of causation and of relation between *Brahman* and the rest.

As already stated in both Advaita and Viśiṣṭādvaita, *Brahman* is considered as *upādānakāraṇa* for the world. *Brahman* is sentient and the world is non-sentient. *Brahman* is a thinking substance while the world is not so. Therefore, one cannot be the material cause for the other. To overcome this, Advaita brings in *avidyā* which consists of *sattva, rajas* and *tamas* that are known in Sāṁkhya tradition. *Brahman* associated with *avidyā* is *upādānakāraṇa*. However, the whole effect is *vivartta* a projection on *Brahman.* Neither *avidyā* nor its effect, the empirical world, has any reality of its own.

Brahman is *adhiṣṭhāna*, the basis of *avidyā,* and its effects are *āropa*, i.e., projection. The relation between the two is *adhyāsa*, a projection. It is only in the capacity of *adhiṣṭhāna,* as the ground, that *Brahman* is considered as *upādānakāraṇa. Brahman* does not undergo any modification to develop into the world. It is only *avidyā* that does so. This kind of causation without modification is called *vivartopadāna*.

The entire world consisting of name and form, *nāma* and *rūpa* (नाम and रूप), is a projection. The basic projection is known as *mūlavidyā* and the projections at different levels of the evolution of the empirical world is called *tulavidyā*. But at all these levels what lends even empirical reality to the world is *Brahman* which is *adhiṣṭhāna* all along.

अस्ति भाति प्रियं रूपं नाम चेत्यंशपञ्चकम् ।
आद्यत्रयं ब्रह्मरूपं जगद्रूपं ततो द्वयम् ॥

asti bhāti priyaṁ rūpaṁ nāma cetyaṁśapañcakam ।
ādyatrayaṁ brahmarūpaṁ jagadrūpaṁ tato dvayam ॥

Even *Brahman*'s functional level as *Īśvara* is a projection. The souls are projections. The reality of these is only functional. The pure *Brahman* is *adhiṣṭhāna,* i.e., the ground. The relation between pure *Brahman* and the rest, including *Īśvara* is a projection.

Thus, the concept of *Brahman* in Advaita has a pure level, i.e., the *pāramārthika* level, and a functional level, i.e., the empirical world and the souls. The latter is a projection according to Advaita. It has no reality. Therefore, Brahmadvaita, i.e., the *Brahman* is the only reality in the Advaita concept of *Brahman.*

V

Viśiṣṭādvaita describes the causation of *Brahman* and its relation with the world and the souls in a different way.

According to Viśiṣṭādavaita, *Brahman, jīva* and *jagat* constitute one complex. He is of the nature *cidacidviśiṣṭa* (चिदचिद्विशिष्ट). Its subtle stage, i.e., *sūkṣmacidacidviśiṣṭa* (सूक्ष्मचिदचिद्विशिष्ट), is the cause while its gross stage, i.e., *sthūla cidacidadviśiṣṭa* (स्थूल चिदचिदद्विशिष्ट), is the effect. The metaphor of the soul and body is utilized to describe the status of *jīva, jagat* and *Brahman* in this complex. *Brahman* is *śarīrin* and *jīva* and *jagat* are *śarīra*. When the cause develops into the effect, it is the body aspect that undergoes a change. This change is described as *avasthāntara* (अवस्थान्तर). Keeping this in mind, *Brahman* is described as *upādānakāraṇa* (उपादानकारण). He is the agent in bringing about this change. Hence, he is *nimittkāraṇa* (निमित्तकारण). In this way Viśiṣṭādvaita manages to develop the cause and effect relation without involving the development of the non-sentient from the sentient. This process is illustrated by a child developing into a young boy and then into an old person. The soul of the child does not change. It is only the body that changes.

Dvaita solves this problem in another way. According to Dvaita the sentients, viz., *Brahman* and *jīva* are quite distinct from each other and also from the material world. *Brahman* is not *upādānakāraṇa* (उपादानकारण) for the world. He is agent only. The world develops out of *prakṛti*, i.e., primordial matter. The relation between *Brahman* and *jīva jagat* is explained by the metaphor of *bimba* and *pratibimba*, i.e., the archtype and prototype. The nature of this relation is explained as *tadadhīnatve sati tatsadṛśatvam* (तदधीनत्वे सति तत्सदृशत्वम्।) *jīva* and *jagat* are similar to God as well as dependent upon God. This dependence is with respect to the very existence, function and cognition. Though *jīva* and *jagat* are quite distinct, these are intimately connected by this relation. There is not much difference between the *śarīra-śarīrī* (शरीर-शरीरी) metaphor and the *bimba-pratibimba* (बिम्ब-प्रतिबिम्ब) metaphor. Both accept the distinction between *jīva* and *Brahman* but connect them with an intimate relation.

From the above explanation it is clear that the problems, (i) whether from the sentient cause the non-sentient can arise and vice-versa, and (ii) whether a holistic concept of the universe can be maintained if the sentient and the non-sentient separate, are solved by the three schools of Vedānta in different ways:

(i) Advaita considers the sentient *Brahman* only as the ultimate reality, i.e., *pārmārthikasat* (पारमार्थिकसत्). The rest has no ultimate reality. It is in this sense that the universe is holistic.

The non-sentient is projected over the sentient, therefore the question of its arising from the sentient does not arise. The mind is real and the matter is projected.

(ii) Viśiṣṭādvaita considers the mind and the matter as one complex and maintains the holistic nature of the universe. It is only the matter aspect that assumes the effect stage from its subtle stage. The sentient aspect does not undergo any change.

(iii) Dvaita considers the mind and the matter as distinct. The non-sentient world develops from the primordial matter.

However, its very existence and functionning is entirely dependent upon the mind, i.e., *Brahman.*

In the introductory remarks, we noted the *Śvetāśvatāra* statement mentioning some early views. Dvaita recalls those views and declares that all these so-called causes are under the control of *Brahman* as he is the ultimate cause of all cause.

द्रव्यं कर्म च कालश्च स्वभावो जीव एव च।
यदनुग्रहतः सन्ति न सन्ति यदुपेक्षया॥

dravyaṁ karma ca kālaśca svabhāvo jīva eva ca ।
yadanugrahataḥ santi na santi yadupekṣyā ॥

8

Vyāsa's Mahābhārata and Vālmīki's Rāmāyaṇa
Some Observations

R. P. Goldman

WE speak conventionally and often without reflection of the *Rāmāyaṇa*'s being — like the *Mahābhārata* and indeed the *Iliad* and the *Odyssey*, etc., — an "epic." But that term does not correspond clearly to any of the carefully defined and classified literary genres treated by the *alaṁkāraśāstrins*. We know the text as a piece of — indeed the reputed first example of — the genre of *belles lettristic* texts called *kāvya* or *sāhitya* in Sanskrit but that is a very broad category indeed encompassing gnomic verse, long narrative poems, all forms of drama, much prose composition, and the like. But then again, the great Kashmiri rhetoricians Ānandavardhana and Abhinavagupta, who were among the first to apply a strictly literary type of analysis to the *Rāmāyaṇa*, also refer to it by the genre term *itihāsa*, or historical saga, a term chiefly thought of in connection with the *Mahābhārata* and itself not very clearly delimited in its scope as witnessed by its being commonly included under the rubric of the compound term — *itihāsa-purāṇa*.

But although the *Rāmāyaṇa* and the *Mahābhārata* are clearly closely affiliated and bear many characteristics — both formal and substantive — in common, they also exhibit a number of significant differences. Among these differences one needs to consider, in the context of the present discussion, differences of scope, theme and purpose.

Let us consider first the question of scope. Although both texts are very large and cover a broad spectrum of concerns, the *Mahābhārata* is a much larger and far more inclusive text than the *Rāmāyaṇa*. Where the latter largely restricts itself to the poet's goal of providing a lengthy but generally focused answer to Vālmīki's framing question

> *ko na asmin sampratam̐ loke guṇavān kas ca vīryavān* ।
> *dharmajñaś ca kṛtajñaś ca satyavākyo dṛḍhavrataḥ* ॥
> *caritreṇa ca ko yuktaḥ sarvabhūteṣu ko hitaḥ* ।
> *vidvān kaḥ kaḥ samarthaś ca kaś caikapriyadarśanaḥ* ॥
> *ātmavān ko jitakrodho dyutimān ko 'nasūyakaḥ* ।
> *kasya bibhyati devaś ca jātaroṣasya sam̐yuge* ॥[1]

in the form of his own inspired poetic elaboration of *devarṣi* Nārada's concise account of Rāma's biography, Vyāsa's work betrays the much grander ambition of its author.

Indeed the latter work revels in its self-proclaimed status as a virtual encyclopedia of history, law, cosmology, mythology, science, theology, and, yes, philosophy, as these topics were known at the time of the formation of the epic. Thus the poet's boast,

> *dharme cārthe ca kāme ca mokṣe ca bhāratarṣabha* ।
> *yad ihāsti tadanyatra yan nehāsti na tat kvacit* ॥[2]

---

1. *Vālmīki Rāmāyaṇa* (henceforth *VR*) 1.1.2-4. All references to the *VR* are to the Critical Edition [*The Vālmīki Rāmāyaṇa: Critical Edition* (1960-75), 7 vols., Baroda: Oriental Institute, General ed. G.H. Bhatt and U.P. Shah] unless otherwise specified.

2. *Mahābhārata* (Henceforth *Mbh*) 1.56.33. All references are to the Critical Edn. of the *Mahābhārata* [*Mahābhārata: Critical Edition* (1933- →

is, given the limits of the world in which it took shape, by no means an exaggeration.

Thus, the great epic of the Bhāratas is not merely the elaborate history of a family feud and the civil war to which it gave rise, but an attempt, in the format of a grand narrative poem of love, war, treachery, adventure, and spiritual education to disseminate to a broad audience, throughout the vast cultural mosaic of South and South-East Asia the fundamental social, political, and metaphysical ideologies of late Vedic system(s) of thought, belief, and practice that constitute the foundation of the vast and complex edifice we call Hinduism. In this way the text came to be regarded as a kind of appendix to the Vedas, as evidenced by such designations as "the Fifth Veda," "the Veda of the śūdras," and the like.

For this reason, the author and redactors of the saga of the Bhāratas felt moved — even obligated — to include in the capacious confines of the work lengthy disquisitions on metaphysics, *karma*, *yoga*, salvation, etc., showing considerable familiarity with the language and ideology expressed in the Upaniṣads, including early formulations of the tenets we associate with such philosophical schools as *Advaita-Vedānta* (*Uttara-Mīmāṁsā*), *Sāṁkhya*, and *Yoga*. In this way such lengthy passages as the *Bhagavad-Gītā*, the various *Anugītā*s, the *mokṣadharmaparvan*, etc., whatever their date, cannot be considered distracting diversions from the epic theme but rather integral to the grand scheme and purpose of the expanded work itself.

The *Rāmāyaṇa*, by way of contrast, seeks to portray the life of an exemplary person who in his actions and pro-

---

→ 70), 24 vols., Poona: Bhandarkar Oriental Research Institute, with *Harivaṁśa* (1969-71). Critically edited by V.S. Sukthankar *et al.*].

nouncements acts out and elucidates the moral ground and social ideology upon which the edifice of ancient Indian civilizations was erected. Thus, although the characters in the epic — chiefly, but not exclusively Rāma — and, through them, the poet frequently indulges in moral discourse and in perorations on truth, *dharma*, proper political and social conduct (*nīti*), the poem, by its very nature, does not offer great scope for what one would normally call strictly philosophical disquisition.

But in addition to the question of genre that I have touched on, there is a significant difference between the two poems in what one would have to call the theological realm that has, I believe, considerable bearing on the nature and amount of philosophical material in the two poems respectively.

What I am referring to here is the different ways in which the two poets, Vālmīki and Vyāsa, and their principal characters represent and understand the nature and role of their respective divine heroes, the *avatāra*s Rāma and Kṛṣṇa.

Kṛṣṇa is, according to several schools of Vaiṣṇava theology, a *pūrṇāvatāra* of the Lord, perhaps the only such incarnation, as distinct from what is sometimes referred to as an *aṁśāvatāra* or partial incarnation. As such he is fully and at all times conscious — being consciousness itself — of his own nature as not different from the *paramātman*, the doctrine of which forms the essence of the Vedānta or, in more *saguṇa* terms, as it were, he is Puruṣottama, the Supreme Person. Not only is Kṛṣṇa fully self-aware, he actively proclaims his identity with the absolute, most famously in the *Gītā*, and gives, there and at a number of other moments in the narrative, dramatic demonstrations of his divine nature, his *aiśvarya*. Moreover, this divine nature of the hero is not by any means a secret. It is proclaimed by Bhīṣma in the *sabhā* of Yudhiṣṭhira and made clearly manifest in such episodes as the slaying of Śisupāla, Duryodhana's failed attempt to capture Kṛṣṇa, and the like. Indeed, it is only the perverse, ungodly and evil-minded, such as the Cedi prince and Duryodhana himself, who refuse to acknowledge the manifest divinity of Kṛṣṇa. Even they, as in the case of the former, can merge fully with the Lord in salvation even as he punishes them for their apostasy.

It will be noted that whether in the *Bhārata* itself, the *Harivaṁśa Pūraṇa*, the *Śrīmadbhāgavatam*, or any of the texts that narrate the *līlā* of Lord Kṛṣṇa, the *avatāra* — as man, boy, or even seemingly helpless infant — is never at a loss, is never seen to suffer or to be unaware of his divine nature and his divine powers, although those who surround him are generally ignorant of it. As such he is the perfect vehicle for the exposition and the demonstration of the nature of reality, the beginningless, endless, changeless, undecaying *para-Brahman* who, in his compassion for suffering beings trapped in the world of nescience and *saṁsāra*, deploys his *māyā* to engage in his apparent incarnation as a kṣatriya prince, the kinsman, friend and adviser to the Pāṇḍavas and the visible object of human devotion.

How different is the conception of the *avatāra* in Vālmīki. Although the *ādikavi* and we, his audience, are always clearly aware of Rāma's divinity, of his nature as an *avatāra* (*aṁśa* or otherwise) of Lord Nārāyaṇa, a unique aspect of Vālmīki's tale is that — until he has accomplished the purpose for which he took human form — Rāma himself, and, for the most part, those around him do not and cannot know this.

The reasons for this are simple both on the theological-mythological and the didactic levels. Unlike some of his later emulators, the authors of the innumerable re-tellings of the *Rāmakathā* that form so significant an element in the cultures of South and South-East Asia, Vālmīki takes very seriously the theme of the boon of Rāvaṇa. The essence of this boon is that the *rākṣasa* lord is, in effect, invulnerable to gods, *asuras*, and every other class of supernatural being. Therefore, for Viṣṇu to honour his pledge to the gods to kill him and yet not violate the terms of the boon of the Creator, Lord Brahmā, he must not only take on the appearance of a man but the nature of a man — albeit a highly superior man. That means, among other things that Rāma cannot know that he is in fact the Lord of the universe and therefore must suffer like any ordinary man if not more so in the light of his exemplary status.[3]

This unique representation of the *avatāra,* as unaware of his true nature fits not only Vālmīki's sense of mythological propriety but dovetails perfectly with his project of creating a literary rendering of the life of an exemplary man who not only suffers loss, grief, and pain like any mortal, but bears them with a stoicism and nobility that we are meant to admire and, to the extent possible for us, to emulate.

Therefore the *Rāmāyaṇa,* at least in Vālmīki's influential version, presents little scope for its hero to preach on the nature of the absolute or to reveal himself in his *virāṭa rūpa* as Jagannātha, Puruṣottama and, indeed *para-Brahman.* In fact, even after he has accomplished his divine mission by slaying the monstrous Rāvaṇa, and the gods, in their relief and delight, assemble to praise him, Rāma can only express his utter ignorance of such matters telling Brahmā in a famous verse:

---

3. For a thorough discussion of the boon of Rāvaṇa and its role in the representation of Rāma as a divinity and as a man see Pollock, Sheldon, *The Rāmāyaṇa of Vālmīki: An Epic of Ancient India,* vol. III, 3, Araṇyakāṇḍa, Princeton: The Princeton University Press, 1991, pp. 15-43.

ātmānaṁ mānuṣaṁ manye rāmaṁ daśarathātmajam ।
yo'haṁ yasya yataś cāhaṁ bhagavāṁs tad bravītu me ॥[4]

I think of myself only as a man, Rāma, the son of Daśaratha. May the blessed lord please tell me who I really am, to whom I belong, and why I am here.

This said, however, I do not mean to suggest that the text of the *Vālmīki Rāmāyaṇa*, at least in some of the versions in which it has come down to us, is utterly devoid of the kind of metaphysical and philosophical passages of the type discussed above as characteristic of many portions of the *Mahābhārata*. Indeed, given the theological and philosophical climate in which the text became so deeply imbricated in the religious culture of India, it was only to be expected that the text itself, including its later accretions, its rich medieval commentarial literature, and of course, its densely theological, metaphysical, and philosophical reworkings such as the *Adhyātma Rāmāyaṇa*, the *Rāmcaritamānasa*, the *Yogavaśiṣṭhamahārāmāyaṇa*, etc., should be influenced by the emerging currents of thought and belief. With this as a background let me turn now to some of the more explicitly philosophical elements in the poem.

On a very general level and in keeping with the broad definitions of philosophy mentioned earlier, the text and its characters concern themselves deeply with an ongoing discourse on ethical and moral philosophy. The poem itself is a kind of a Dharmaśāstra paying particular attention to social relations (chiefly in the area of hierarchy, deference and *varṇāśramadharma*), the critical question of truth, and a thoroughgoing concern with the nature of human action.

The first of these areas is worked out in the text's unremitting concern with and exploration of the theme of the deference owed by junior to senior figures of authority, by the lower to the higher *varṇa*s, and by wives to their husbands.

This imperative is dealt with by positive and negative examples and in numerous well-known didactic passages throughout the poem and needs no further elaboration here. The second, lying at the heart of the *Rāmāyaṇa*'s concern with ethics is exemplified by the poem's central narrative event — Rāma's dogged insistence on maintaining the truth of his father's promise to Kaikeyī — is part of an ongoing meditation on the nature of truth and the nature of reality itself that comes to dominate much philosophical discourse in India from the time of the Vedas onward. The third area constitutes a discourse that in many ways mirrors Western philosophical and theological debates on the subject of free will and determinism. In Vālmīki's terms, the question is posed as an opposition between what he calls *puruṣakāra,* or human effort, on the one hand, and *daiva,* fate or destiny, on the other, and his story, in which virtuous characters are continually subjected to suffering, provides an ideal vehicle in which to explore the fundamental human concern as to why, in a supposedly justly ruled and ordered universe, bad things happen to good people. Here, as suggested above, this kind of debate is only possible if the hero-*avatāra* is unaware of his divine nature.

In addition to these pervasive themes of social, ethical and moral philosophy, the poem, as we have received it, does have a number of passages that can be viewed as more explicitly metaphysical or, "philosophical," if you will. Let me turn briefly to a few of these.

One well-known such passage occurs towards the end of the Ayodhyā-Kāṇḍa of the poem in the context of the complex ethical debate between Rāma and his brother Bharata as to the necessity, advisability, and propriety of the former's continuing to abide by the vow of their deceased father, Daśaratha.

In the midst of this debate one Jābāli, a brāhmaṇa attached to the Kosalan court, addresses Rāma arguing that he should give up all his lofty ethical and moral notions and adhere to a strictly materialist and instrumentalist philosophy of advancing one's own self-interest. Jābāli's arguments, which the poet tells us at the outset, are at variance with *dharma* (*dharmāpetam*) and are distinctly evocative of the materialist philosophical school summarized in the *Sarvadarśanasaṁgraha*, and which we know as the Cārvāka or Lokāyata doctrine. Particularly noteworthy here is Jābāli's denial of the existence of a higher unseen (*adṛṣṭa*) level of reality, an afterlife, in effect, hope for or fear of which governs the behaviour of people he characterizes as ignorant.

Jābāli envisions a universe in which the pious and the self-indulgent alike are doomed to extinction upon the death of the body. In his view religious rites are ineffectual and the texts that urge people to engage in sacrifice, charity, worship, penance, and renunciation — the hallmarks of the spiritual life from time immemorial in India — are pious frauds composed by cunning men only in their own self-interest.

> *dānasaṁvananā hy ete granthā medhavibhiḥ kṛtāḥ* ।
> *yajasva dehi dīkṣasva tapas tapyasva saṁtyaja* ॥[5]

Rāma, of course, refutes Jābāli's arguments. But it is interesting to note that in so doing he does not directly appeal to what one would anticipate as the appropriate counter-arguments for the existence of the unseen, the world of the gods, and the after life (although belief in these is implicit in his response); but rather falls back on his familiar ethical discourse about proper conduct (*caritram*) and above all truth (*satyam*).

---

4. *VR* 6.105.10.
5. *VR* 2.100.15.

ṛṣayaś caiva devaś ca satyam eva hi menire ı
satyavādī hi loke'smin paramaṁ gacchati kṣayam ıı[6]

There are two further passages found in the received text of the *Rāmāyaṇa*, or at any rate in the most commonly printed versions of the poem, that are, however, distinctly reminiscent of the kind of Upaniṣadic metaphysics that is common place in the *Mahābhārata*.

Perhaps the best known of these is a passage that occurs only in the southern recension of the text at Yuddha-Kāṇḍa 105[7] in which the sage Agastya comes to Rāma just before the latter's final battle with Rāvaṇa and reveals to him a secret teaching (*guhyam*) known as the *Ādityahṛdaya* through which, he declares, Rāma will conquer his foes.

The passage is regarded as a significant hymn incorporated as an integral part of the *Rāmāyaṇa*. Many of the southern commentators consider the piece to be virtually a Vedic hymn, assigning to it, in the manner of the *vaidikas*, a principal divinity, either Brahmā (so Nāgojībhaṭṭa and Mādhavayogīndra) or Rāma in the form of the sun (Śivasahāya), a *ṛṣi* (Agastya) a Vedic metre (*anuṣṭubh*) and an application (*viniyoga*), which includes the elimination of all obstacles, the acquisition of knowledge

---

6. *VR* 2.101.11.

7. The reference here is to the so-called Vulgate text of the poem as it appears for example in such printed edn. as those of the Nirnayasagar Press [*The Rāmāyaṇa of Vālmīki* (1930), 4th rev. edn., Bombay: Nirṇayasagar Press. With the commentary (*Tilaka*) of Rāma, ed. Vāsudeva Laxmaṇ Śāstrī Paṇaśīkar, the Gujarati Printing Press]; The Gujarati Printing Press [*Rāmāyaṇa of Vālmīki* (1914-1920), 7 vols., Bombay, Gujarati Printing Press, With three commentaries called *Tilaka*, *Śiromaṇi*, and *Bhūṣaṇa*, ed. Shastri Shrinivas Katti Mudholkar]; and the Gita Press [*Śrīmad Vālmīki-Rāmāyaṇa* (1969), 3 vols., Gorakhpur: Gita Press]. The passage appears in the Critical Edn., at Appendix I, no. 65.

of the absolute, and the accomplishment of universal victory. These commentators also suggest that the piece, like the Vedas themselves, has ancillary texts, variously described as homage to the radiant sun or to Gāyatrī. In fact, some of the commentators, notably Mādhavayogīndra, Nāgojībhaṭṭa, Śivasahāya, and Maheśvaratīrtha, invest the text with an almost Upaniṣadic quality as the sun, sometimes as Lord Viṣṇu, sometimes as Rāma, and sometimes as the Upaniṣadic *Brahman*.

Govindarāja alone among the commentators who treat this passage seems less than deeply impressed with it. He comments on it in a generally straightforward fashion avoiding the esoteric, etymological, and Upaniṣadic explanations of some of his colleagues. In fact, he expresses some disquiet at the way in which the hymn seems at times to exalt Sūrya, a relatively minor divinity in post-Vedic India, above even Nārāyaṇa, the central focus of *Rāmāyaṇa* devotion. He makes some effort to harmonize these two interpretive approaches in a set of general comments to the *sarga*'s final verse but indicates that he also has some skepticism with regard to the textual authenticity of the passage. He notes that Uḍāli (Varadarāja), whose commentary we believe to be the oldest one extant, does not comment on this *sarga*. Moreover, Govindarāja notes that Uḍāli enumerates one hundred and thirty *sargas*, in the Yuddha-Kāṇḍa and that if the *Ādityahṛdaya* chapter were to be included it would raise the total (in Govindarāja's text)[8] to one hundred and thirtyone.

8. This text is represented in such printed editions as those of the Kumbhakonam [*Śrīmadvālmīkirāmāyaṇam* (1911-13), 7 vols., Bombay: Nirnayasagar Press, also called the Kumbakonam Edn., ed. T.R. Krishnacharya and T.R. Vyasacharya] and Venkatesvara Steam Press [*Śrīmadvālmīkirāmāyaṇam* (1935), 3 vols., Bombay, Lakshmivenkatesvara Mudraṇālaya. With the commentaries of →

Some of the commentators understand that Agastya has come to bolster the confidence of Rāma who is anxious about his ability to kill Rāvaṇa (so Varadarāja and Maheśvaratīrtha). Nāgojībhaṭṭa believes that Rāma (as a omnipotent divinity) merely pretends to be afraid, since he wishes to receive the *Ādityahṛdaya* from Agastya for the benefit of the world. Govindarāja understands that Rāma is concerned about how he is to defeat Rāvaṇa without revealing his nature as the supreme divinity.

The passage consists largely of a *stotra*, or hymn of praise, to Āditya or Sūrya, the sun god, and as such contains numerous names, kennings, and epithets for this central celestial deity. Commentators exercise their ingenuity and demonstrate their devotion by providing many multiple interpretations of these names and terms, often giving both the standard mythological reference as well as a more esoteric "functionalist" interpretation based on the etymology of the name. These secondary interpretations tend to refer to the role of the divinity in the creation and maintenance, the dispelling of ignorance, and the pains of worldly existence, the salvation of devotees, etc.

In short, most of the Vaiṣṇava commentators regard the passage as in some ways similar to passages such as the *Bhagavad-Gītā* in that it reveals the epic hero for what he is, an incarnation of the Supreme Spirit. So that one can appreciate the similarity to such passages, here is our translation of it:

> Then the blessed Agastya, who had come alongwith the gods to witness the battle, seeing Rāvaṇa, exhausted by combat and overcome by anxiety, on the battlefield and

---

→ Govindarāja, Rāmānuja, and Maheśvaratīrtha and the commentary known as *Taniślokī*, ed. Gangavishnu Srikshanadasa] editions.

positioned in the forefront for further combat, approached Rāma and said, "Rāma, great-armed Rāma, now hear this immemorial secret teaching by means of which, my child, you shall conquer all of your enemies. One should constantly intone this holy Ādityahṛdya, which destroys all one's enemies, brings victory, and which is everlasting and supreme blessedness. It is the auspiciousness of all auspicious things and it destroys all sins. It calms anxiety and grief, and it is the greatest means for the extension of life. So worship Visvasvant the sun god, bringer of light, the lord of the worlds, rising with his halo of rays, worshipped by the gods and *asuras*. He is the essence of all the gods. Filled with blazing energy, he brings all beings to life with his rays. With his rays he protects the gods, the *asuras*, and all the worlds. He is Brahmā, Viṣṇu, Śiva, Skanda, and Prajāpati. He is great Indra, Kubera, the bestower of wealth, Time, Yama, the god of death, Soma, and Varuṇa, lord of the waters. He is the ancestors, the Vasus, the Sādhyas, the two Aśvins, the Maruts, and Manu. He is Vāyu, the god of wind, Agni, the god of fire. He is all creatures, the breath of life, and the sun, bringer of light and author of the seasons. He is Āditya, the child of Aditi, Savitṛ, impeller of beings, Sūrya, the sun god, he who moves through the sky, Pūṣan, the nourisher, and he is the many rayed sun. He is the being as radiant as gold, he the golden seed, the maker of day. He is the thousand-rayed lord of the bay steeds, the master of seven horses, and he has myriad rays. He is the dispeller of darkness, he is Śambhu the auspicious one, he is Tvaṣṭṛ and Mārtaṇḍa, of many rays. He is Hiraṇyagarbha, the golden embryo, the cooling one, the scorching one, Ravi, the bringer of light, Son of Aditi, he bears Agni, the god of fire, in his womb, he is Śaṅkha, he brings the winter to a close. He is the lord of the heavens, dispeller of darkness, master of the *Ṛk*, *Yajur*, and *Sāma* Vedas, friend of the waters, he is the source of torrential rains, he flies across the path of the Vindhya mountains. He is the scorching one, the great orb.

He is death, the golden one, who scorches all beings. A sage, omnipresent, of immense blazing energy, reddish in hue, he is the source of all existence. He is lord of the constellations, planets, and stars, giver of light to all, most radiant of all radiant beings. As you are, I do homage to you, you of the twelve forms. Homage to him who rises on the eastern mountain and who sets on the western mountain. Homage to the lord of the hosts of heavenly luminaries. Homage to the lord of day. Homage, homage to the victorious one, to him of the bay horses, who offers victory and auspiciousness. Homage, homage to him of the thousand rays. Homage, homage to Āditya. Homage to the fierce warrior. Homage, homage to the swift one. Homage to him who makes the lotus bloom. Homage, homage to Mārtaṇḍa. Homage to Sūrya, the luminous sun god, the lord of Brahmā, lord Śiva, and the imperishable Viṣṇu, whose radiance is that of Āditya and who in his fierce form, devours all creatures. Homage to the banisher of darkness, and the bringer of the thaw, to that immeasurable one, the god who slaughters his enemies and destroys the ungrateful, the lord of heavenly luminaries. Homage to Viśvakarmā, the maker of all things, to fire, whose lustre is that of burnished gold. Homage to Ravi, eye of all the worlds, dispeller of darkness. He is the lord who destroys the creation, and then creates it anew. With his rays, he dries up, scorches, and inundates the world. Lodged within all beings, he remains awake while they sleep. He is the *agnihotra* sacrifice as well as the reward of those who perform it. He is all the Vedas, all sacrifices, and the reward of all sacrifices. He, lord Ravi, is everything. He is every action that is done throughout the worlds. Even if a man be in distress, difficulty, or danger, or if he be lost in the wilderness, he shall not, Rāghava, so long as he praises the sun, succumb to any harm. Therefore, with a focused mind, you should worship that god of gods, the lord of the worlds, for having intoned this hymn three times you will be victorious in all your battles. This very hour, great-armed

> warrior, you shall slay Rāvaṇa. 'Then, when he had spoken in this fashion, Agastya departed just as he had come. When immensely powerful Rāghava had heard that, he became free from care and, concentrating his mind, greatly pleased, he memorized it. Gazing at Āditya, the sun god, and intoning that hymn, he attained supreme happiness. Sipping water three times and having thus become purified, the mighty warrior took up his bow and his eyes fixed on Rāvaṇa went forth to battle with delighted heart. Exerting himself to the utmost, he was determined to kill him. Then Ravi, the sun god, himself, surrounded by the hosts of gods, anticipating with a delighted mind, the destruction of the lord of the night-roaming *rākṣasa* gazed upon Rāma and in great excitement said, "Make haste!"

This passage, highly venerated though it is, has been shown on sound text-historical grounds not belonging to the oldest stratum of the epic text. Indeed, given the mythological and theological issues discussed above, the analysis to which it is subject by the commentators does not seem to fit well in the epic narrative as it appears to bring this kind of metaphysical discussion (albeit in the form of a hymn to Sūrya) into the drama before completion of the avatāric mission.

There is one final passage that is believed to be noteworthy in the context of a discussion on the philosophical content of the epic. It is the one in which the gods at last reveal to Rāma his true nature after he has carried out, in his role as a human prince the terms of Brahmā's boon by killing Rāvaṇa.

> Then King Kubera Vaiśravaṇa, Yama, the god of death, dragger of his foes, great Indra of the thousand eyes, Varuṇa, god of waters, scorcher of his foes, the great god, majestic Śiva, with his halt-six eyes and the bull on his banner, Brahmā foremost of those who know the Vedas, the creator

of the entire universe: All these assembled in their flying chariots as radiant as the sun, and coming to the city of Laṅkā, they approached Rāghava. Then raising their broad arms covered with bracelets, the foremost of the thirty gods addressed Rāghava who stood before them, his hands cupped in reverence. "How can you the creator of the entire universe, the most ancient one, foremost among those possessing supreme knowledge, stand by and watch as Sītā falls into the fire, eater of oblations. How can you not realize that you are the foremost of the hosts of the gods? Long ago, you were the Vasu Ṛtudhāman, the progenitor of the Vasus. You are the primal creator of the three worlds, the untrammelled lord. You are Rudra Śiva the eighth among the Rudras and you are fifth among the Sādhyas. The twin Aśvins are your ears, the moon and the sun your eyes. You are present before the beginning and after the end of the universe, scorcher of your foes. And yet, like some ordinary man you ignore Vaidehī. Now when Rāma Rāghava, the lord of the world, was addressed in this fashion by those guardians of the world, that foremost of those who uphold righteousness said to the foremost of the thirty gods: I think of myself only as a man, Rāma, the son of Daśaratha. May the blessed lord please tell me who I really am, whom I belong to, and why I am here. To Kākutstha, who was speaking in this fashion, Brahmā, foremost amongst those who know the Vedas, said, "Truly valorous Rāma, now hear the truth from me. "You are a god, the majestic Lord Nārāyaṇa, weilder of the discus. You are the single-tusked boar, conqueror of your enemies, past and future. You are the imperishable *Brahman*, existent in the beginning, the middle, and the end. You are the highest governing principal of all the worlds, the four-armed Viśvakṣena. You are the wielder of the horn bow, you are Hṛṣīkeśa, the primal person, the supreme spirit. You are Viṣṇu, the invincible wielder of the sword, and you are Kṛṣṇa of immense strength. You are the leader of the hosts. You are the leader of all beings. You are intelligence, strength, forbearance, and self-control. You are the origin and the dissolution. You are Upendra, Indra's younger brother, and Madhusūdana, slayer of the *asura* Madhu. You are the author of Indra's deeds. You are the lord of the great gods. You are the lotus-navelled god. You are the destroyer of your enemies in battle. The divine great seers call you fit for refuge and refuge itself. You the great bull of a thousand horns and a hundred tongues that is the Veda itself. You are the sacrifice, the sacred utterance *vaṣaṭ*, and the sacred syllable *oṁ*, scorcher of your foes. No one knows your origin or your end, wondering, Who are you? You are manifest in all creatures, brāhmaṇas and cows and also in all the directions, the sky, the mountains, and the forests. You are the majestic Lord of the thousand feet, thousand heads, and a thousand eyes. You support all beings as well the earth with all its mountains. At the end of the world, you manifest yourself resting on the great serpent on the waters. You support the three worlds, Rāma, along with their gods, *gandharva*s and *dānava*s. I am your heart Rāma, your tongue is the goddess Sarasvatī. It is I, Brahmā, O Lord, who made the gods who are hairs on your limbs. When you close your eyes, it is night; when you open them, it is day. Your ritual practices are the ordinances of the Vedas. Without you, there is nothing. Your body is this world, your steadiness the surface of the earth. Agni, the god of fire, is your wrath, Soma, the moon, your gentleness, O bearer of the *śrīvatsa* mark. In ancient times, you spanned the three worlds, with as many strides. After confining the great *asura* Bali, you made great Indra king. Sītā is Lakṣmī; you are god Viṣṇu. You are Kṛṣṇa. You are Prajāpati, lord of creatures. It was in order to slay Rāvaṇa that you entered a human body here. Thus have you accomplished our purpose, foremost of upholders of righteousness. Rāvaṇa has been slain. Now please return to heaven in delight. Your strength and might have not been in vain, nor has your valour. Nor will men who are devoted to you ever fail

> of their purpose. Those who are firmly devoted to you, the ancient god and supreme spirit, those men who praise you, will never fail in any way.[9]

This passage, which belongs to the oldest recoverable strata of the text, is (except for the fact that its message must be revealed to the *avatāra* rather than by him) very similar to the sort of passage I referred to earlier in my discussion of the *Mahābhārata*.

Its existence here is, I believe, testimony not only to the care with which Vālmīki has constructed his narrative around the legend of the boon of Rāvaṇa, but also to the philosophical and metaphysical world-view in which both epics took shape.

The Upaniṣadic-Vedāntic philosophy that is so evident in many portions of the *Mahābhārata* is not, I believe, absent from the mind of the *Rāmāyaṇa*'s poet, but has been judiciously subordinated to the demands of his narrative.

In conclusion it would be appropriate to say that while both works, the *Rāmāyaṇa* and the *Mahābhārata* share the same metaphysical, theological and philosophical bases, their expression of these systems differs to a considerable extent as a direct result of two significant factors.

The first of these is the differing scope and purposes of the two works. Vyāsa's great work purports to serve as an all-inclusive guide to every aspect of ancient Indian life, thought and society by narrating a multi-generational family saga replete with examples of the best and the worst kinds of human behaviour. The author and his heirs have further expanded and embellished this tale with numerous myths, legends and stories drawn from Vedic and popular sources and enriched it with many moral, spiritual and philosophical

9. *VR* 6.105.

discourses. By war of contrast, Vālmīki's monumental poem seeks to teach us how to live a dhārmic life in the contexts of family an society by recounting in great detail and with tremendous emotional power and poetic skill the remarkable biography of an exemplary figure, the God-become-man, Rāma Dāśarathī. The *Mahābhārata* then is simply a much larger work with a much broader agenda and its authors have filled its larger space with many more things than the *Rāmāyaṇa* was designed to contain.

The second major factor that has led to the relative paucity of explicitly philosophical discourse in the *Rāmāyaṇa* when compared to the *Mahābhārata* is the different conception of the two great Vaiṣṇava *avatāra*s the two works put forward. Śrī Kṛṣṇa in the *Mahābhārata*, as in the *Śrīmadbhāgavatam* is at all times fully aware of his identity with the Supreme Spirit and both he and his devotees fully and freely expound the doctrine of the *avatāra* as non-different from the *paramātman* and the value of *bhakti* or devotion to the Lord as the surest path to salvation.

Vālmīki however, ever mindful of the particular terms of Rāvaṇa's boon of invulnerability to divinities is careful to maintain the fiction that his hero Rāma is merely a man who has no full consciousness of his own identity with the eternal *para-Brahman* until he has completed his mission of the destruction of the *rākṣasa* lord and is "enlightened" as it were to his true nature by the lesser divinities on whose behalf he was acting.

In this way, although the two great poet-seers Vyāsa and Vālmīki share the same philosophical understanding of the nature of the absolute, the degree to which they express it in their immortal poems must, of necessity, differ significantly.

9

Ecology and Conservation in the Bhūmisūkta of the Atharvaveda

Shashiprabha Kumar

I

THE Vedas though the oldest source of Indian culture and tradition, propound the most complete and holistic perspective of the universe. In the present state of ecological imbalance on this earth, it is necessary to draw upon this fund of ancient knowledge so that some integral path towards the goal of sustainable growth can be prepared. The present paper is a modest attempt in the same direction.

Ecology is the study concerned with the interrelation of living organisms and their environment while *conservation* means management, protection and preservation of the earth's natural resources and environment.[1] In the Vedic world-view all life in the cosmos is interrelated and interwoven; the process of transmutation and cyclic degeneration and regeneration of life is an accepted postulate. The man-nature relationship is at the centre of Vedic vision enunciated through sacred incantations and articulated as rituals for repeatedly reminding us of the need to sustain and foster the ecological balance of nature.

1. Collins Reference Dictionary, *Environmental Science*, pp. 90, 140.

II

The *Bhūmisūkta* of the *Atharvaveda* is one of the oldest and the most important sources of information on the relationship of man to his environment and his duty to preserve it. In the sixty-three verses of this hymn, the seer Atharvan has presented a beautiful picture of Mother Earth which is the source of our sustenance as also a symbol of the entire environment. The verses reflect the symbolic significance of a sensitively comprehended ecology and conservation.

Bhūmi, i.e., the earth is invoked here as the personified Mother Goddess; she supports us with her abundant endowments and riches; it is she who nourishes us all like a loving Mother nourishes her children.[2] What could be a more intimate depiction of the intrinsic relationship of Man to the Earth. These sentiments clearly denote the bond between the Earth and the human beings and exemplify the true relationship of human beings to other forms of life.

In fact, the Earth in the *Bhūmisūkta* does not merely mean the land; she rather represents all that is part of the environment. She symbolizes the three principal components of the environment: the solid, the liquid and the gaseous. She is described here as born out of the waters of ocean. Surrounded by space, she is the creator and sustainer of the world.

In her solid form, *bhūmi* is the land and abode of living and non-living beings as also the guardian and protector of all that is born and is to be born.[3] She supports and sustains all, furnishes wealth and is the foundation of the world.[4] Rocks,

---

2. *Atharvaveda* (*AV*), 12.1.10.
3. *Ibid.,* 12.1.1.
4. *Ibid.,* 12.1.5.

stone and dust constitute the earth; her soil is brown, black and variegated.[5] The ascents, advances and planes of land belong to the earth.[6]

On the liquid side of the environment, *bhūmi* is the sustainer of oceans, rivers and waters;[7] she is the wife of the clouds and is enriched by the rains.[8] Various resources of water, such as the seas, rivers and waterfalls flow on the earth.[9]

The gaseous aspect of earth is brought out through the observation that the air, "Mātariśvan," blows on the earth and the light of the flame follows the wind which is blowing forward and backward. All the birds and bipeds fly to the earth.[10] She bears whatever lives, breathes and stirs.[11] All the four quarters belong to her.[12]

Bhūmi is called *agnivāsā*,[13] having fire as her covering. She also represents the energy or the element of fire in the environment. She bears with her the universal fire which is present in the herbs, waters, stones, men and horses.[14] Agni gives heat and shine to the earth. The earth also has rich treasures of gold, gems and metals.[15] She carries along with her the seasons brought by the Sun,[16] her companion.

---

5. *Ibid.*, 12.1.26.
6. *Ibid.*, 12.1.2.
7. *Ibid.*, 12.1.8.
8. *Ibid.*, 12.1.42.
9. *Ibid.*, 12.1.9.
10. *Ibid.*, 12.1.51.
11. *Ibid.*, 12.1.3.
12. *Ibid.*, 12.1.4.
13. *Ibid.*, 12.1.21.
14. *Ibid.*, 12.1.19.
15. *Ibid.*, 12.1.44.
16. *Ibid.*, 12.1.48.

The physical aspect of the earth includes agriculture. The fertility of the earth is symbolized here through the image of the brimming vase, the bowl of plenty. Foliage and lotus emerge from the bowl. Waters flow as the life-giving forces of regeneration. The energy of the sun blossoms as vegetation which is the sap of life. She bears herbs of various varieties. Foodstuffs, such as rice and barley, come into being on the earth.[17] In this way, the earth is a figure of fecundity.

The earth is the source of life. She is the world of living beings. The five races of men belong to her. They are her children. She has people dwelling at places, using different languages and practising diverse customs and manners.[18] The great trembling and stirring vibrations of the earth render the diversity into a close-knit unit. All are born on the same land and all move on the same land, and she treats them all like a cow treats her calves, alike.

Not only human beings, ferocious animals also are children of the same Mother Earth. Serpents and scorpions lie hidden in a torpid state. Worms too stir in the early rainy season in lively forms. Man-eating lions, tigers, jackals, wolves scorpions and reptiles — all are on the earth.[19] The seer, however, wishes that they should not harm or crawl on man, mainly because all of them should live together harmoniously. According to this integral view, nothing in this universe is without its utility; each and every species has to be protected for its own sake so that the equilibrium of nature is not disturbed.

It is against this background that the land, water, air, fire, plants, animals, humans and divine beings come together in the various images of the Goddess Bhūmi, Mother Earth. The

17. *Ibid.*, 12.1.2, 4.

18. *Ibid.*, 12.1.45.

19. *Ibid.*, 12.1.46.

heaven, the earth, and the atmosphere have given this vastness of vision to the seer while the fire, the sun, the waters, and the gods have given him wisdom.[20] He, therefore, gratefully reveals the sublimity and divinity of *bhūmi,* the all-encompassing principle of nature and its resources.

III

We have taken a long stride since the Vedic age. At the turn of the twentieth century, environmental issues have emerged as a major concern for the survival and welfare of mankind on this planet. With the rapidly advancing technology and the fast growing economic system the modern civilization is under increasing threat from its own activities causing pollution of air, water and soil.[21] The ozone hole, acid rain, nuclear and other toxic wastes, chemical and pesticide industries, the fear of global warming, pollution of rivers and oceans, deforestation and the consequent soil erosion and the loss of bio-diversity are just a few highlights of the developmental models adopted across the globe which cause economic concerns.

The multiplying demands upon the ecosphere, which supports life on this planet, are rapidly exhausting the resources. The list of ecological threats is increasing by leaps and bounds. The prevailing world order has linked much of its productive economy to energy-intensive techno-culture which is ecologically destructive. We stand at the verge of an unprecedented environmental disaster never faced by man before. Man indeed has used his power not to transform, but to destroy the environment. As an eminent thinker observes in the context of India:

20. *Ibid.,* 12.1.53.

21. C.K. Varshney, *Environmental Challenges,* New Delhi: Wiley Eastern Limited, 1993, p. 10.

> Even more than the population explosion, the imbalance in the environment and ecology is the greatest threat to the continent. We may be able to control the first, but the process of devastation we have begun in the second may bring final doom.[22]

In fact, what Plato said of Attica in the fourth century BC, "Our land compared with what it was is like a skeleton of a body wasted by disease," could very well apply to India with her increasing arid, semi-arid and dry-humid areas totalling about five billion hectares.

IV

This brings us to point where we have to pause and ponder over the ecological imbalance threatening the modern world as well as over the ways and means to cure and curb them. The question is what are the diverse components of the disturbance and what methodologies and strategies were suggested and adopted in the past to sustain the ecological balance. Can we, even at this crucial stage, learn any lesson from the Vedic lore for equipping ourselves suitably to face the human predicaments of today?

First and foremost is the pollution of the land. Fouling the air and poisoning the water are not our only trespasses against the elements. Nor were they the earliest. "Man's first onslaught was against the Earth itself."[23] The Earth is a unique planet, most beautiful and bountiful. It is the floating ball beneath the most gleaming membrane of a bright blue sky. What,

---

22. Kapila Vatsyayan, "Ecology and Indian Myth" in *Indigenous Vision* (ed. Geeti Sen), New Delhi: Sage Publications, 1992, p. 158.
23. Sridath Ramphal, *Our Country, The Planet,* London: Lime Tree, 1992, p. 5.

however, have we done to it? Arid lands have increased, the soil which was venerated by our ancestors has been eroded, and infertile sand and salt have taken over. It is estimated that in this sub-continent alone, a million hectares are being turned into desert each year. The desecration of the bowels of the Earth through excessive quarrying has become common. Man's power has asserted its most destructive tendencies and his collective greed has hollowed the centre of life. Consequently, *bhūmi,* the eternal mother, now stands polluted and desecrated beyond all measurements.

Related to this is the massive, unprecedented deforestation. Consequently, the soil's capacity to absorb and hold water has diminished. The disturbance in the ecological system of the earth, water, vegetation, river and mountain is threatening the existence of all types of life. Man has disturbed the cosmic order, the rhythm of the movement of the earth, water, air, ether and Agni, i.e., the five elements whose interaction and interdependence are the basic rules of nature.

In the Vedic view, the sustenance of ecological balance is regarded as the first and last duty of man, since only then the moral order of the world, i.e., *ṛta* can be sustained. The idea of *ṛta* has much to do with the law of ecological balance as envisaged by the Vedic seers. The emphasis is both on the notion of cosmic regularity as also on purity and non-pollution. The Vedas dedicate many hymns to Varuṇa who is considered the great superintendent of the moral order. He is the guardian of *ṛta.* He sees all that is there between the Earth and the Heaven and even what lies beyond them.[24]

There is another prayer in the *Atharvaveda* which draws our attention once again to the ecological balance and how

24. *AV,* 4.16.5.

the Earth, like Varuṇa, is herself the upholder of moral order. Truth and moral order sustain her.[25] She is called the sacred environment, "Devayajani."[26] Man has been given the capacities for its conservation and growth which would promote his own developement also. The conception of the earth as the Mother in the *Bhūmisūkta* even goes further and prescribes that we should always recount without forgetting the glories of Mother Earth in all assemblages and meetings of the people,[27] since she prefers virtuous men of great abilities to those who obstruct the good.[28]

This is to warn us that we have "only one earth." Our science may increase its bounty and our husbandry make its resources go further but its capacity to support life cannot be indefinitely extended. As such, our generation, as cusodians of the present and trustees of the future, must take responsibility to sustain it. If life on the earth is to be sustained, we shall have to take care of it and share to a greater extent the responsiblity for its conservation. No longer do we live in a world endowed with an infinite amount of ecological resource. We must be conscious of the ecological bottom-line. The time is now ripe to give back to Mother Earth what we have taken from her because whatever comes from nature, must go back to her many times over. This is the message of the Veda. This "Good Earth" would not get better tomorrow unless we act today. Now that we are aware of our wrong doings and their consequences, we must change the mode of our response to nature.

---

25. *Ibid.*, 4.16.3.
26. *Yajurveda*, 3.5.
27. *AV*, 12.1.56.
28. *Ibid.*, 12.1.37.

V

The ecological implication of the relationship between man and nature is deep-rooted in the history of mankind, while man's sense of responsibility towards it is tied up with the knot of conservation. The theory of conservation has to be the science of totality which moves from segmental knowledge to the integrative wisdom of our Vedic seers. This means that the earth and its resources have to be protected for their own sake and not merely to preserve their potential for man's development. The concern for conservation or stewardship of natural resources is linked with the notion that man's respect for nature is lost today in the pursuit of material gains. The greatest challenge that confronts the present generation is the sustained development and intelligent management of the planet earth. Fundamental to this sustainable development is the concept of inter-generational equity which is the mainstay of Indian culture; it teaches one to meet the needs of this generation, without compromising the privileges of future generations to meet their own needs. It reminds us that the primary responsibility for our common future on this unique earth is, in a very real sense, in our own hands. As has been remarked very succinctly by Dieter Frisch, Director General of the Development Commission of the European Community (Brussels), "We have not inherited the land from our ancestors, we have borrowed it from our children."[29]

The seer Atharvan of the *Bhūmisūkta* has also expressed the same feeling when he prays to the Mother Earth that we and our children may live long and be free from sickness and

---

29. Dieter Frisch "Report of Development Commission of the European Community," *The Courier*, No. 133, May-June, 1992, Belgium, p. 2.

consumption.[30] For that, he clearly remembers his own obligation and says :

> Whatever I dig from thee, O Mother Earth,
> May it have quick growth again! Purifier,
> We may not injure thy vitals or thy heart.[31]

This conditional qualification about living according to the eternal law of nature clearly implies that the course of the development of human history is open-ended. Man has been given the freedom to make this earth a paradise by aligning himself with the divine design, but there is a clear realization that he has to carve his future through his conduct today. The Veda declares that "for the one who lives according to eternal law, the winds are full of sweetness, the rivers pour sweetness. So may the plants be full of sweetness for us."[32]

Many of us consider that ecological awareness has developed in man only in the recent past. This notion becomes unfounded, however, when one reads the *Bhūmisūkta* of the *Atharvaveda* alone, not to talk of the whole of the Vedic literature. It is probably the first of its kind of scriptures among all living traditions on earth which presents such a wide spectrum of noble ideas on ecology and conservation. It aims at conserving the environment not only on the physical level, but also on the moral, mental, religious, spiritual and above all the cosmic level and that too not merely by checking or controlling pollution, but also by changing the attitudes and perceptions of people towards nature. In this way, the *Bhūmisūkta* creates an attitude of environmental

---

30. *AV*, 12.1.62.
31. *Ibid.*, 12.1.35.
32. *Yajurveda*, 13.27.

stewardship and eco-spirituality which is scarcely to be found in any other tradition.[33]

The *Bhūmisūkta* envisages that the whole world can be redeemed only by redeeming the character of man. This is possible only if ecological thinking, instead of being confined to the plane of expediency, delves deep into philosophical thought as well as religious sensibility. This has become all the more important today when the earth is teaching us a moral lesson through ecological crisis. The very opening verse of the hymn states that the earth is sustained *by truth, by eternal order, consecration, penance, knowledge and sacrifice.*[34] These are the six qualities which sustain the earth and its firmness. In other words, love of the earth is grounded in certain ethical and religious notions. An austere life of discipline devoted to the pursuit of higher values, such as truth and *ṛta,* makes this love of earth really significant and valuable. Truth and *ṛta* presuppose *Brahman* or knowledge and *dīkṣā* which result in *tapas* and *yajña.* These six values are enumerated here as the basic principles on which ecology has to be founded. These factors make us understand that the earth has a certain divinity about her and that we must protect it by means of sacrifice and self-control. Such a spiritually charged and protected earth alone can bestow strength, lustre and authority on the nation.[35] Mother Earth, representing nature as a whole, is presented here not only as a source of sustenance but also as a means of spiritual enlightenment.

---

33. O.P. Dwivedi, in *Environmental Stewardship and Sustainable Development* (ed. R.B. Jain), New Delhi: Friedrich Ebert Stiftung, 1997, p. 279.
34. *AV,* 12.1.1.
35. *Ibid.,* 12.1.8.

According to the modern environmental science, conservation comprises three steps, viz., preservation of natural resources, environmentalism and global citizenship.

Preservation of Natural Resources

There are again two views about the preservation of natural resources, viz., utilitarian conservation and bio-centric preservation.

UTILITARIAN CONSERVATION

According to this idea, natural resources should be used for "the greatest good of the greatest number and for the longest time."[36] In this view, man is the focal point of the universe. According to it the purpose of saving forests is not because they are beautiful or provide shelter for wild animals but because they provide homes and jobs for men.

BIO-CENTRIC PRESERVATION

It emphasizes that nature deserves to exist for its own sake, regardless of its usefulness to humans. In this view, habitat protection is the fundamental right of other species as well as of the humans.

The *Bhūmisūkta* of the *Atharvaveda* combines both these aspects in its implicit concept of conservation. There is interdependence between human beings and other forms of nature, but being dominant, human beings have destroyed the environment out of their greed and uncontrolled desires. Over-consumption and the wasteful habits of man could ultimately be the cause of elimination not only of other species but also of their own race. Unless human beings change their attitudes towards the earth and its resources,

---

36. William P. Cunningham, *Understanding Our Environment*, Oxford: Wm. C. Brown Publishers, 1994, p. 11.

damage and destruction will continue. Those who protect natural resources are showered with divine blessings.[37] But those who pollute the environment and indulge in hatred, violence and selfishness, have to be controlled. Such control plays an important role in shaping our attitude towards the earth and its resources. This step of conservation has to be taken by one and all.

Environmentalism

It is concerned with the entire environment, created as well as natural and emphasizes the links between science, technology and society. It aims at promoting a sense of interdependence amongst all the elements of creation. The *Bhūmisūkta* also throws some light on this side of conservation by mentioning that cities should be planned in such a manner that the earth remains full of prosperity and natural beauty fascinating even for the gods.[38] Those who destroy the environment of Mother Earth and prove detrimental to the growth of her flora and fauna are asked to run away; she herself has brushed aside all such persons in the same way as the horse shakes off dust from its body.[39] The robustness of the sense of environmental purity of seer Atharvan can be judged from the fact that "he provides for punishment to the extent of banishment of the exploiter of the earth."[40]

The prayer for the preservation of the original fragrance of the earth borne by herbs and waters and shared by all the creatures including men and women, horses, deer and elephants[41] also suggests that we should not exploit the natural

37. *AV*, 12.1.7.
38. *Ibid.*, 12.1.43.
39. *Ibid.*, 12.1.57.
40. *Ibid.*, 12.1.58.
41. *Ibid.*, 12.1.23-24.

resources beyond a certain measure. This fragrance is not the physical odour which is also a specific characteristic of the earth. It signifies the bewitching loveliness of the land, mixed with honey[42] or the nourishing aspect of nature. This has to be shared by all.

Global Citizenship

The third step of conservation lies in taking care of the systems which support the life of the planet. A key concept in this regard is one of sustainable development which is a term introduced and defined to meet the needs of the present generations to meet their own needs. United Nation's Conferences such as the "Earth Summit" held at Rio de Janeiro in 1992 have been organized to attract the attention of the governments to this vital problem of environmental protection.

The *Bhūmisūkta* of the *Atharvaveda* goes a step further when it propounds that every entity and organism is a part of one large family presided over by the eternal Mother Earth. The Mother has always supported her children and has been the source of fulfilment of their unending desires. Never has she demanded anything in return. But we, her children, must not exploit her and violate her line of control. These sentiments denote a family bond not only between the Earth and the human beings, but amongst all forms of life. The *Bhūmisūkta* enjoins us to have a universal code of conservation so that the case of God's creation is undertaken in right earnest. In fact, the traditional Indian ideal of *vasudhaiva kuṭumbakam,* i.e., the whole world being one single family is even wider than that of global citizenship. In the cosmic vision of the Vedas, all animate beings and inanimate things are operated by one and the same principle. This concept has been well enunciated by

42. *Ibid.,* 12.1.7.16.

Dr. Karan Singh when he says that "the planet we inhabit and of which we are all citizens, 'Planet Earth' is a single, living and pulsating entity, and the human race, in the final analysis, is an interlocking extended family, *vasudhaiva kuṭumbakam* as the Vedas have it."[43]

To sum up, it may be said that the *Bhūmisūkta* of the *Atharvaveda* is a lucid expression of the emotions of a true son of the soil. Mother Earth is depicted here as a symbol of natural resources bestowed upon man and it is desired that the same may remain steadfast, gracious, pure and propitious.[44] *Bhūmi* is worthy of homage. Never does she decay. She fulfils all our wishes.[45] The Prajāpati furnishes her with whatever she lacks in.[46] It is the duty of us, human beings that we should never trouble her whether we are sitting, standing or striding forth, with our right or left feet.[47] May she bless us with all that is good. May God, the Lord of the universe, make this Mother Earth of ours pleasant in every quarter.[48] May that Mother Earth, thus prospering, enhance our prosperity.[49] But for that we have to be watchful, cautious and ready to sacrifice our best for her, the Mother Earth :

vayaṁ tubhyaṁ balihṛtaḥ syāma.[50]

---

43. Karan Singh, *Brief Sojourn*, New Delhi: B.R. Publishing Corporation, 1991, p. 123.
44. *AV*, 12.1.17.
45. *Ibid.*, 12.1.61.
46. *Ibid.*, 12.1.61.
47. *Ibid.*, 12.1.28.
48. *Ibid.*, 12.1.43.
49. *Ibid.*, 12.1.13.
50. *Ibid.*, 12.1.62.

10

Interflow of Art Between India and Japan

Lokesh Chandra

Asuka Period (AD 538-644)

Prof. Hajime Nakamura wrote in 1961: "As Buddhism originated in India, most of the Japanese regard India as their spiritual motherland." It began in AD 538 when the first Buddhist images and *sūtra*s were sent to Japan by the Korean kingdom of Paekche. These votive images had experienced influences of the great traditions of India, Central Asia, China and were given Korean modes of expression. In AD 552 the king of Paekche gifted a gilt bronze image of the Buddha to Emperor Kimmei of Japan, along with the words: "This doctrine is the most excellent among all doctrines . . . it leads on to a full appreciation of the highest wisdom." The same kingdom deputed to the Japanese Emperor monks, a nun, a Buddhist image-maker and an architect in AD 577. In AD 584 a stone image of the Maitreya, the Buddha-to-be, arrived from Paekche. Buddhist images were made as an offering to cure the illness of Emperor Yōmei in AD 587. More monks and a painter arrived from Paekche in AD 588. Painters, sculptors, monks and scholars brought with them ideograms, new ideas, and noble ideals of human relationship. Civil war followed the death of Emperor Yōmei. During one of the battles Shōtoku vowed to build a temple to the *Caturmahārājika*, if he won. Empress Suikō succeeded in AD 593 and Shōtoku was appointed Regent. He gave lectures at the palace on the three classics of Buddhism: *Vimalakīrti-nirdeśa, Mālādevī-siṁhanāda-sūtra,* and *Saddharma-puṇḍarīka-sūtra*. In AD 597, Prince Asa of Paekche came to Japan as a master-painter. In AD 604, Shōtoku promulgated the Seventeen-Article Constitution wherein the *triratna* (Buddha, Dharma and Saṅgha) were a fundamental factor, for the well-being of all beings. Buddhism became the grass-roots of good government and high morality. Tori Busshi was the first sculptor of Japan. In AD 606 he set up a great Buddha and an embroidery at the Gangoji temple. Empress Suikō was highly pleased and decorated the sculptor.

Prince Shōtoku spread the splendour of Buddhism in the Land of the Rising Sun by constructing several Buddhist monasteries, among which the Horyuji "The Temple for the Flourishing of Dharma" (*Dharma-vardhana-vihāra*) near the city of Nara is the most ancient wooden building in the world. Its mural paintings were modelled after those found in the monastic universities of India. Its great Buddhas and *bodhisattva*s to which the centuries have given a rich dark patina evince a particular purity of line, surface and decoration, and a desire to see humanity, flesh and blood, fused in the most abstract of deities. the Horyuji Monastery has yielded one of the most ancient Sanskrit manuscripts of the *Uṣṇīṣavijayadhāraṇī* in the Gupta script. Avenues, trees, play of the curves of the roofs, like a great heron's wings resting among trees, lend it an impression of calmness and serenity, embodying and reflecting a unity of the history of Asia. Horyuji is a unique repository of the earliest Buddhist art of Japan, including monumental bronzes, shrines painted in lacquer, sculptures and paintings that evince older continental traditions. A bronze statue of Bhaiṣajyaguru was consecrated at Horyuji in AD 607, which had been vowed several years earlier to cure the illness of Emperor Yōmei. In the same year, a scholar was sent to China to study Chinese culture.

To pursue the *sūtra*s in seclusion, Prince Shōtoku was attracted by the Ikaruga hamlets far away from the Imperial capital. Here he started the construction of his palace and the Horyuji temple, whose sheer splendour captured the hearts of all men. The multiple buildings of the austere dormitories for the monks, the *kondō* or golden hall, the *kōdō* or *sūtra* auditorium, with their woodwork painted bright cinnabar red, the roof tiles scintillating in the sunlight, gilded surfaces glittering against the sky, wind-bells hanging from the eaves singing melodiously as they swung in gentle breeze, the nine golden rings atop the towering *pagoḍā*, the buildings vast in scale: all evoke wonder and awe. Away from the din and turbulence of everyday life, confronted by profound beauty a devotee could visualize the unstained purity of the human spirit. The octagonal Yumedono or "Dream Hall" today commemorates the site where Prince Shōtoku once lived. The roof ornament in gilded bronze is the *cintāmaṇi* jewel with beams of light radiating in all directions, resting on a lotus flower and a vase (*kalaśa*) covered with a canopy. It symbolizes this sacred hall as a centrum whence radiates the divine force of *dharma*. In the hall stands an image of the Avalokiteśvara modelled after Prince Shōtoku, which was given his body length. In his hands rests the flaming *cintāmaṇi*, the emblem of the *Bodhisattva*'s power of liberation. In AD 623 Tori Busshi's Triad of Śākyamuni, accompanied by two *Bodhisattva*s, was enshrined in the Horyuji so that Prince Shōtoku might reach the "Land of Bliss."

The kondō or golden hall of the Horyuji is adorned with murals whose style has close affinities to those from India. Its special importance lies in reflecting the artistic achievements of seventh-century India. In the years AD 643-46, 648-49, and 657-61 the entourage of the Chinese envoy Wang Hsüan-ts'e copied the frescoes on the walls of monasteries in India. Later on these paintings were compiled in 40 fascicules. Some of them were taken to Japan by the Korean artist Honjitsu, and they are said to have been the models for the Horyuji murals.

The earliest preserved painting of the first half of the seventh century is the Tamamushi Shrine which has scenes of the worship of the sacred relics of the Buddha, sacrifice for a stanza, sacrifice to a hungry tigress, Mount Sumeru, the self-sacrificing deeds of the *Bodhisattva*s which earned them the merits of their *karma* to Buddhahood. The root texts are the *Svarṇaprabhāṣa* and *Mahāparinirvāṇa-sūtra*. Buddhism, a religion of peace and moral grandeur, contributed to far-reaching political, social and spiritual advance. Its ascendance was a victory of novelty over a tradition whose grass-root customers, popular cults, practices and deities were merged into the new *dharma*. It was a challenge to the latent intellectual capabilities of Japan, an opportunity for potential literacy and an impressive asset to cultural outflow.

Statues of the Guardian Kings of the Four Directions (*Catur-mahārājika*) stand on the main altar of the Horyuji. The figure of Virūpākṣa is inscribed with the name of the sculptor Yamaguchi no Ōkuchi who was commissioned to carve an image in AD 650. These figures are distinctive in style in the schematic design of the garments, a tendency to natural proportions, and free hanging draperies.

A beautiful wooden sculpture of the Avalokiteśvara at the Horyuji temple dated to about AD 660 shows a development in modelling.

The paintings of those reborn in paradise, at the base of the Tachibana Shrine, are the most Indian of any in Japan.

They present a seductive charm with their freer postures, expressive faces, and languid eyes.

Painter Motozane made a copy of the Buddha's footprints while in China. These had been brought to China from India by Wang Hsüan-ts'e. A stone at the Yakushiji shows this Buddha-pāda.

Remarkable life-size clay sculptures of the Twelve Yakṣa Generals of Bhaiṣajyaguru in Shin Yakushiji are the culmination of the art of the Nara period. A gilt bronze head of Bhaiṣajyaguru, originally the main image of Yamada-dera is 98.3 cm, dated to AD 685, is now in the Kofukuji at Nara. It must have been a monumental image of majestic proportions.

The Hasedera plaque of AD 686 representing Śākyamuni and Prabhūtaratna Buddhas follows the T'ang style. It pictures the fifteenth chapter of the *Saddharma-puṇḍarīka-sūtra*'s conception of the eternity of *dharma* and of the infiniteness of the Buddha. The middle panel has the manifestation and teaching on Mount Gr̥dhrakūṭa.

Sugiyama speaks of the Gupta influence on the two *Bodhisattvas*, Sūryaprabha and Candraprabha, flanking Bhaiṣajyaguru in the triad at Yakushiji monastery. He opines that the contraposition seen in these statues goes back to the images of the Gupta period carved in India. In AD 697 the monumental gilt bronze statue of Bhaiṣajyaguru, 255 cm high, was enshrined in the Golden Hall of the Yakushiji, Nara. It is the basic jōroku-size of sculpture, one of the most popular sizes, two and a half metres for seated figures and twice that for standing ones. They represent the unification of idealization and realism in sculpture. The faces of all the three statues are wonderfully modelled, though the original gilding has peeled off. The triad were to cure the pains of illness and to relieve emotional pressures. The main image is a spiritual rendering of the human form as well as an idealized expression.

The Lady Tachibana shrine stands on the altar of the Horyuji, and it is generally dated to AD 710. It represents the culmination of the bronze technique. The paintings on the sides of this shrine "seem more Indian than either Japanese or Chinese" (Robert Treat Paine).

Taima-dera was founded late in the seventh century at the foot of Mt. Nijō with a statue of Maitreya as the main image. The present clay figure of the Maitreya and the dry lacquer figure of the four *lokapāla*s date from around AD 710. The axis of the temple was changed to accommodate a large *maṇḍala* as the main image. The Taima Maṇḍala is based on the *Amitāyur-dhyāna-sūtra*. It represents, for instance, the five *dhāraṇā*s of the *Gheraṇḍa Saṁhitā* and other texts on *yoga*. The *pārthivī dhāraṇā, āmbhast dhāraṇā, āgneyī dhāraṇā, vāyavī dhāraṇā*, and *ākāsi dhāraṇā* are concentrations on the five elements.

Around AD 711 new materials and techniques were introduced from China: the technique of using a wooden armature and making the statue with wet clay. The clay permitted the *busshi* "Buddhist sculptors" to produce finely modelled forms. The aesthetic intuition and mastery of the materials resulted in the perfection of undulations in the drapery folds, visible muscular structure, more powerful expression and realistic forms. This wave of stucco sculputre had Indian origins. The stucco techniques of India reached the oasis temples of Central Asia, Tun-huang, Maichishan, and the metropolitan cities in China, and finally Japan in the eighth century.

Nara or Tempyō Period AD 711-81

In AD 710 the capital was shifted to Nara which was laid out with broad streets, palaces and temples on the pattern of

Ch'ang-an, the capital of China. This period is called Nara after the city of Tempyō after the famous regnal period (AD 729-48) in which the Daibutsu was made.

The earliest clay images are the four groups of figures of AD 711 in the *pagoḍā* of Horyuji. They illustrate the *nirvāṇa* of the Buddha on the north, sacred relics on the west, paradise of Maitreya on the south, and the discourse of Vimalakīrti and Mañjuśrī on the east. The statues of the two Guardians in the central gate were also sculpted in AD 711. The polychrome clay image of the *nirvāṇa* of the Buddha shows his physician Jīvaka. Kneeling in front, he took the Buddha's pulse and announced his passing away. In these scenes the imagery has descended from the abstract to the real.

In Japan, Sarasvatī (Benten or Benzaiten in Japanese) figures along with Lakṣmī in the eighth century. In the annals of the Todaiji monastery it is said that the first ceremony of *Kichijō-gekka* celebrating the worship of Lakṣmī and Sarasvatī was held for the first time in the year AD 722. This may well be the year in which the two images were first consecrated. Ever since, the *Kichijō-gekka* has been an annual celebration at the Todaiji at Nara. The Todaiji image of Sarasvatī belongs to the "serene" (*śānta*) type in contrast to the "violent" (*krodha*) manifestations of divinities. The *śānta* aspect is reflected in the modelling of the graceful narrow eyes and placid lips. This Sarasvatī image originally had eight arms, out of which five arms survive, with none of the original attributes. Her eight hands once held the bow, arrow, sword, trident, axe, *vajra, cakra* and noose. The image was a casualty of the catastrophic fire that broke out in AD 954. Both the images were reduced to a whitish clay colour, revealing that they were of unbaked clay. The height of the Sarasvatī's image is six and a half feet.

Dry lacquer statues of the Eight Classes of Beings from the mid-Nara period in the hall of Kofukuji were done with sensitivity. The eight were: *deva, nāga, yakṣa, gandharva, asura, garuḍa, kinnara* and *mahorāga*. They were for the divine protection of the State. The five-storied *pagoḍā* was completed by AD 730, and the images for the West Golden Hall were begun in AD 734. The images of the Śākyamuni flanked by Mañjuśrī and Sāmantabhadra, the aforesaid Eight Classes, the statues of Brahmā and Indra, and several others formed an impressive array in the hall.

The Hokkedō was put up by AD 733 for priest Rōben. It was sanctified by Amoghapāśa Lokeśvara, Brahmā and Indra, the Four *lokapālas*, and the Two Door-guardians or Niō. In AD 743 a vegetarian feast was held at the temple for reverence to the *Suvarṇa-prabhāsa-sūtra*. The sculptures of Brahmā and Indra show a harmony between spiritual peace and physical form.

The Tempyō, "Peace under Heaven," was meant to be an era of peace, but political conditions were not stable. Hirotsugu led an uprising against the central government. The *Avataṁsaka-Sūtra* was invoked to suppress the rebellion. Twenty days after the recitation of the *Avataṁsaka*, Hirotsugu was captured and executed.

In AD 740 Emperor Shōmu saw a colossal Rocana at Chishikiji near modern Osaka. He said, "we have the most sincere desire to create one ourselves" (as recorded in the *Shoku Nihongi Annals*).

Floating in a sea of verdant woods is the golden ornament of the imposing roof of the Daibutsu-den, "the hall of the Great Buddha," of the Todaiji monastery. Daibutsu-den enshrines the *virāṭ rūpa* of Rocana, in the form of a gigantic statue, in the national temple of eighth-century Japan. Emperor Shōmu had vowed to raise this statue to a height of 48 ft to symbolize the power of the profane and the profound. Twelve years and immense materials were spent in casting the Daibutsu. On 9 April 722 AD it was consecrated in a sumptuous ceremony, which was presided over by Bodhisena, the first historic Indian to have visited Japan. He was a brāhmaṇa of the Bhāradvāja *gotra*. Inspired by Mañjuśrī, he went to China to Wu-tai shan mountains sacred to Mañjuśrī. At an Imperial invitation, he arrived in Japan in AD 736 where he was warmly welcomed. The people knew him as the Baramon (brāhmaṇa) Archbishop. On 25 February 760 AD he entered in eternal *samādhi* and his disciple Shuei (*Taisho Shinshū Daizōkyō* 51: 987a) wrote: "On his death we felt as though, the main prop of the house were broken and we deplored, we could hear his virtuous voice no more. . . . His wisdom, vast as the ocean, always pours over us without ever being dried up." In this Todaiji temple consecrated by the brāhmaṇa Archbishop, we can view an expressive range of Nara sculptures of Brahmā, Indra, the four *lokapāla*s, Sūrya, Candra, Sarasvatī and Śrīlakṣmī which have escaped the ravages of fire. In front of the Great Buddha Hall stands the eighth-century octagonal bronze lantern adorned with the musicians of heaven on its grilled open work amid a florid array of cloud patterns and swirling drapery. The world's largest statue in the world's largest wooden building was intended to express a spirit of devotion in all its grandeur and magnificence and at the same time to give concrete embodiment to national solidarity of all classes of the population. It was a major step towards the democratization of *dharma*.

To this day the Todaiji and other monasteries and museums of Japan have masks which were used in the Bugaku or Gagaku dance and music which was introduced to Japan by Bodhisena. There are the masks of Baramon (brāhmaṇa), *garuḍa, sagaranāgarāja, yakṣa,* Indra, Brahmā, Sūrya, Kubera,

Agni, Vasiṣṭha *ṛṣi*, *Īśvara*, Lakṣmī and others, used in dances performed in temples and in the Imperial Palace at banquets. These forms have been preserved as ceremonial dances for national celebration. Some of the musical pieces pertain to Bairo or Bhairava. I had the pleasure of listening to Japanese sacral music at Ann Arbor, Michigan (USA) and was charmed by the depth of its perceptivity.

A few yards from Yakushiji is the Toshodaiji monastery, where the aura of Classical times lingers to this day. It was built for the Chinese *bhikṣu* Ganjin who had been invited to Japan in AD 753 to strengthen monastic discipline in the opulent monasteries of Nara. He succeeded in giving birth to forces which were to correct laxities and extravagances. The severity, calm and purity of Ganjin's character is reflected in his realistic statue. The array of statues in the *kondo* of this temple expresses the power and grace of the pantheon, with Rocana seated in the centre, the origin of all in the cosmos. The wooden figures of Brahmā, Indra and the four *lokapāla*s made an imposing phalanx of statues. When I visited the *stūpa* of Ganjin in September 1970, along with Swami Omanand Sarasvatī, at the door stood a lady who later disclosed herself as Mrs. Fusano Okada the wife of a textile magnate. While we circumambulated the *stūpa* and pondered over the flown centuries, Mrs. Okada gazed at us, absorbed in a reverie. As we came out of the door, we presented her a sandal incense-stick. Prof. Chikyo Yamamoto interpreted her innermost thoughts: "She is so happy to see an Indian priest. It is in ten thousand years that one may have this pious privilege." So deeply was she moved that she composed a poem on the spot. Memories of eighth-century Nara became alive in a sacral realism of the present.

The largest dry-lacquer statue of the thousand-armed Avalokiteśvara, 18 ft high, is in the Toshodaiji which was founded in AD 759, and where Ganjin lived till his *nirvāṇa* in AD 763. Its majestic proportions exuding power, the thousand arms remind one of the *Puruṣa-sūkta* of the *Ṛgveda*.

The *vīṇā*, under its Japanese form *biwa*, is an integral characteristic of the Japanese Sarasvatī. The most ancient *biwa* known today is preserved in the Shosoin Repository, dating to AD 757.

The Shin Yakushiji houses the clay statues of the twelve *yakṣa-mahāsenāpati* of Bhaiṣajyaguru. They have been dated to AD 760. Once the renowned photographer Mr. Ogawa shone a spotlight on the head of one of the statues, it caused the violent, wrathful face to appear as if it was floating up out of the darkness. The light emphasized the wide open eyes, the flaring nostrils, the tensed tendons of the face, a violent expression, and an iron will to root out sin. The *Manyu-sūkta* of the *Ṛgveda* came alive in it.

Sculpting projects continued at the Horyuji till the late eighth century. The clay statues of Brahmā, Indra, the Four *lokapāla*s were housed in the refectory, and belong to the AD 760s. They evince the beautiful touch of the artist and are exquisitely rendered. The refinement of modelling and the beauty of their facial expressions remind us of T'ang Buddhist sculptures.

The Saidaiji monastery was constructed to house the Four *lokapāla*s in fulfilment of a vow of Empress Shōtoku taken in AD 764. Four bronze statues were commissioned to quash the rebellion of Nakamaro Fujiwara, based on the *Suvarṇa-prabhāsa-sūtra* which teaches that the Four Kings favour a ruler who governs the nation properly. None of these statues remains today, except the demons beneath their feet. Only a wood-core dry lacquer polychrome statue of Lakṣmī, datable to about AD 790, exists by chance.

In AD 770 empress Shōtoku had one million mini-*pagoḍā*s made, each with a Buddhist *dhāraṇī* wood-printed on paper. The technique of wood-block printing must have come from China. Wang Hsüan-ts'e had brought stamped pictures from India in AD 660.

Empress Shōtoku ordered in AD 767 that the worship of Lakṣmī be held in all the provincial temples (*kokubunji*) to "bring peace, timely rains, good crops and happiness to the people." The first special service was held at Yakushiji in AD 770. The painting used in this service has survived. It is painted in varied colours on hemp, with complicated lines, a sensitive rendering of transparent gauze garments, and it emphasizes feminine beauty.

Early Heian or Jōgan Period (AD 782-897)

The Jingoji temple in Kyoto has many sculptures in the Jōgan style. It was established around AD 800 and its main image of Bhaiṣajyaguru was of heavy proportions.

In AD 804 Kōbō Daishi sailed to China in quest of the "ornamental heart of mystery" of Esoteric Buddhism, Shingon or Mantrayāna. It was the new denomination which had gained vogue in the Imperial metropolis of T'ang China which was the golden epoch of the ever-new glory on the secular and spiritual planes. Indian teachers, at the Imperial court and in monasteries, lent resplendence to the times. Their sonorous recitiation of *mantra*s in Sanskrit accompanying gorgeous tāntric rites emanating from the philosophical subtleties of Mantrayāna was the new dimension that had attracted the young Kōbō Daishi (then known as Kūkai) to Ch'ang-an' the cultural centre of Asia. It was here that Kōbō Daishi met his master Hui-kuo (AD 746-805), the patriarch of Esoteric Buddhism in China. Hui-kuo was disciple of Amoghavajra (Chin. Pu-k'ung, AD 705-74) who had inherited the *dharma* from

Vajrabodhi (d. 741). Master Hui-kuo was highly esteemed as the successor to Amoghavajra.

When Kōbō Daishi called on his *guru*-to-be, Hui-kuo was full of joy and assurance that the great Mantrayāna had a glorious future. This dramatic encounter is narrated by Kōbō Daishi himself:

> I called on the abbot in the company of five or six monks from the Hsi-ming Temple. As soon as he saw me he smiled with pleasure and joyfully said, "I knew that you would come; I have waited for such a long time. What pleasure it gives me to look upon you today at last. My life is drawing to an end, and until you came there was no one to whom I could transmit the teachings. Go without delay to the altar of *abhiṣeka* with incense and a flower." I returned to the temple where I had been staying and got the things which were necessary for the ceremony. It was early in the sixth month then that I entered the altar of *abhiṣeka* for primary initiation.

Kōbō Daishi mastered all that Hui-kuo had to offer, as one would "pour water from one jar into another." The final instructions of Hui-kuo to Kōbō Daishi were:

> Now my existence on earth approaches its term, and I cannot long remain. I urge you, therefore, to take the *maṇḍala*s of both realms and the hundred volumes of the teachings of the Diamond Vehicle, together with the ritual implements and these objects which were left to me by my master. Return to your country and propagate the teachings there. When you first arrived, I feared I did not have enough time left to teach you everything, but now I have completed teaching you, and the work of copying the *sūtra*s and making the images has also been finished. Hasten back to your country, offer these things to the court, and spread the teachings throughout your country, to increase the happiness of the people.

Hui-kuo had the Twin Maṇḍalas drawn for him by the famous painter Li-chên assisted by more that ten other artists. They were polychrome. They found full efflorescence and fruition in their new milieu. Though the original paintings of the *maṇḍala*s brought by Kōbō Daishi are now lost, from them were painted the Takao Maṇḍalas in AD 824 in gold and silver lines on purple damask silk in polychrome. These are now preserved at the Jingoji monastery.

Kōbō Daishi studied Sanskrit under the Indian teachers Prajñātara and Muniśrī. He learnt the calligraphy of *bīja*s and *mantra*s which are still an integral part of Shingon.

Versed in the new learning, endowed with treasures of books, holy images, ritual implements, Kōbō Daishi reached his country in the tenth month of AD 806. This was the beginning of a new age in Japan. Kōbō Daishi towers over the culture of his land. Alphabet, architecture, bridge-building, painting, democratization of education, poetics and profound philosophical thought: all bear the impression of his deep insights and intimate commitment to the human condition. The life of Kōbō Daishi is pervaded with Sanskrit, from the Sanskrit script to its multi-dimensional expressions. He wrote commentaries on Sanskrit *bīja*s or symbolic syllables, for example, *Unji-gi* or the "signification of *hūṁ*." The Sanskrit alphabet symbolized the profound to Kōbō Daishi. He elaborates on it in his *Hizō hōyaku* "The Precious Key to the Secret Treasury":

> [I take refuge] in the Silent One (Mahāvairocana) who is
>
> KA [*kārya*], *CA* [*cyuti*], *ṬA* [*ṭanka*]
>
> *TA* [*tathathā*], *PA* [*paramārtha-satya*], and *YA* [*yāna*]

Here the alphabet is the *dharma-maṇḍala*, evolving (*KA*), involving (*CA*), majestic (*ṬA*), Suchness (*TA*), the Ultimate Truth (*PA*), and the absolute Vehicle (*YA*) on which all are being carried.

In the Twin Maṇḍalas is mirrored the realm of Shingon or Mantrayāna infused with Hindu deities. It is a complex empyrean populated with Gods and *ṛṣis*, spirits and furies, the inexhaustible beauties, potentialities, activities and mysteries of the world transformed into celestial personages. Here is the deep link of the *mantra* with the arts: by sacred gestures (*mudrā*), wealth of symbolism, liturgy, music, incense and song we return to art. Hundreds of deities of Indian origin are represented in the Twin Maṇḍalas of Japan, representing abstractions of thought and recondite *mikkyō* or esoteric doctrine around Vairocana "the Great Light." This great art is *koreru ongaku* or "frozen music" of manifest forms, awaiting one who has attained the summit, the *himitsu shogon shin* or the "Ornate Heart of Mystery." They inspire a sense of hidden meaning into the onlooker. Kōbō Daishi has said "people can be made to feel truth by means of forms and colours."

The outermost quarter of the *Garbhadhātu-maṇḍala* shows several Hindu deities, for example, Gaṇapati or Vināyaka. The Japanese names of Gaṇapati are Binayaka, Shōden and Kangiten. Binayaka is the most usual appellation in the *Hizōki*. Kangiten (Nandikeśvara) denotes the god of happiness,

prosperity, and well-being. Shōden can be rendered into Sanskrit as Āryadeva. Besides, specific manifestations have individual names. There is a lovely illustration of this Gaṇapati with an axe and a radish in a ninth-century scroll, kept in the Daigoji monastery at Kyoto, drawn in AD 821.

Gaṇapati is still worshipped in Japan. At the Jingoji monastery of Takao a special Temple is consecrated to the esoteric Twin Gaṇapati and every year a worship is held in his honour. In other Mantrayānic monasteries too special shrines are dedicated to Gaṇapati. Homes in Koyasan are hallowed by Gaṇapati. On the last day of my stay at Koyasan, I sat on a bench for the bus to the railway station. Curiosity took me inside the shop and there was a graceful image of a standing Gaṇapati in white wood. My repeated entreaties to the shopowner to give it to me only evoked smiles and polite bowings. Alas for my vain desire! The overflowing bounty of the grace of Gaṇapati still glimmers in the adoring hearts of Japan.

The *trimūrti* of Brahmā, Viṣṇu and Maheśvara appears in the outer quarter of the Taizōkai or Garbhadhātu-maṇḍala. Brahmā with four faces (Jap. Bonten), Narāyaṇa (Jap. Naraen-den) on a Garuḍa, Umā and Maheśvara (Jap. Uma-hi and Daijizai-ten) each of them riding on a separate bull in the drawings of Ken-i (AD 1030) are the purity of line and the rhythm of grace. How very Japanese they are, in their bold and charming strokes. Umā has her hair tied back like a daughter of Japan, with the perfume of the earth still lingering about her. (Illustrations on the next page.)

Sarasvatī or Benzaitan appears with a *vīṇā* or *biwa*, sprung from the very soil of Japan. The Japanese representations of the Gods express a deep respect for the dignity of the human form, a love of purity and a vivid feeling for life. According

to a Japanese text: "Sarasvatī is the compassionate Mother of all sentient beings. Her virtuous merits pervade the three thousand worlds. She bestows treasures. She is wondrous wisdom. She grants longevity and happiness. As she presides over music and eloquence, she is also called "Beautiful-sound Devī." As she is a goddess of profit, virtues and knowledge she is also known as Guṇa Devī. She grants desires to those who pray for treasures or profits, eloquence or music, dexterity or wisdom. (Illustration shown above)

In Japanese paintings and woodcuts we find the representation of several brāhmaṇa sages, for example, Vasiṣṭha, Aṅgiras, Gautama, Atri, Bhṛgu. Presented here (on the next page) are the line-drawings of Vasiṣṭha, Aṅgiras and Atri with their consorts from the Taizōkai Maṇḍala of AD 806.

After Kōbō Daishi had established the monastery at Koyasan, in AD 823 he was given control of the Kyō-ō-gokoku-ji or the "Temple for the Protection of the Country through the Noble Dharma," popularly termed Toji or Eastern Temple. This was the establishment of Mantrayāna in the capital of

Vasiṣṭha (Jap. Basu-sen)

Aṅgiras and consort

Atri and consort

Japan itself. The 21 statues in the lecture hall at Toji arranged in a *maṇḍala* paradigm are an impressive monument to a ceremony that was performed in the ninth century for the well-being of the country. Among them are the imposing statues of Brahmā, Skanda Kārttikeya, Sarasvatī and others, besides deities of ferocious appearance whose profound and mysterious sculptures radiate irresistible power. This monastery has preserved the oldest Gyodo masks employed in ceremonial dances. To name a few: the masks for Brahmā, Indra, Sūrya, Kubera, Agni, Vasiṣṭha and Īśvara.

Till recent times, Koyasan forbade the presence of women, while Muroji welcomed them and thus was destined to be a more popular place for pilgrimage, known as the "Koya for women." There is a large image of the Maitreya Buddha on the face of the cliff on the road which leads to this temple. While it reminds us of its prototypes at Bamiyan, it is a delicate line engraving on the cliff. The central image of Śākyamuni at Muroji is flanked by Bhaiṣajyaguru and Kṣitigarbha on the left and by Mañjuśrī and Avalokiteśvara to the right. The Muroji temple was famous for the *maṇḍala* of Indra as the lord of rainfall, painted on a wooden wall at the back of the main sanctum. On numerous occasions prayers have been offered for rain during serious droughts. In AD 824 Japan's most accomplished rain-maker Kōbō Daishi performed *pūjā* for rain which was a resounding success. The holy lake at Muroji is shaped like the Siddham-nagarī letter *vaṁ* representing Vairocana, the prime principle of the universe: for crossing over from *saṁsāra* into *nirvāṇa*.

The Jūni-ten "Twelve Devas" were featured on sets of paintings or sculptures, as well as in the *Garbhadhātu-maṇḍala*. They govern the ten points of the compass (E, S, W, N, NE, SE, SW, NW, zenith and nadir) and the two luminaries Sun and Moon. They are Indra, Agni, Yama, Nairṛti, Varuṇa, Vāyu,

Kubera, Īśāna, Brahmā, Pṛthivī, Sūrya and Candra. There is a beautiful set of the Twelve Devas from the Saidaiji Temple at Nara.

Fudō Myōō or Acala Vidyārāja is the main deity of Japanese *homa* (*goma*). He is surrounded by flames and is a manifestation of the power of Vairocana. He is very popular in Japan. The Red Acala of Myooin of Koyasan sits on a rock with a background of flames, indignation glares from his eyes to terrify away all evil. His esoteric name Vajrānala reminds us of the epithet of the cosmic form of Lord Kṛṣṇa *vajrānalārka-dyutim aprameyam* in the *Bhagavad-Gītā*.

Heian 2, Fujiwara Period (AD 898-1184)

The Fujiwara family, whose regency continued from the ninth century up to the twelfth, were prolific builders of temples. The greatest builder among them was Michinaga. In 1019 he began the construction of a wide hall to enshrine nine large images of Amitābha and named it Muryoju-in which was focused on the Sukhāvatī doctrines of meditation on Amitāyus. In 1022 the main Golden Hall and the Hall of Five Vidyārājas (Godaido) were completed and the entire monastery was named Hojoji. In 1030 his daughter Shoshi (AD 988-1074) built a sub-temple in Hojoji. In its meditation hall she enshrined Amitābha with four acolyte *Bodhisattva*s: Avalokiteśvara, Mahāsthāmaprāpta, Kṣitigarbha and Nāgārjuna. The main image of its Golden Hall was a ten metre statue of Mahāvairocana, flanked by Śākyamuni, Bhaiṣajyaguru, Mañjuśrī, Maitreya, Brahmā, Indra, and the four *lokapāla*s. The Hojoji became the supreme monument of the Fujiwara regents, and exerted tremendous influence on the architecture, statues and paintings of later times. The genius of the sculptor Jōchō at the Hojoji was so distinguished that he was honoured with a Buddhist title. In his sculpture the tranquillity of the Absolute harmonizes with the compassion (*karuṇā*) for the finite.

The major temple constructed under the influence of the style of Hojoji was the Byodo-in. In 1052 Yorimichi dedicated the image of Vairocana as the principal object of worship. The next year, he dedicated the Amitābha Hall, now called Phoenix Hall (Jap. Hoodō), which recreated the Pure Land of Amitābha in tangible form. The central image has the rich glow of gold, its beautiful lotus seat retains its brilliant original colouring, and on the pedestal is a disk inscribed with Sanskrit *mantra*s in the *siddham* form of the Nāgarī script. The pillars, bracketing, ceiling and other woodwork is decorated in appealing coloured designs. The upper part of the walls have fifty-two adoring *Bodhisattva*s in wood, floating on clouds.

Kiyohira from a branch of the Fujiwara family dedicated the Chusọnji in 1126 to ensure the peace and prosperity of the nation and to lead the souls of victims of the earlier Nine Years and later Three Years Wars to the Sukhāvatī Pure Land. The main image was of Śākyamuni, besides a *sūtra* repository which had the complete *Tripiṭaka* written in gold and silver on indigo paper. Its bronze bell hung in the bell house weighed 300 kg. Chusonji was to rival the glories of the capital Kyoto. The white colour *Ekākṣara Cakravartin* has a charm of features in its life-like realism.

In 1013 Ganshin commissioned the painting of a "Maṇḍala of Welcome to Amitābha's Paradise of Sukhāvatī," known in short as *Raigo* in Japanese. It is the descent of Amitābha, the *Bodhisattva*s and the monks from paradise to welcome dying supplicants. It was inspired by Genshin's reading of *sūtra*s, millions of recitations, copying *sūtra*s, and making Buddhist images. The Raigo paintings on the door of the Phoenix Hall are of the Genshin school and vividly executed. The Phoenix

Hall paintings served as models for subsequent Raigo depictions. Yamagoshi Raigo or paintings of an outsized Amitābha encouraging the supplicants from beyond the western mountains became a preference for their rapid motion. The popularity of the Raigo pictures led to Raigo representations in wood. In 1045, Prince Atsuakira (d. 1051) enshrined the Raigo statues.

Shokai, a monk who practised lotus meditation at the Kofukuji, made the Shokai *maṇḍala* in AD 989. It was "woven from lotus fibres" indicating that it was a tapestry. Tradition says that later on the lotus flowers appeared from the fibres and they were copied as an addition to the outer border. This *maṇḍala* is based on the *Amitāyur-dhyāna-sūtra.* Against a background of a temple and the lotus pond, is a dominant Amitābha with Avalokiteśvara and Mahāsthāmaprāpta. On the left-hand border are the sixteen ways to meditate as preached by the Buddha to Vaidehī, the mother of Ajātaśatru.

Japan has preserved the tradition of model books for accuracy of iconography in the icon-rich theogony of Mantrayāna or Shingon. The earliest model book is the *Gobushingan* which was drawn under the personal supervision of Śubhākarasiṁha who was in China from AD 716-35 till his death at the age of 99 years. This has Sanskrit captions, with drawing indications in Chinese. Kakugen, who lived 1000-65, has left drawings of *homa-kuṇḍa*s. The Indian monk Sūryayaśas (1017-73) wrote the *mantra*s of deities in Sanskrit and drew illustrations of 428 *mudrā*s. One of the outstanding iconographers of Japan is Shinkaku (1117-80) who wrote his *Besson-zakki* in 57 scrolls with text and over 300 illustrations. Shōchō (1205-81) wrote a vast compendium *Asabashō* in which ritual and iconography (in colour) are treated at length, running into 228 scrolls. Dhyānabhadra, the Indian teacher, has left 291 illustrations of demons causing illnesses, with Sanskrit *mantra*s to ward them off. From the twelfth century, by the inspiration of Emperor Shirakawa and his guru Kakuyū, commenced an uninterrupted tradition of iconographic model books.

Kamakura Period (1185-1332)

The Kamakura period was a crucial turning point in the history of Japan. In the long bloody war of 1180-85, Yoritomo (1147-99) defeated his rivals and established the capital of his military government (*bakufu*) at Kamakura away from Kyoto. In this turmoil, an innovative style of Buddhist sculpture arose under the brilliant sculptor Unkei (d. 1233). He was born in a *busshi* family, which had produced statuary for Buddhist monasteries for generations of master and disciples. The burning of the Kofrukuji and Todaiji monasteries by the Taira chieftain in 1180 aroused the antipathy of the nation as these two temples had been the pride of Japan since the eighth century. This tragedy came as a shock to Kokei, and his son Unkei, and to other Nara *busshi*. Unkei had the *Lotus Sūtra* transcribed at this time to petition the Buddha's grace. Seven of the eight scrolls of this *Lotus Sūtra* commissioned by Unkei have survived. The shafts of the scrolls were made from the wood of the charred pillars of the Todaiji. Unkei was the chief sculptor at the Jorakuji monastery and also worked at Kofukuji. Unkei was living with and working for battle-scarred warriors in a simple and virile atmosphere. Overflowing with vitality, he was shaping a stirring and heroic style. He was endowed with a richly creative spirit and he fast created a sculpture appropriate to the age of warriors. His sculptures of the patriarchs of the Hosso sect or *cittamātratā* sect were based on the *vijñānavāda* of Maitreyanātha, Asaṅga, Vasubandhu and Dharmapāla. The statue of Maitreya with lacquer and gold leaf over wood at the Kofukuji displays the developed style of Unkei, so perfectly formed that we can sense that he had penetrated to the very depths of his art. The statues of Vasubandhu (Jap. Seishin) and Asaṅga (Jap. Muchaku) completed in 1208 at the northern circular hall of the Kofukuji are strikingly imaginative portraits. As we gaze at them, we want to cry: here at last is real sculpture. They are the greatest of his masterpieces. These two great masters of Buddhist thought stand life-size, as if alive, impressive in the simplicity of their handling, in the natural hang of the garments, and their eyes with a realistic sparkle.

In 1191 Shōga drew the paintings of the Twelve Gods at the Toji monastery. The twelve are: Indra, Agni, Yama, Nairṛti, Varuṇa, Vāyu, Kubera, Īśāna, Brahmā, Pṛthivī, Sūrya, and Candra. They are standing figures in profile. They are drawn with a fluency of line which buckles and fluctuates from the broad to the thin. They reflect a new type of iconography and stylistic change.

Kaikei was a fellow apprentice with Unkei and he learnt the techniques of carving Buddhist statues from Kokei. People of his time hailed him as "a man with almost no equal." Kaikei and Unkei were competing in speed and skill. Kaikei was always looking for new horizons. During his youth, his signature was unusual in that it used the Sanskrit character *oṁ*, pronounced *an* in Japanese. His signature read: "The *kosho* (skilled artist) Kaikei of the Buddhist name. An (written in *siddham* script) Amida Butsu" or *oṁ amitābha buddha.* His style came to be called the Annami style (*oṁ namaḥ* style). It was unique and overflowed with intellectual beauty and realism. This was his individual style, distinct from the Kei school. One of his early works is the Maitreya at the Boston Museum of Fine Arts, sculpted in 1189. It is a wooden statue completely covered with gold, charming in its modulations in the draperies and its mundane directness of the Kamakura period. His style reached its perfection in the painted wood statue of

Kṣitigarbha in the Todaiji, Nara. The brilliant carving of the robes and the expression on the face combines dignity with grace. The celebrated statues of the two Guardians (Niō) of the Southern Main Gate of the Todaiji were carved in 1203 by Kaikei and Unkei. Rising to an imposing nine metres they are heroic statues. Kaikei carved the statues of the Ten Great Disciples of the Buddha (Jap. Jū Daideshi) at the Daiho-onji in Kyoto. They are full of charming daintiness, a beauty with which any one could feel intimate. Kaikei and Unkei are the most representative of those who created the sculpture of the Kamakura period.

The zenith of the Unkei-style sculpture found in the Kamakura region is the Kamakura Daibutsu, the colossal bronze image of Amitābha, 11.5 m high. Its casting was begun in 1252 under the sponsorship of monk Joko. He raised funds among the people instead of getting a donation from a rich potentate. The robes mulded in thick, deep folds create a vivid impression of flowing movement. The serene face has an expression of ineffable calm. Its size and workmanship mark it out as a prominent masterpiece. It is deservedly the symbol of Japan today, constructed with the contributions of the devotees of the Sukhāvatī sect. Five centuries ago, a tidal wave swept away its hall and since then it has sat under the open sky. Despite its immensity, the statue has an aesthetic fluencey. It gazes downward with an aura of divine compassion (*karuṇā*) while the devotees chant adoration to Amitābha "Infinite Illumination," *namo amida butsu*, so that there shines the light of illumination.

A statue of Sarasvatī (Jap. Benzai-ten) was carved in wood in 1266 and enshrined in the Shrine of Music in Kamakura as the goddess of music. Her arms are positioned to play a *vīṇā*. Its important feature is that a nude body is shown in the sculpture. Nude statuary was popular in Kamakura. It bestowed earthly charms on heavenly beings. The Kamakura period had masks for the Bugaku dance. These masks covered only the face, and were derived from India or Champa.

The popularity of the meditative Zen sect was swiftly growing during the entire thirteenth century. It was centred on Kamakura, where Zen temples were concentrated. This art had very distinctive features. The paintings of the great masters were given much importance, as they were looked upon as the embodiment of *dharma*. These paintings were called *chinzo*, in which an absolute fidelity to the master's features was the prime requisite. The "Red-Robed Bodhi-dharma" by an unknown artist in 1271, is a superb work, and registered as a National Treasure. It is one of the finest Buddhist paintings of the Kamakura period. It occupies a position of isolated grandeur in the evolution of Zen painting. The colophon in the painting reads:

> He [Bodhidharma] was the youngest son of the King of Kanchi.
>
> And follower of Prajñātāra's eminent line.
>
> He came to China, and the strange five-petalled flower blossomed.
>
> The fragrant doctrine was transmitted on to Japan.
>
> The auspicious signs like sands of the river.

The Raigo paintings gained immense popularity in the Kamakura period. They showed the descent of Amitābha across the mountains over a panoramic landscape. Amitābha and his two great *Bodhisattvas* were resplendent in gold. They were expressive of the devotees who embarked on the boat of Amitābha's vow to be "able to cross over the turbulent sea of birth and death, and arrive at the shore of the Pure Land. The dark clouds of worldly passions will then hasten to clear away, for the enlightening moon of truth begins to shine"

(Tannishō). These paintings show King Bimbisāra and his Queen Vaidehī's vision of the Paradise of Amitābha. Amitābha was sometimes accompanied by the twenty-five *Bodhisattvas*, who personified the twenty-five steps of *samādhi*. After the thirteenth century, these *Bodhisattvas* became an orchestra and dancing troupe to greet a devotee awaiting rebirth.

Nambokuchō Period (AD 1333-91)

In 1333 the Japanese artist Mokuan went to China to paint in the Zen ink style. The Zen monks used ink sparingly and boldly. The pure ink monochrome was a reminder of the Zen dictum: "many colours blind your vision." Eccentric figures, idealized landscapes, unfilled space, a suggested sense of artistic balance in an asymmetric composition reflected the Sanskrit *rūpaṁ śūnyatā, śūnyatā eva rūpam*. These ink paintings, known as *sumie* in Japanese, were the creations of religious and serene minds.

The cultural forms that evolved in Zen had seven characteristics which are of equal significane and in their inseparability form a perfect whole. The seven characteristics are:

1. No rule, Asymmetry
2. No complexity, Simplicity
3. No rank, Sublime Austerity, Lofty Dryness
4. No mind, Naturalness
5. No bottom, Profound Subtlety, Subtle Profundity
6. No hindrance, Freedom from Attachment (*asaṅga*)
7. No stirring, Tranquillity (*śamatha*).

Hajuin calligraphed MU in grass style. MU appears in a well-known *koan*, used as an aid to attain Awakening. A monk once asked Master Chao-chou if a dog has the Buddha-nature.

The Master simply retorted: MU "no." But this reply transcends "no" in the word's ordinary sense. When the meaning of MU is realized truly, the True Self, the Formless Self, is awakened. In other words, far from simply meaning "no," MU is Zen itself. Although this character imparts an impression of grotesqueness, it rather attains the quality of Sublime Austerity (characteristic 3), replete with strength, constancy and a masculine vigour. Both the form of the character and the tone of the ink express Subtle Profundity (characteristic 5).

When these characteristics permeate every aspect of human expression, they become alive and vital, vivid and refined in unique cultural forms, that bring about the union of man with the "flower-heart" (*hana no kokoro*) and "the universal heart." The modern gadgetry of three-in-one derives from the "Principle of Three" in Ikebana, namely, heaven, earth and man. Man is a channel for the spiritual as well as the earthly: the three form the unbroken Three-in-one. They converge into endeavour in its twin aspects: the metaphysical and the practical, the trans-rational and the logical, the *prajñā* and *vijñāna* aspects of Buddhism. The "Principle of Three" was expressed in flowers by Buddhist monks in Japan to reflect the profound meaning of *karuṇā* or compassion for *all* life and cosmic law of growth. Hereby, flower-heart, man's heart and the universal heart were the deep expression of life. The "artless art" was the Environment, touched by the breath of the spirit, its creativity.

India's austerity was Japan's elegance: minimum of lines to express plenitude of form. It is the aesthetic appreciation of stark poverty, of austere form, the *saṁnyāsa* of *rūpa*. Haiku is the incarnation of loneliness, of minimal words. The dusty leaf-hut of India is repeated in Japan as a hut with not a single particle of dust. Zen has transformed the primitive into an exquisite flower. The same is done by Japan to modern technology. The emptiness of the phenomenal world, called the ocean of existence or *bhavasāgara*, is the sand garden at Ryoanji, the *kare sansui* "dry landscape," traversing the seas of illusion towards the shores of *satori*, "illumination," to cross over the sandy ripples of the ocean of existence.

Muromachi Period (AD 1392-1572)

As the Zen influence increased, paintings expressed the Zen ideal of union with the infinite. The Zen painter sought the "truth" of a landscape in sudden enlightenment. After long contemplation he seizes the inner truth in a sword-like stroke of the brush. The Zen artists turned away from accurate detail, and remarkable imaginative depth was achieved in the economy of black ink, the *suiboku* (water ink) paintings. The *suiboku* art found its best in landscape painting. Minchō (1352-1431) painted "The Hermitage by the Mountain Brook" with a lonely cottage over a stream, the solitary retreat of a Zen monk, in communion with nature. It was the ideal of the *tapovana* with towering cliffs, gnarled roots of the pine, the hut consciously over-emphasized, with a quality of mystery and awe.

Sesshū was a Zen priest who lived from 1420 to 1506. He brought *suiboku* painting to its fullest efflorescence. He is the greatest master of the *suiboku* style who captured the mists enveloping the hills, the whiteness of the sand, a Buddhist temple lost in the foliage, in the shimmer of his softer and warmer ink-tones. Zen aesthetics was the perception of beauty in the most lowly object, in the most humble type of work like the decoration of the ridge of one's humble straw roof.

Chip Buddhas (koppa-butsu) of Enku (1632-95)

Enku was born as the son of an unknown farmer in central Japan. He entered a temple near his home and was given the

Buddhist name Enku, "complete emptiness" (*śūnyatā*). He climbed Mount Fuji and prayed for the fulfilment of his vow to carve a hundred thousand Buddha images. The ground began to tremble, and the *avatāra* of the mountain appeared and handed a hatchet to Enku. From gnarled and knotted timbers, from disfigured blocks he created images of sacred deities. At the back of several figures he wrote Sanskrit letters. He carved *garuḍa*s for protecting temples, Indra (Jap. Indara Taisho), Sarasvatī with attendants, Maheśvara and Buddhist deities. On the image of the Sarasvatī carved in AD 1686 he wrote the poem:

> Each day this mind grows purer,
> The moon in the sky and myself
> Round and full.

The sculptures of Enku sleep in tiny shinto shrines and unattended Buddhist temples. They were a prayer for him, a form of meditation. Mind and hand united in spontaneous creativity. The *koppa-butsu* or tiny chip Buddhas were Enku's invention. They combined function and material, the concept and vow of his *lakṣapūjā*. The sinewy grain and swirling knot were allowed to play in inspiration and execution. It took him twenty-eight years to carve 100,000 images and by this time he was fifty-nine. The inscription on Enku's tomb at the Maitreya Temple in Mino Province says that he died in 1695. He asked for a hole to be dug beside the river. The hole done, he sat in it, someone covered it with earth, and put a bamboo tube in the hole so that he could breathe. He had taken *samādhi*. Tall oak and cherry trees entwined with wisteria vines now stand at this spot of his *nirvāṇa*. People living in the village say that these vines will bleed if anyone cuts them.

Japan's art is *koreru ongaku*, "frozen music of forms." a product of the Japanese soil from the Indian seeds of Bodhi, in an Indian hut with Japanese bamboos. In the graceful line and colour of Japanese paintings over the centuries, the Buddhas and *Bodhisattva*s, *deva*s and *dharmarāja*s, *graha*s and *nakṣatras, rāśi*s and *ṛṣi*s gleam in aspects that range from serene enlightenment to ferocious combat with forces of evil and ignorance. Herein the Japanese painters and sculptors have concentrated their efforts in expressing in human terms a calm exterior and an intense introspection. Even the multiplicity of arms and heads is resloved into the rhythm of form. Here is the world of Indo-Japanese Art which, in the words of an eighth-century inscription,

> Calms us, gives us a tranquil mind
> Every vulgar shadow is dissipated
> And caprice is subdued.
> Joy, yes, and Harmony.

The Japanese Okakura Tenshin stayed at the home of poet Rabindranth Tagore in 1902. This led to the cultural renaissance of India. Out of his talks with the Indian poet, Tenshin crystallized his essay on *The Ideals of the East,* his first publication in English. Tenshin, "The Heart of Heaven," launched the idea "Asia is one." Havell, Tagore, and Coomaraswamy responded. The pioneers of modern Indian painting, Abanindranath Tagore, Nandlal Bose, and others, used Japanese brushes and colours and reflected the diaphanous aura of Japanese paintings in their new creativity. The sketch manuals of Japanese iconography inspired the rise of Neo-Classical Indian art. The sino-Japanese brush is an expressive instrument. It was invented by General Meng Tien who supervised part of the building of the Great Wall of China. Deer's hair covered with goat's hair: a responsive brush tipped with a fine point. It was to expedite the construction of the Great Wall to defend culture against the barbarians. Two thousand years later, India's visual culture came alive with Japanese brushes. Tenshin had said: "Mind speaks to the mind. We listen to the unspoken, we gaze upon the unseen." Likewise did Coomaraswamy say: "It is the work of poets to make the heart free." It was echoed in the researches of Coomaraswamy who found parallels for Vedic texts in Japanese art in his *Elements of Buddhist Iconography* published by the Harvard University in 1935. This cultural encounter left a deep impression on our national ethos. India linked freedom with Japan. Some of our revolutionaries sought refuge in Japan.

To comprehend the subtle mind of Japanese art, we may take the great monk poet Saigyō (1118-90) who was "a mind both obeying and at one with nature." To him we and nature are companions, and a vast and subtle music speaks to us from nature. Saigyō identified himself with the inside-out of the Yoshino mountains, whose blossoms were a way into the inner depths, of journeying to the Himālayas:

> Do the white blossoms
> On my mountain take the place of
> Snow on the holy Himālayas?
> I wish to enter the profound
> Inner depths of Mount Yoshino.

Saigyō means "West-go" (*sai* "West" + *gyō* "go"), and his poems speak of his mind emptied of all darkness, moving closer to the mountains in the West. West means India. His name symbolizes his perennial pilgrimage (*gyō*) to India (*sai*), with the Moon as a fellow pilgrim. The scrolls and statues, *sūtra*s and poems were the mind language of Japan, the energy of illumination, journeying to find the pulsing of a heart dyed in the syntax of the Himālayas.

11

Aesthetics and Ideology
The State of the Art

Makarand Paranjape

> To set aside or to ignore rather than to reinvigorate India's past is to deny it any distinctive entry into the future.
>
> — Balachandra Rajan, *Under Western Eyes* 210

THE title of my paper harks back quite self-consciously to an essay by Peter Brooks that appeared in the *Critical Inquiry* in Spring 1994.[1] In fact, both essays have the same title. Luckily, my subtitle is different and, so, I hope, is my argument. Notwithstanding the claim to be *au courant* or the latest, I would not like seriously to press this sense of the phrase "state of the art." After all, the "state of the art" will keep changing and whatever is the "latest" statement about it will, at least in letter, if not in spirit, allude to it. My subtitle, instead, points to the state of the art not just as its condition of coming into being or existing, but also to the manner and method of its production and consumption. To put it a little differently, what

---

1. The essay was reprinted in a book by the same title edited by George Levine, New Brunswick, N.J.: Rutgers University Press, 1994. Another book edited by Michale Sprinker, *Imaginary Relations*, shares the same subtitle, *Aesthetics and Ideology in the Theory of Historical Materialism*, London: Verso, 1987.

concerns me is not only its *estate* or class, but also its relationship to the state, to patterns of sponsorship and circulation, patronage and transmission. All of these, it seems to me, must be taken into account to determine "the state of the art."

But more of that later. Right now, I would like to refer to Brooks' essay, which may as well serve as my point of departure. Brooks, then Tripp Professor of Humanities and Chair of Comparative Literature at Yale University, looks back to Northrop Frye and also mentions an exchange that he had with a critic called Clement Greenburg at a *Partisan Review* conference at Boston University in 1979. Using these two references, Brooks asks questions about the function and practice of criticism in the early 1980s. I propose to ask similar questions later, but first, like Brooks, wish to allude to the inaugural meeting, held last year, of the proposed Delhi Forum on Criticism. . . . I say proposed, because there has been no second meeting so far. Vikram Chandra, the Indian English novelist and featured speaker, gave a reading and offered some observations on the craft of the novelist. He said that he wanted to write books that people enjoyed reading, just as he wished to teach and read books that gave him aesthetic pleasure. I instantly recognized that Chandra was making an important appeal to reinstate the category of the aesthetic into the main agenda of a liberal arts curriculum, to recall it from its banishment into a politically incorrect wilderness to which it had been consigned by various forms of ideologically engaged critical practices. Chandra seemed to say that what makes literary texts, and hence their study distinctive, is their beauty, which when apprehended, is capable of giving pleasure and solace. To him, the literariness of literature lay precisely in its aesthetic qualities which it shared with other fine arts, as opposed to its discursive qualities that it shared with non-literary prose.

In his argument with Greenburg, Brooks stands, a la Jonathan Culler, for poetics, a formalistic science of reading based on linguistic models. Greenburg, on the other hand, still considers critics as responsible for aesthetic judgements, for "the discrimination of the beautiful and significant in art" (511). Brooks makes a case in favour of the structuralist position that always tries to examine specific textual processes in terms of larger systems of meaning and correspondence. The *real* debate in the essay, however, is revealed only later. It is between what Brooks considers a reductive and arrogant "ideologization of the aesthetic" (513) that through a sort of bad conscience, forces the critic and the reader to assume an oppositional social and political praxis or be damned to the position of a displaced academic.

While Brooks quotes approvingly from engaged Marxist critics such as Eagleton, especially from the latter's *Ideology of the Aesthetic*, his sympathies really lie on the side of idealist and conservative thinkers and writers like Friedrich Schiller, Matthew Arnold, T.S. Eliot, and more recently, Charles Taylor. Brooks, like Schiller in *On the Aesthetic Education of Man* (1795), considers the aesthetic a core principle, a part of a programme of liberal education. The aesthetic, according to Schiller, refines the physical while retaining its contact with the concrete and sensuous; it is an integrative principle that helps to overcome alienation, and is an effective counter to egotism, fragmentation and mechanization (516). Quoting Schiller, Brooks says, "Its core principle" called "the 'play-drive' [Spieltrieb] is 'directed towards annulling time within time, reconciling becoming with absolute being and change with identity'" (516). As an aside, we may notice how a very similar notion of the centrality of the aesthetic shaped Rabindranath Tagore's philosophy of education. Much later, Sri Aurobindo and the Mother considered the aesthetic as the best means not just of refining, sensitizing, and training the senses, but also of purifying the vital. Brook's overall argument may be summed up in his own words: "Constantly trumping the aesthetic by the ideological and political . . . making the aesthetic simply a mask for the ideological . . . risks losing a sense of the functional role played by the aesthetic within human existence" (517). To this extent, he is closer to Greenburg than he thinks or cares to acknowledge, the poetics that he advocates serving more or less the same political needs as the more particularistic, critical judgement of Greenburg. Both positions may be firmly located in a conservative bourgeois ideology that believes that the function of the liberal arts is not to contest regimes of power and knowledge, but to develop certain skills and competences that will help subjects make a useful transition from the academy to the marketplace.

Brooks' argument anticipates that of other influential critics like Harold Bloom who lined up to oppose the "Balkanization of literary studies" (517) and the overthrow of the Western canon. In his influential book, *The Western Canon,* Bloom rues the institutionalization of those whom he calls "resenters." Resenters wish to downgrade or dismiss aesthetic value in favour of ideological readings of literature. Describing the resenters variously as "Feminists, Afrocentrists, Marxists, Foucault-inspired New Historicists, or Deconstructors" (20) or as "Feminists, Marxists, Lacanians, New Historicists, Deconstructionists, Semioticians," (527), he argues that they are, lemming-like, in a self-destructive flight from the cardinal aims of the profession. That is the reason, he believes, why students of literature have become amateur political scientists, uniformed sociologists, incompetent anthropologists, mediocre philosophers, and overdetermined cultural historians. . . . They resent literature, or are ashamed of it, or are just not fond of reading it. (521)

Bloom sums up his argument by declaring:

> Either there were aesthetic values, or there are only overdeterminations of race, class, and gender. You must choose, for if you believe that all value ascribed to poems or plays or novels and stories is only a mystification in the service of the ruling class, then why should you read at all rather than go forth to serve the desperate needs of the exploited classes? — 522

My argument repudiates not just this bipolarity of Bloom's but also Brooks' call to empower a depoliticized poetics of reading as a key to literary education, but also denies the sort of polarity that is inherent in his, and indeed, in many other accounts of this debate. Very simply put, I would urge that the phenomenology of art does not deny its specific historicity and vice versa. Art calls for a complex hermeneutics that has both paradigmatic and syntagmatic, synchronic and diachronic components. An art criticism bereft of the political dimension will only support the *status quo*; on the other hand, one that is merely political will rob the richness and pleasure of the art experience. The four clear, *sūtra*-like, propositions that I outline below may serve as a summary of my position:

1. Art has, or points to, something irreducible, even transcendent in it, even though it may be considered epiphenomenal in the classical Marxist sense.
2. Art is not entirely autonomous, as idealists would like to argue, but definitely contingent and determined by economic and social forces.
3. Yet, these determining factors do not exhaust what art is or has to offer.
4. In present times, simplistic and monocausal ideas of patronage or state sponsorship will not be sufficient to understand the complexity of the economic forces

> that shape art, let alone account for all its forms and (dis)contents.

What I have tried to propose is that the aesthetic dimension of a work of art is irreducible to its economic, political, or cultural matrix of production. Significant art, in other words, erupts in the excess that generates an ever-changing surplus value that we may call pleasure, jouissance, *rasa*, or *ānanda*. That is what keeps the text alive in an interpretative community. Even if the language in which the text is written dies, the text persists in a sort of afterlife, through translations or other means of extension, precisely because of this surplus or excess. Roland Barthes, in the passing, makes a similar point in *Pleasures of the Text*:

> The *brio* of the text (without which, after all, there is no text) is its *will to bliss*: just where it exceeds demands, transcends prattle, and whereby it attempts to overflow, to break through the constraint of adjectives. . . which are those doors of language through which the ideological and the imaginary come flowing in. — 12-14

Barthes is of course struck not so much by the excesses of the text as its very texture of possibilities, which he finds so erotic.

That is why it becomes equally important, I believe, to remember that a text is not autonomous or self-contained, shut off from or immune to its conditions of production. Even if it is, as Cleanth Brooks put it, a well-wrought urn, it shows traces of its origins and comes inscribed with the conditions of its creation. It bears the stamp of history in the Marxian sense, that is, it reflects a certain class-consciousness that arises from a specific historical conjuncture. Every text, then, invites us to place it in various systems of power or discursive orders, be they imaginary or symbolic, spatial or temporal, geographical or historical.

II

D.D. Kosambi attempted precisely such a reading of one of India's most enduring literary texts, the *Bhagavad-Gītā*. In an essay called "Social and Economic Aspects of the *Bhagavad-Gītā*," published as the inaugural essay in *Myth and Reality: Studies in the Formation of Indian Culture* (1962), he argues at great length that the *Gītā* is a text of "slippery opportunism" whose utility "derives from its peculiar fundamental defect, namely dexterity in seeming to reconcile the irreconcilable." Composed between AD 150-350 and inserted into the *Mahābhārata* corpus later, the *Gītā*, according to Kosambi, served a peculiar class function which made so many leading exponents of Indian culture, including Śaṅkara, Rāmānuja, Jñāneśvara, Gandhi, Tilak, Aurobindo, and others, return to it again and again. Kosambi believes that:

> **The *Gītā* furnished the one scriptural source which could be used without violence to accepted brahmin methodology, to draw inspiration and justification for social actions in some way disagreeable to a branch of the ruling class upon whose mercy the brahmins depended at the moment.** — Emphasis in the original

In other words, the *Gītā* is a synthetic text that manages to incorporate a wide diversity of complex and, often, contradictory doctrines. Kosambi believes that such a text could only be written at a certain period during which the competition over the surpluses produced wasn't so intolerable as to result in class conflict:

> **Fusion and tolerance become impossible when the crisis deepens, when there is not eno1ugh of the surplus product to go around, and the synthetic method does not lead to increased production.** — Emphasis in the original

Analysing the career of Jñāneśvara, the author of the influential commentary *Jñāneśvarī*, Kosambi says:

> The conglomerate *Gītā* philosophy might provide a loophole for innovation, but never the analytical tools necessary to make a way out of the social impasse. Jñāneśvara's life and tragic career illustrate this in full measure.

In other words, though the *Gītā* provided Jñāneśvara with some ammunition against the ills of his times, it could not afford him a full-fledged blueprint for revolutionary action. That is why, according to Kosambi, "there was nothing left for him [Jñāneśvara] except suicide."

Kosambi concludes his paper with the following observations:

> Modern life is founded upon science and freedom. That is, modern production rests in the final analysis upon accurate cognition of material reality (science), and recognition of necessity (freedom). A myth may grip us by its imagery, and may indeed have portrayed some natural phenomenon or process at a time when mankind had not learned to probe nature's secrets or to discover the endless properties of matter. Religion clothes some myth in dogma. "Science needs religion" is a poor way of saying that the scientists and those who utilize his discoveries must not dispense with social ethics. There is no need to dig into the *Gītā* or the Bible for an ethical system sandwiched with pure superstition. Such books can still be enjoyed for their aesthetic value. Those who claim more usually try to shackle the minds of other people, and to impede man's progress, under the most specious claims.

It is interesting how this conclusion is built upon a whole series of binary oppositions such as science *vs.* religion, modern *vs.* traditional, reality *vs.* myth, progress *vs.* superstition, and so on. The cure for all social ills for Kosambi lies not in "theology but in socialism." The essay ends with a ringing reaffirmation of the revolutionary doctrine: "the material needs could certainly be satisfied for all, if the relations of production did not hinder it."

I have chosen Kosambi's essay on the *Gītā* not because it is especially "exasperating" . . . as the title of another collection of his work suggests . . . but because it is symptomatic of both the benefits and pitfalls of a particular approach to art. Kosambi's rigorous materialist and historicist analysis certainly adds something to our understanding of the *Gītā*, but, as I have argued earlier, it does not exhaust the possibilities of that text. A few years after Kosambi's death in 1966, western India, where he himself lived for several years, witnessed a widespread peaceful social upheaval triggered by a movement called *svādhyāya*. It is no surprise to me that this social movement, about which I have written elsewhere, was inspired by the same complex and heterogeneous text that Kosambi considered incapable of guiding any genuine social change. The slogan of this movement is "Jai Yogeśwar," one of the many names of Kṛṣṇa that we find in the *Gītā*, and which is also enshrined in the very last verse of the *Gītā*:

यत्र योगेश्वरः कृष्णो यत्र पार्थो धनुर्धरः ।
तत्र श्रीर्विजयो भूतिर्ध्रुवा नीतिर्मतिर्मम ॥१८-७८ ॥

yatra yogeśvaraḥ kṛṣṇo yatra pārtho dhanurdharaḥ ।
tatra śrīr vijayo bhūtir dhruvā ṇītir matir mama ॥18.78 ॥

Where there is Krsna, the Lord of yogas, and where there is Partha, the wielder of the bow, there are fortune, victory, prosperity and unfailing prudence. Such is my conviction.
— Swami Gambhirananda's translation
from the *Gītā* Supersite

Also known as the *ekaśloki Gītā*, or the *Gītā* in one *śloka*, this verse is supposed to bestow the benefits that come of reading the whole scripture. The *svādhyāyīs*, with their notion of *kṛti bhakti* or an activist devotion, have fanned out in thousands upon thousands, on *bhakti pherīs* reordering human relationships and social organization on an unprecedented scale. The idea that God is both within me and beside me in my struggles has become a living reality for several million *svādhyāyīs* who give their time and talent to this cause. This assurance, contained in the *Gītā*, has been convincingly conveyed to large masses of people by the inspirer of the *svādhyāya* movement, Pandurang Shastri Athavale. I heard him myself in a very large gathering of about 250,000 people at Kurukṣetra a few years back. I had never experienced anyone expound the *Gītā* in that fashion and, for the first time in my life, the text came alive to me in a unique and moving manner.

I have deliberately chosen a sacred text to illustrate the point that while a materialist reading may be very illuminating, it need not rob the text of its aesthetic, even scriptural, affects.

III

Let me end by asking how our own work has been affected by the material conditions in which it was engendered. If we think of sponsorship as one of these material conditions, we would have to ask if our sponsors, I don't of course mean just those who pay our salaries, but also those who fund our research, travel, seminars, even enable publications, dictate what we should say? Probably not, but as any Marxist would point out, the process of determination is not so simple. It is a matter of how the discourse is framed. As Foucault would remind us, what sorts of things are excluded, for instance, or emphasized? The idea that each of us is free to say whatever he or she wishes is, then, to be questioned rather than accepted.

In other words, our class backgrounds, religious beliefs, economic status, geographical and cultural location, and so on will have shaped what we have had to say. Paradoxically, while we are programmed to think that we are free, we are actually produced by larger systems and forces. That is to say those who think they are free are not, but those who know that they are not, are . . . to that extent . . . free. Thus, it is that in an overall sense our words and worlds are determined, not autonomous. But as I have argued, a certain kind of limited and contingent space for action, a space that has to be earned through a struggle against precisely those forces that work to preclude it, is possible. That is why I believe that art . . . or those who interpret it . . . usually have the option to earn such a positional effectiveness through an interrogation of its given circumstances of production.

It has been one of the premises of this paper that to try to annex India's past, in this case, the history of its arts, to any grand narrative of interpretation would tantamount not only to a denial of India's difference, but also result in the kind of epistemic violence that one wishes to avoid. The uniqueness of the object of study demands that we search for unique tools of interpretation. As critics isn't it our role to examine these systems and how they influence the discourse that we produce? There is, at times, a naïve assumption that somehow intellectual activity occupies an autonomous sphere that is free to scrutinize and criticize, even if it is state — or industry — sponsored. We need very quickly to move beyond that kind of assumption. Especially those of us who believe that art is somehow a mask for ideology, or, *is* ideology concentrated, must also acknowledge that academics and intellectual endeavour is subject to the same charge. Are we, then, as intellectuals in a privileged and impossible Archimedian place, from where we can unmask the hidden ideologies of the arts, but remain safe from such unmasking ourselves? Or should we at once acknowledge that there are no such places of privilege and that we, like the writers and artists that we study, also function in a realm that is shot through and through with the anxieties of location and moral dilemmas of collusion? We know and admit that we might in fact be collaborators in the very regimes of capital that we profess to resist. What does such a knowledge and admission of guilt imply as far as our cultural praxis is concerned? At the very least, it means that we will argue from contingent locations, from strategic positions, not from fixed and reductively oppositional categories.

Let us look, for a moment, at the world in which we live. Are we not all subjects of an empire that, to all appearances, has no centre and no circumference, but has conquered the whole world in ever widening circles of penetration and inclusion? What kind of resistant coalescences might be mounted against such a monotheistic empire of economic paramountcy is hard to conjecture. Since this empire is elusively transnational, the resistance will also have to be multiform and scattered across the globe. One of the key weapons in our arsenal will be precisely the sense of difference, cultural and otherwise, with which this regime of capital contends. A precise articulation of difference, then, will be the *petits recits* of Lyotard's that interrupts and even overthrows, howsoever intermittently, the grand narratives of the triumph of capital. In other words, criticism, at least most of it, is itself compromised. Its cry of outrage or its whine of protest are both signs of its complicity and defeat. We are like chained dogs who can only bark but not bite the thief or the intruder. The more unreasonable and uncompromising the objection, the more secure the chain that binds the conscientious objector. Criticism must be read symptomatically just as art or literature are. Criticism can do very little to alter the world because however much we may shout ourselves hoarse to the contrary, the world is not a text. Textual practice cannot be equated with changing the power structures in the real world. In most instances, there is a curious cohabitation and collaboration between the two: they are like parallel and mutually reinforcing hegemonies. The dominance of criticism is supported by the dominance of the very rule of capital that it professes to overthrow.

Authority cannot obliterate the subject, but produces a splitting, doubling, hybridity which then creates a site for resistance. The compelling logic of modernity, and one of its especially powerful subsets, dialectical materialism, may similarly split the colonial subject as might the unrelenting dominance of capital. Absolutist regimes have produced "great" art and philosophy, the result of which is not at all politically progressive — Dante's *Divine Comedy* or Milton's *Paradise Lost*. Likewise, some art has been classified as imperialistic or fascist, Wagner, for example, but does that make it bad art? The aesthetic, then, may not be rejected, even if merely as an opiate of the classes. Even Kosambi grants the *Gītā* such a role: "Such books can still be enjoyed for their aesthetic value," he concedes.

What, then, of criticism? At worst, it is entirely self-serving and parasitic; at best, it is merely aesthetic, like art. Did I say "merely"? I should take that back. Because the aesthetic is that specially charmed space that will not yield all its secrets to the economic, wrung dry though it may be. There will be some degree of slippage and evasion that will not be exhausted by the probing, however relentless. From this point of view, whatever little autonomy the aesthetic may still retain is also the last resort of criticism.

Note: An earlier version of this paper was presented at the Conference on Performing Arts, State and Society, Carleton University, Ottawa, 23-24 November 2001.*

I would like to thank Professor Harsha Dehejia, Dr. Sudha Dehejia, Dr. Vivek Dehejia, and Dr. Rajiv Dehejia for their support. I would also like to thank Ms. Sharon Pillai for her careful reading of this paper and her comments on it.

References

Barthes, Ronald, *The Pleasures of the Text*, tr. Richard Miller, New York: Farrar, Strauss & Giroux, 1975.

Bloom, Harold, *The Western Canon*, New York: Hartcourt Brace, 1994.

Eagleton, Terry, *The Ideology of the Aesthetic*, Oxford: Basil Blackwell, 1990.

Gītā, Supersite, http://www.Gītāsupersite.org/

Levine, George, ed. *Aesthetics and Ideology*, New Brunswick, N.J.: Rutgers University Press, 1994.

Kosambi, D.D., *Myth and Reality: Studies in the Formation of Indian Culture*, Bombay: Popular Prakashan, 1962.

Rajan, Balachandra, *Under Western Eyes: India from Milton to Macaulay*, Durham, N.C.: Duke University Press, 1999.

"Social and Economic Aspects of the *Bhāgavad-Gītā*," the entire essay is found on the website: http://www.crosswinds.net/~bhupi/ddk/mar/mar1.htm.

Sprinker, Michael, ed., *Imaginary Relations: Aesthetics and Ideology in the Theory of Historical Materialism*, London: Verso, 1987.

12

Loss, Recovery and Renewal of Texts in Indian Traditions

Kapil Kapoor

THROUGH the sciences that were the earliest to develop in India — Phonetics, Vyākaraṇa (grammar), Nirvacana (etymology), Mīmāṁsā (textual analysis) — and through *pāṭha* (the systems of text-permutations) and Śāstra *paddhati* (interpretation of meaning), India has maintained its knowledge texts for almost five thousand years, if not more. The *Ṛgveda* is the oldest extant Indo-European poetry and the *Brāhmaṇa*s are the oldest Indo-European prose. Evidently, the community attached great value to knowledge and made enormous intellectual effort not only to possess these as relics, but also to comprehend the texts that embodied the knowledge. Though there are records of the "texts," the knowledge has been "lost" more than once — they disappeared or got fragmented and dispersed, or became opaque because their tradition of learning was terminated. The text-internal dynamics (change in language over time, for example) and text-external circumstances (war or natural calamities or invasions) disrupted the tradition and rendered the texts inaccessible, incomprehensible or incoherent. It is also recorded that the community assiduously sought to recover and/or renew these seminal texts and developed a number of mechanisms for the purpose over a period of time, such as re-enunciation, recension, redaction, adaptation, translation, commentary, popular exposition and recreation. There have been several cycles of loss and recovery and these are embodied in what the tradition calls the Vyāsa *paramparā*. The last cycle, we posit (for the tradition has yet to incorporate a record of this cycle) began in and around the eleventh century, when under the impact of waves of invasions, the tradition of learning broke up, texts got dispersed, fragmented, lost, and the Indian knowledge systems became esoteric and almost dried up. The processes of reconstruction and renewal of texts/knowledge began in the "modern" times (eighteenth century onwards), outside India, in Europe. The history of reconstruction and dissemination of the classical Indian (Sanskrit, Pāli, Prākṛt) intellectual tradition in the last two hundred years or so is truly an example of a successful *viśva yajña* (global effort) to maintain and sustain what is, in fact, the heritage of mankind. Reconstructed Indian thought has influenced and shaped much contemporary thinking. All the major European minds of the nineteenth century, Humboldt, Fichte, Hegel, Goethe, Schopenhauer, Kant, Nietzsche, Schiller, Schelling, de Saussure, Roman Jakobson, Trubetzkoy, were either Sanskritists or, of their own admission, deeply involved in Indian thought. Their work has inspired various thought movements -- Idealism, Romanticism, among others — which have shaped the contemporary mind. For example, structuralism owes much to the work of de Saussure who was a professor of Sanskrit at Geneva before he came over to Sorbonne. And Structuralism today underpins what are virtually global thought-movements right up to post-Modernism. A large number of Indian texts have become available across cultures through translations and these have enabled and strengthened Indian studies. However, the diffusion and dissemination of texts and their "modern" study has created a new challenge for the Indian scholar, to defend the tradition and his "traditional" reading of the texts. Knowledge formation, storage and dissemination in the oral tradition is radically different from that in the scriptural/written traditions and it has monumental intellectual achievements to its credit. It needs to be defended and sustained. We take a look at what motivates these processes and mechanisms of continuity, indeed, at what they are and what they have achieved.

I

What does the "continuity" of a civilization imply? We ask this question because the "continuity" of Indian civilization is etched in the public cognition and enshrined in the folk vocabulary. Puṇḍit Bhagvata Sastriji of Pune once used the metaphor of a river for this knowledge-centred civilization — *bhāratīya jñāna paramparā sanātana gaṅgā pravāha*, which means that the Indian knowledge tradition is timeless and continuous like the flow of the river Gaṅgā.[1] *Sanātana* (age-old/ancient/ timeless) and *śāśvata* (given, unchanging, always true) are, in fact, the two almost fixed adjectives for this *sanskṛti* (culture) in the ordinary speech of the people. The "continuity," therefore, is of the thought and the texts that embody that thought and "tradition" is the mechanism of transfer of ideas from one generation to the other.

Knowledge has always enjoyed a primary, privileged status in India. It is to be noted that culture is understood here as Tantra (a set of systems or "grammars") on which various institutions of a society are founded. Indian culture has, for example, systems/grammars of dance, language, music, polity,

---

1. At a lecture in the Department of Sanskrit, Sagar University, Sagar, 1995.

ethics, arts, crafts, painting, sculpture, literature, etc. These systems are expressed in compositions, and texts, and their whole network constitutes the knowledge or culture of that community and may be cumulatively referred to as Indian Knowledge Systems.

The sheer amount of knowledge-literature, available in Sanskrit is amazing.[2] The tradition has several knowledge typologies for this large body of literature, in order to classify and arrange these compositions in a hierarchy of validity according to their status as discourses of valid knowledge. There is, therefore, a range of knowledge discourses with relative validity and no one discourse of knowledge. All rational discourses are placed on different clines of validity and all compositions are classified into categories intermediate between those that have "contingent" knowledge and those that contain "non-contingent" knowledge. There is, for example, the fundamental division between Śāstra and Kāvya. In such typologies, the Vedas are assumed to be repositories

---

2. We get some idea of this from the fact that despite losses due to calamities and vandalism, more than a million Sanskrit manuscripts are still in existence. They are sometimes preserved carefully, as is the case with European collections, but more often they are just stockpiled and stored in private collections and public libraries, with a large number of them not even catalogued yet. The Sanskrit word for literature is *vāṅmaya*, compositions in words/language. The primary texts in this *vāṅmaya* span a large number of disciplines — philosophy, medicine, grammar, architecture, geography, literary theory, political economy, logic, astronomy and mathematics, biology, military science, sociology, metallurgy, agriculture, mining, ship-building, veterinary science and commerce besides the sixty-four arts and crafts that are conventionally enumerated and include, for example, sculpting, bangle-making, etc.

of "non-contingent" knowledge, knowledge that is independent of time, place and person, the kind of knowledge that is coded in the laws of science. We have the other well-known three-fold division of all *vāṅmaya*, verbal discourse, into Śruti-Smṛti-Kāvya. Śruti is directly apprehended knowledge, totally non-contingent. This covers the Vedas and the Upaniṣads — texts that handle metaphysical questions. Smṛti is next in degree — it is non-contingent knowledge but one that is recalled and therefore has the intervention of a thinker. This applies to the primary texts of philosophy and the six auxiliary sciences. Kāvya is knowledge that is contingent on an individual, their particular perception and their location in time and space. Pāṇini (seventh century BC), the celebrated grammarian, sets up a five-fold typology — *dṛṣṭa, prokta, upajñāta, vyākhyāna* and *kāvya*. He substitutes *dṛṣṭa* (grasped by visual perception) for Śruti (grasped by aural perception) and divides Smṛti into two categories, *prokta* (restated by someone else) and *upajñāta* (found/constituted again). This division distinguishes between *Nyāyasūtra* of Gautama and *Aṣṭādhyāyī* of Pāṇini, which is itself a re-formulation and extension of the knowledge available in the long line of earlier grammarians. He adds a new category, *vyākhyāna* (commentary), which establishes the importance of this kind of "renewal" literature in the Indian intellectual tradition. There is also a clear opposition made, as we have noted above, between Śāstra (knowledge/texts) and Kāvya (imaginative/literary texts).

It is also to be noted that contrary to the popular impression, knowledge in India has not been confined to learned texts, nor has it ever been, a repository of the few. Along with the learned, scholarly tradition, there has always been a parallel *kathā, pravacana paramparā* (popular tradition of narration and exposition of texts), which has throughout mediated between the learned tradition and the ordinary masses. Even Ādi Śaṅkarācārya, one of the greatest minds, besides having composed numerous intellectual texts, was also a *pravacanakāra* (a popular expounder), who travelled through the length and breadth of India addressing village congregations, explaining and sharing with them his understanding of Advaita Vedānta.[3] In fact, there is strong reason to believe that Śaṅkara's learned commentaries originated in his popular discourses. Similarly, Śrī Rāmānujācārya expounded his Viśiṣṭādvaita philosophy for twelve years in Tamil, the people's language, in the village of Melkoṭe near Mysore.

In the learned texts, *dṛṣṭānta* (illustrations) and *upamā* (analogies), borrowed from the day-to-day activities and ordinary lives of the people, such as from the sphere of *śṛṅgāra* (ornamentation), cooking, family relationships and obligations, as well as activities such as digging wells, etc., abound. In the five-step syllogism, the third step is *udāharaṇam*, a real life example, the applied example "characteristic of India's practical outlook and its practical conception of proof" (Heimann 86-87). Both these attest to the fact that in India, knowledge is not a privileged discourse, nor a discourse of the privileged. And what decisively attests to the non-esoteric and non-elitist nature of knowledge, and above all, to its continuity, is the fact that what was once the learned vocabulary of Indian thought is today a part of the ordinary language of the people. Trans-disciplinary philosophical terms such as *jaḍa*, *cetana*, *jīva*,

---

3. In a personal conversation with Śrī Śaṅkarācārya of Śārdā Pīṭha, Śṛṅgerī, it was confirmed that, in the seventh century, apart from the fact that Sanskrit was a very widely understood language, the Indian speech community was covered by five Prākṛts, and that Śrī Ādi Śaṅkaracārya gave his discourses in Prākṛt followed later by his compositions in Sanskrit, the pan-Indian language of learning.

ātman, saṁsāra, dhyāna, kṣamā, dayā, maitrī, karuṇā, aṇu, jñāna, jñānī, citta, buddhi, pratyakṣa continue to be present in almost all Indian languages and, what is more significant, are present as ordinary words in the speech of the people. Not only terms of philosophy, even technical terms of grammar, *saṁjñā*s, such as *vṛddhi* and *guṇa*, are high frequency words in the ordinary speech of people of almost all Indian languages. Even the conceptual propositions[4] are a part of the ordinary thinking of the people as maxims. It is not just a question of words or clauses being present, it is a matter of ideas permeating and continuing to be alive. It is also an example of what can be unequivocally termed as the true democratization of thought in India. This democratization makes the possession of right knowledge[5] — a civilizational value in India.

Thus, great value has always been attached to knowledge, and tremendous intellectual effort has gone into maintaining the texts of knowledge. As has been noted elsewhere[6] even

---

4. Such as "death is certain for the born" (*Bhagavad-Gītā* 2.27).

5. As we have said elsewhere,

   The goal of knowledge in the Indian tradition therefore is so very different — it is to promote the freedom of the individual. Of course, what constitutes "freedom of the Individual" in our thought has to be clearly understood. For true individual freedom, the only goal has to be *mokṣa*. So the individual seeks/pursues his *mokṣa*. But the instrument or means of *mokṣa* is Knowledge. But what Knowledge? That which promotes *dharma*, which is defined in the *Mahābhārata* as that which promotes the general welfare of mankind. So the individual has to seek knowledge that promotes what the *Bhagavad-Gītā* calls *loka-saṁgraha*, the collective well-being. Knowledge informed by dharma binds the individual and the society. (Kapoor, "Knowledge, Individual and Society in the Indian Tradition")

6. See Kapil Kapoor, "Some Reflections on the Interpretation of Texts in the Indian Tradition."

though Hindu culture is not bibliolatrous, it has accorded a special status to certain texts, the texts of knowledge, and made them perennial objects of study. The difference, however, is that there has been a complete freedom to come up with numerous, even competing, interpretations. A distinction therefore has to be made between the conformist, undifferentiated study of a single sacred text and a freely interpretive study of an intellectually important text (such as the *Ṛgveda*) that generates a multiplicity of what are often the contending interpretations.[7] Śruti and Smṛti texts, as texts of knowledge, have been objects of perennial study. The two dominant metaphors for these texts are,

(i) *kāmadhenu*, and

(ii) *kalpavṛkṣa*.

The first metaphor suggests that they are sources of endless knowledge, and the second that they yield the desired fruit, whatever is the *iṣṭa*, conducive to the happiness of the community/individual.

But it has not been simple, this successful maintenance of texts. Various processes have been involved in this — loss, recovery and renewal. Some texts, many in fact, have quite possibly been irretrievably lost. A text is lost when it —

(i) gets dispersed and portions of the text become unavailable for the time being,

(ii) grows asymmetrical with new known facts and so ceases to be relevant or grows outmoded, that is obsolete or anachronistic, and

(iii) becomes opaque and no longer makes sense.

---

7. Bhartṛhari says, "Monism, Dualism and any number of points of view (*pravāda bahudhā mata*), all equally valid, are all rooted in and argued from the Veda" (*Vākyapadīya* 1.8).

The Indian tradition records repeated loss and recovery of its seminal cultural texts. Even in known/written history we can observe the operation of both, loss, and, of various text-recovery/renewal mechanisms. Renewal needs to be understood as a different process, one that in the course of recovery or maintenance involves extension or deepening of the thought. These processes deserve to be studied, though the evidence is scarce and culture-specific.

It has been earlier affirmed that culture is a Tantra or a set of systems or "grammars." These systems, with the passage of time, may, due to various factors, be lost. Thus, when a text grows asymmetrical[8] with what it seeks to explain and loses its relevance and position as a primary text in a given domain of knowledge, it may get dropped.[9] Or, through a sudden external event or process, texts (and their knowledge) may be physically destroyed or lost (as would happen, for example, in case of a great war or upheaval such as the *Mahābhārata*, in which even great grammarians were made to drive chariots).

However, dynamic communities do not allow their systems of thoughts to die. A civilization such as India's, that puts a premium on knowledge, would strive and develop techniques for maintaining its texts. As has been described elsewhere,[10]

8. As would be the case of a book dealing with medicinal plants which have since become extinct.
9. Particularly in the oral tradition, where texts occupy space in the mind and that space has to be economically used according to priorities.
10. See Kapil Kapoor, "*Vyāsa Paramparā*, Text Renewal Mechanisms, Max Müller and European Scholarship" 117-35. The discussion of the "Recovery" process here in section II is based on this paper. But I make a distinction in this paper between "Recovery" and "Renewal" mechanisms.

oral cultures have in-built mechanisms for the recovery of texts. As it is, strong cultures resist both kinds of loss — those due to the text-internal factors and those due to the text-external, contextual factors — to preserve culturally central systems of ideas. A culture may, therefore, employ one or any of the following seven text maintenance/renewal mechanisms to keep the thought alive and re-contextualized:

(i) ***Commentary*** : Such as Kātyāyana's *Vārttika*, 350 BC; Patañjali's *Mahābhāṣya* second century BC; *Kaśikā* seventh century AD and Śaṅkara's *Bhāṣya*;

(ii) ***Recension*** (a critical revision) : Such as *Candra Vyākaraṇa*, fourth century AD, a Buddhist recension of the *Aṣṭādhyāyī* that interestingly eschews what it believes to be its philosophically loaded technical vocabulary; *Jainendra Vyākaraṇa/Śabdānuśāsana*, composed in fifth century AD by Devanandin or Siddhanandin), and *Aṣṭāvakra Gītā*;

(iii) ***Redaction*** (a re-arrangement) : Such as *Rūpamālā* of Vimala Saraswati, *Siddhānta Kaumudī* of Bhaṭṭojīdīkṣita, sixteenth century AD and *Laghusiddhānta Kaumudī* of Varadarāja, eighteenth century AD;

(iv) ***Adaptation*** : *Hemaśabdānuśāsana* by Hemacandrācārya, eleventh century AD, an adaptation of Pāṇini's grammar to describe Prākṛt, contemporarily spoken Prākṛts, or Śaṅkaradeva's Assamese adaptation of Vālmikī *Rāmāyaṇa*, and such other adaptations in almost all the Indian languages from the thirteenth and fourteenth centuries onwards;

(v) ***Translation*** : For example, the many translations of major literary and philosophical texts in almost all the modern Indian languages from roughly the fourteenth century onwards; Hindī paraphrase of *Aṣṭādhyāyī* by

Shri Narayan Misra and the English translation of the text with incorporations from *Kaśikā* by Shri S.C. Vasu, 1898;

(vi) ***Popular exposition*** : The *kathā, pravacana paramparā*, a hoary tradition, has been chiefly instrumental in both the maintenance and renewal of texts of thought.[11] The two parallel traditions, the learned and the popular have been present throughout, and even today are mutually enriching each other and contributing in equal measure to the development of thought, through processes of paraphrase, explication, verification, falsification, illustration, etc.; and

(vii) ***Re-creation*** : The *Mahābhārata*, for example, is in addition maintained by repeated creative use of its themes and episodes. Recreations based on the *Mahābhārata* date back to the ancient Sanskrit playwright Bhāsa, who wrote a number of plays on epic characters and episodes including his portrayal of the dilemma of Karṇa in his play *Karṇābhāra*. Another powerful attempt at recreation of the themes and characters of the epic is seen in the stage performances of Kathakalī in Kerala. Modern Indian literature has been lately flooded with re-tellings of the epic. In the Malayālam novel, *Anuyatra* by S.K. Marar, Kuntī is portrayed as suffering like the "Mother Earth" herself.

---

11. This *kathā, pravacana paramparā* continues to be vigorous and alive even today, with many distinguished expounders of Upaniṣads, Vedānta, *Bhagavad-Gītā* and *Rāmāyaṇa* drawing huge crowds in their live discourses and having millions of devoted followers across the country. Shri Asaram-ji Bapu and Shri Murari Bapu are just two examples. Their discourses are learned but *sarasa* and in the functional mode laid down by the *Nāṭyaśāstra* they make profound thought accessible to the people.

Shivaji Sawant's *Mṛtyuñjaya* discusses Karṇa's ethical predicament. This Marāṭhī novel glorifies Karṇa and justifies his actions through a psychological framework. Another Malayālam novel, *And Now Let Me Sleep*, by P.K. Balakrishnan also attempts to see Karṇa as a person suffering from a grave identity crisis. A very notable re-telling of the *Mahābhārata* is the English novel by Shashi Tharoor, *The Great Indian Novel*. Tharoor borrows the structure of the epic, employs the technique of subversion and parodies the general schema. The various re-tellings show that the great epic is renewed through re-interpretation and re-contextualization. All these renewals restore the dynamics of a text that may otherwise lose its vitality. In this they align with commentary or the *ṭīkā* mode.

II

How is the loss due to external conditions handled? This "external process" is a very complex phenomenon and has several articulations. For example, when the Nalanda library was burnt, some Buddhist *bhikkhus* (monks) fled to Tibet with whatever texts they could take with them. (The library's massive collection, it is said, burnt for months; so only a small fraction could have been saved.)

Many texts were irretrievably lost. One text, Diṅnāga's *Pramāṇasamuccaya*, has an interesting and representative history of recovery. In 1968, Masaaki Hattori translated, annotated and published the section on perception, the *Pratyakṣapariccheda*, from the Sanskrit fragments and the Tibetan versions. In 1987, Richard P. Hayes, published an English translation from Kanakavarman's Tibetan translation and Vasudhārakṣita's translation of the text. He prepared explanatory notes on the basis of the *ṭīkā* (sub-commentary) by Jinendrabuddhi (also known as Jitendrabudhi, eighth century AD). Jinendrabuddhi's sub-commentary is more useful as a guide to Diṅnāga's thought as it offers an explanation of nearly every phrase in *Pramāṇasamuccaya*, both for the verses and the prose auto-commentary. Further, Hayes notes in his introduction:

> To all of the passages translated I have added my own commentary, which not only contains information on how Diṅnāga's arguments were interpreted by such philosophers as Uddyotkara, Jayamisra, Pārthasārthimisra and Jinendrabuddhi, but also ventures occasionally to express the line of argument used by the Indians in a way intended to make them a little more acceptable to modern readers.
>
> — Hayes, 223

The *Pramāṇasamuccaya* text has had an interesting history in Tibet where it was taken by the monks. The Sanskrit original is no longer available but three Tibetan translations were made from the original. Burston records that a *puṇḍit* by the name of Candrarāhula was invited to Tibet and that he and the Tibetan translator Ting nge dzin Bzang Po translated *Pramāṇasamuccaya* and other works in the middle part of the eleventh century. The second of the two surviving translations of the *Pramāṇasamuccaya* was done by the Tibetan scholar Dad pai shes rab in collaboration with an Indian *puṇḍit* named Kanakavarmana (Kser kyi go ch). Kanakavarmana's translation of Diṅnāga's work is, generally speaking, clearer than the translation by Vasudhārakṣita and Zha ma seng ge and more in line with the grammatical analysis and philosophical expositions given by Jinendrabuddhi. In cases where a fragment of the original Sanskrit passage has survived, a comparison of this fragment with the two Tibetan translations most often shows that Kanakavarmana's work shows more finesse and accuracy than the other translation.

As for the original text, only the first chapter of the *Pramāṇasamuccaya* by Diṅnāga (AD 480-540) is available at the Government Oriental Library, Mysore. This first chapter, *Pratyakṣapariccheda*, on perception as a means of valid knowledge, consists of forty-eight verses while the total number of verses in this text has been reported to be two hundred and forty-seven. This is an example of the partial recovery of a text in recorded history in an allied cultural tradition at a time when the traditional modes of storing the text in the mind in various permutations had been disrupted. In what is today referred to as "pre-history," it was possible to reconstitute the texts within the tradition and though we have no means to assess the degree of reconstitution, the authenticity of reconstitution is implicitly accepted.[12]

III

The process of recovery of texts has been institutionalized in the tradition as Vyāsa *paramparā*. Vyāsa *paramparā* is a record of the recovery of texts. Understanding this involves questions such as the nature of evidence.[13] As mentioned above, we are

12. We are referring to the elaborate and complex *pāṭha*-tradition which analysed and re-organized texts in various permutations and combinations which when stored in the mind in different arrangements/combinations ensured accurate re-construction of the texts even when, and if, all the exteriorized, written versions were to be destroyed. The texts have been maintained intact and uncorrupted through intricate techniques of mental storage and oral transference.

13. We rely on Purāṇa narratives. It is said that Purāṇa narratives are metaphorical, not literal. But on that count we cannot reject their evidence. *Mīmāṁsā-Sūtra* clearly says that *rūpaka* is the mode of statement in the Vedas and goes on to interpret, to attribute, content to them. Further, to call thirty different ṛṣis, scholars, by the same nomenclature, Vyāsa, is itself an act of metaphoricization.

different from the West in our understanding of notions such as "authenticity," in our sense of time, and in our *itihāsa-purāṇa* (modes of recording what happened/what is likely to happen). It is enshrined in the *Mahābhārata* and in the different Purāṇas that in India's long tradition, the central codes (Vedas, contingent *vāṅmaya* and *vidyās*) were lost and re-constituted or enounced anew at least thirty times, and then renewed and subsequently elaborated. For the latter, we have the attested example of *Aṣṭādhyāyī*, and for the former, we have cited the example of *Pramāṇasamuccaya*, a culturally central code of Buddhist epistemology. Many Western scholars would discount these formulations given their assumptions and their methodology for in no other tradition do we have such efforts at reconstituting and renewal. But in the case of the Indian tradition even those belonging to other traditions have worked assiduously to reconstruct texts and renew them, as, for example, the German and French scholars did in the nineteenth and twentieth centuries with the Sanskrit texts.

An Indian scholar, Dr. Kunwarlal Vyasashishya, has pointed out,

> Western writers do not even accept the existence of Parāsharya Vyāsa [the author of the *Mahābhārata*], so what value can they attach to the twenty-nine Vyāsas who preceded him? Today, Parāsharya Vyāsa is the source of *Vedavānmaya* [the entire body of Vedic literature. By rejecting the existence of Vedavyāsa] the Western writers have dug up the very root of authentic Indian history just as Kauṭilya had dug up the very root of the Nanda dynasty. But the roots of Indian *itihāsa* go into the very *pātāla* [the netherworld] 'and so they have not succeeded in plucking them out completely.' So the famous Purāṇa scholar, Pargiter, though unable to grasp the whole truth, did apprehend the

> truth that Vyāsa enounced the texts before the *Mahābhārata* war.
> — 35, 37; my translation[14]

Far beyond the limited chronology of the West, Vedic literature has existed in India since time immemorial. Moreover, it has been, for various reasons, repeatedly in need of re-statement, re-constitution, defence. It has happened thirty times. The span of time over which it has happened need not concern us here, as it is not pertinent. What is pertinent is the phenomenon of loss and recovery through restatement or reconstitution. We know for example from the *Mahābhārata* text itself that it was constituted in Janmejaya's *nāga-yajña* at the Nigamabodha Ghāṭa, a tell-tale name, of the then Indraprastha, modern Delhi. This was obviously an assembly of the learned, convened by Janmejaya to reconstitute texts that were lost in the great convulsion, with the purpose of recovering the Nigama texts.

We must comment on the nature and the cause of loss. As Max Müller has noted[15] texts in the oral tradition are stored and maintained in the memory.[16] This mode assumes an

14. The author quotes Pargiter: "He (Vyāsa) would probably have completed that work of Vedic (recension) about a quarter century before the Bharata battle" (Pargiter 318; as ctd. in Vyāsaśiṣya 37).
15. "This may sound startling, but what will sound more startling, and yet is a fact that can be easily ascertained "at the present moment, if every MS of the *Ṛgveda* was lost, we should be able to recover the whole of it — from the memory of the *śrotriya*s in India. Here then we are not dealing with theories, but with facts, which — anybody may verify. The whole of the *Ṛgveda*, and a great deal exists at the present moment in the oral tradition" (*India: What Can It Teach Us* 131).
16. Orality, as a mode of constituting and maintaining knowledge, organizes knowledge in the mind, as against the literate traditions in which knowledge is maintained externally, exteriorized with attendant consequences for knowledge formation, storage and dissemination. For some more details, see Kapil Kapoor, "*Texts of the Oral Tradition*" 27-31.

ordered, stable society. If there is a major disturbance, such as the long twelve-year drought just before the ninth Vyāsa (*Mahābhārata*, Śalya Parva, *adhyāya* 51), the scholars can think of nothing but their very existence and the texts go into the background. Or if there is a war such as the *Mahābhārata*, or if there is a massive invasion such as that of the Śakas at the turn of the era or of the Islamic armies in the tenth, eleventh and twelfth centuries of this era.

The scholar we have already cited lists by name the thirty Vyāsas on the basis of evidence in the Purāṇas and the *Mahābhārata*, and describes the function they performed. While the earlier Vyāsas are credited with the first enunciation of the texts, the ninth, the tenth, the nineteenth, the twenty-fifth and the thirtieth Vyāsa are explicitly recognized as those who re-constituted the texts.

> *Saundarānanda*, 7, records:
>
> *sārasvato yatra suto'asya yajñeya na hasya vedasya punaḥ pravaktaḥ* ।
>
> Sarasvatī's son Sārasvata was born, who re-constituted the Vedas that had been lost.

It is also recorded that there was a continuous drought for twelve years and sixty thousand *ṛṣi*s congregated in the Sārasvata Āśrama (hermitage), and afflicted by hunger and thirst, they forgot the Vedas. Sārasvata then reconstituted them and taught them again. Aśvaghoṣa in his *Buddhacarita* again recorded the same fact:

> *sārasvat cāpi jagād na ṣṭam vedaṁ punartha dadr. . . urṇapūrve.*
> — I.42
>
> At the destruction of the world, Sarasvata (*ṛṣi*) reconstituted/ restored the Vedas to their earlier form.

It is noted by the Purāṇas and Itihāsas that Veda-Śruti has been lost or been seized or forgotten several times and that it has been "rescued" time and again by great minds. For example, it is widely recorded that the *asuras*, Madhu-Kaiṭabha, had seized the Vedas and Hari (Viṣṇu) had to rescue the texts.

Harivaṁśa Purāṇa records a similar conribution of *ṛṣi* Dattātreya in restoring the Vedas and Vedic sacrificial rituals:

> *dattātreya'na e u vede u prakriyāsu makhe a ca* ।
> *saha yajñakriyā vedā pratyānī tā hi tena vai* ॥
> — I.41.4-5, 7

> Dattātreya — at the destruction of the Vedas and Vedic practices with effort restored both ritual practices and the Vedas.

Vāyu Purāṇa also records it with some variation:

> *tretāyuge tu daṁame dattātrayo vabhéva ha* ।
> *na e dharma caturthañca mārkaṇḍeya purassaraḥ* ॥

> In *Tretāyuga*, for the tenth time, when Dharma was destroyed, Mārkaṇḍeya, as a Vyāsa, re-constituted the Vedas with the help of Dattātreya.[17]

The names of the Vyāsas, from that of the eleventh to that of the thirtieth, are known but details are available only about the nineteenth (Bhāradvāja), the twentieth (Vājaśrava, the father of Naciketā), the twenty-fifth (Ṛkṣavālmikī), the twenty-seventh (Parāśara), and, of course, the thirtieth Kṛṣṇadvaipāyana Vedavyāsa, the contemporary of Śāntanu, whose contribution is acknowledged by Pargiter, as noted

---

17. It is to be noted that in the early texts and tradition, the term Veda encompasses not only Śrutis but also all *Brāhmaṇas* and all Smṛtis, and *vidyās*. Later the term got restricted to Śruti texts, at some point of time.

above. In many Purāṇas and in the *Mahābhārata* this is acknowledged, viz.,

sarvavedavidaṁ śreṣṭho vāsaḥ satyavatisutaḥ
— Śānti Parva 2.9

It is said that the *Vedavāṅmaya* composed in the earlier ages became disordered and dispersed. Vedavyāsa, seeing that human intellectual abilities had declined, put together the essence of all the Veda Saṁhitās in the form of the four Vedas because of which he came to be called Vyāsa (Ādi Parva 63.87-88).

This entire text-renewal institution of Vyāsa needs to be studied as against the needs of those times.

There are thus various functions of this institution of Vyāsa, such as re-establishment, recovery and reconstitution, extension (viz., 21 *śākhā*s of the *Ṛgveda* by the disciples of the Vedavyāsa) and propagation. What is of importance is the evident knowledge-centredness of the Indian community. So immense is the value attached to these texts of knowledge (Vedas) that repeated efforts have been made by great minds to keep these texts intact. In this sense, Ādi Śaṅkara could also be called a Vyāsa as he re-established, re-interpreted and propagated Vedic knowledge after it had been restricted and overshadowed by Buddhist thought for almost one thousand years.

From these narratives, another convention emerges. Such monumental work as the different Vyāsas did, could not have been achieved by any one individual — several thinkers must have been involved in what perhaps took the shape of a vigorous intellectual movement. So what the later recorders do is to identify one of them as the leader of that movement, call him Vyāsa, and name the several other thinkers who performed limited, specific tasks, as his disciples. This is how Vedavyāsa's disciples are known — one of them, Paela, engaged himself with the *Ṛgveda* and later twenty-one of his disciples developed the twenty-one schools of the *Ṛgveda*. One can trace this kind of intellectual progression and relationship even in the history of the evolution of Advaita. Thus, the subsequent thinkers such as Rāmānujācārya of Viśiṣṭādvaita would be counted as a *śiṣya* (disciple) of the Vyāsa — Ādi Śaṅkara. And in the same vein, one may recognize the contribution of Yāska, more than fifteen hundred years before Ādi Śaṅkara. We know from his *Nirukta* that the Vedic texts had become so opaque with the passage of time that materialist skeptics such as Kautsa asserted that Vedic *mantra*s were meaningless. Yāska took up the gauntlet, developed the science of *nirvacana* — etymology — restored meanings to the Vedic texts and thus renewed them. He initiated the science of interpretation and came at the head of a line of scholars culminating in Jaimini and his *Mīmāṁsāśāstra*. He may be attested as the thirty-first Vyāsa with Ādi Śaṅkara as the thirty-second.

In this manner time and again, a number of *dṛṣṭa*s/*ṛṣi*s rescued the Indian Knowledge Systems from being submerged and destroyed, very much like Lord Viṣṇu rescued the *gaja* (elephant) from the fatal clutches of the *graha* (crocodile).

IV

Now we come to (i) the availability of the text, (ii) the ability to understand the text, and (iii) the relevance of the text. The continuous and cumulative *ṭīkā paramparā* (the commentary tradition) ensured all the three — availability, comprehensibility and contextual relevance of the texts.

The commentary tradition is a cumulative tradition, i.e., a number of commentaries on a given text follow each other in succession, with every succeeding commentary taking into account and building on the preceding ones. Almost all the major texts have been cumulatively commented upon.[18]

These commentaries take many forms, from *pañjikā* (bare annotation) to *mahābhāṣya* (exhaustive, encyclopedic analysis).[19] What K.A. Subramania Iyer says about the purpose and value of commentaries is true of commentaries in general:

> [These] 'supplied the context and brought out the full implications of the main idea' [they also explain] the logical sequence [of topics and ideas] '[handing down the old

---

18. For example, the commentaries, *ṭīkā*, on Jaimini's *Mīmāṁsā-Sūtra*: *Śābarabhāṣya* (AD first century?); Kumārila Bhaṭṭa's *Ślokavārttika* and *Tantravārttika* (sixth century/seventh century AD?) commentaries on *Śābarabhāṣya*; Prabhākara Miśra's commentary on *Śābarabhāṣya, Bṛhati* (seventh century AD?); Śālīkanātha's commentary on *Bṛhati, Ṛjuvimala* (ninth century AD); Pārthasārathī Miśra's *Śāstradipikā* (fourteenth century AD?); Madhvācārya's *Nyāyamālā* (fourteenth/fifteenth century AD); Appayadīkṣita's *Upakramaparākrama*, Apadeva's *Mīmāṁsānyāyaprakāśa*, Khaṇḍadeva's *Mīmāṁsākaustubha*, Gaṅgabhaṭṭa's *Bhaṭṭacintāmaṇi*, Nārayaṇa Bhaṭṭa's *Mānamayodya* all in the seventeenth century; Kṛṣṇayajavana's *Mīmāṁsāparibhāṣā* (eighteenth century AD). The commentary literature is indeed endless; we have mentioned here only those that are most frequently cited and discussed. Indeed there are commentaries on these commentaries (which is what makes the tradition "interlaced"), such as the two major *Ślokavārttika* commentaries, *Kaśikā* by Sucharita Misra and *Nyāyaratnākara* by Pārthasārathī Miśra, the *Tantravārttika* commentaries, *Nyāyasudhā* by Someśvara Bhaṭṭa, and *Tauttatitamatatilaka* by Bhavadeva Bhaṭṭa, to mention only two. (For a complete list, see Gaṅgānātha Jha's introduction to his translation of *Ślokavārttika*.)
19. Rājaśekhara, in his *Kāvyamīmāṁsā* (ninth century AD) in chapter 1, lists eight forms.

> tradition] was also one of the original motives of those writers' [they also placed the text in the context of the totality of philosophical systems]. — 50-51

Above all, as Vāmana-Jayāditya say in the first *kārikā* of their *Kaśikā*:

> The purpose is to bring together and unify the 'knowledge that lies scattered in *vṛttis*, *bhāṣyas* and all *śāstras*.'

Thus, over a period of time, texts (i) grow opaque, and/or (ii) become asymmetrical with the context, and/or (iii) their connection with the tradition of knowledge in that domain becomes incoherent. If the intellectual texts have not become "dead" and are still studied in the learned, though now relatively esoteric, tradition, it is because the *ṭīkā paramparā* has kept them alive and pertinent. As we have already noted, some of India's most brilliant minds have been exegetes — Yāska (ninth century BC), Śabaraswāmin (first century AD), Kumārila Bhaṭṭa (sixth century AD), Ādi Śaṅkara (seventh century AD), Śrī Rāmānuja (eleventh century AD), Madhvācārya (thirteenth century AD), Sāyaṇacārya (fourteenth century AD), Jñāneśvara (AD 1400-1500), right down to "The Great Moderns," Śrī Aurobindo, Mahatma Gandhi, Radhakrishnan, Vinoba Bhave (who all wrote commentaries on the *Bhagavad-Gītā* in the illustrious line of Śaṅkara and Rāmānuja). As already noted (*Vākyapādīya* 1.8-10), the existence of this continuous, cumulative tradition of interpretation, apart from attesting to society's commitment to knowledge, also attests the freedom of mind that the culture allows the individual to exercise in reaching different, competing and self-validated interpretations/constructs. Freedom to interpret means freedom to think. Above all this tradition ensured continuity of the habits of the mind, of what is called the culture of a community.

Commentary is the major form that *artha-nirdhāraṇa* (interpretation), takes in the tradition. The interpreter seeks to establish meaning at the level of *yathārtha* (meaning at the apparent level) and at the level of *tattvārtha* (significance or purport). As texts can be highly complex even at the surface, we need canons and instruments of interpretation. Faced with transparent, discontinuous, repetitive, contradictory, tautological, implausible, non-coherent, apparently meaningless texts, Indian exegetes developed, over long stretches of time, a system of interpretation that employed the following ten strategies or instruments of exegesis:

A. *śabda pramāṇa* (verbal testimony) — *śruti, darśana, itihāsa-purāṇa, jñāna mīmāṁsā* (established epistemologies, perception, inference, etc.),

B. *sārvabhauma siddhānta*, major assumption of text-domain,

C. *saṅgati* (coherence), *paribhāṣā nyāya* (meta-rules; rules of interpretation), *laukika nyāya* (judgements employed in ordinary life), *vyākaraṇa* (grammar),

D. *nirvacana* (etymology; exposition of word-meaning), *śabda-śakti* (theories of meaning, including *dhvani*, [suggestion] and *lakṣaṇa vṛtti* [figurative meaning]).

It is instructive to study the great exegetes and see how they employ these instruments of interpretation and how they differ from each other in their preferred instruments. For example, while Śrī Rāmānuja dominantly uses verbal testimony in his *Gītā Bhāṣya*, Śrī Śaṅkara's dominant epistemology is inference.[20] In his commentary on the second chapter of the

20. For a detailed statement of Śrī Śaṅkara's method in his commentary on the *Gītā*, chapter 2, see Kapil Kapoor, "*Some Reflections*" 264-71.

Gītā, his argument is presented in the given *vāda* tradition — the *pūrva-pakṣa* (the opponent's point of view) is presented first, and then controverted, and finally the *sva-siddhānta* is argued. Ādi Śaṅkara employs all the instruments of interpretation in an exposition that displays a concentric enlargement of the argument built around the one keyword, *aśocya* (un- or non-mournable).

In this part of his commentary Śrī Śaṅkara achieves a remarkable reconciliation of what had been posited since the Upaniṣads as the three contending means of *mokṣa* (liberation) — *jñāna* (knowledge), *karma* (action) and *bhakti* (devotion). The *Bhagavad-Gītā* is important in the Indian history of ideas because it investigates the cause of suffering in relation to a real life situation, a drastic situation that involves the issues of killing and/or getting killed and also one that epitomises all the dilemmas that a person may encounter in this life. The great sage Vyāsa examines this question and to give it authority makes Lord Kṛṣṇa the spokesman. Ādi Śaṅkara's seminal commentary articulates and establishes Lord Kṛṣṇa's *siddhānta* for attaining *mokṣa* (freedom from suffering): *niṣkāma karma* (unattached action) leads to *citta śuddhi* (the purification of the self), which leads to *vairāgya* (wise indifference), which leads to *viveka* (discriminating faculty), which leads to *viśuddha jñāna* (pure knowledge) which then leads to *mokṣa* (freedom from suffering).

The commentary tradition remained alive, though restricted, even in the period of great disruption following the eleventh century.

V

Owing to the upheavals in Indian history in the eleventh century and the vandalism that followed, Indian learning/

knowledge got excluded, suffered, dispersed. It went "underground," with some families of scholars secretly continuing to engage with particular parts and portions of this body of knowledge. The Bhaṭṭojidīkṣita family of Varanasi, for example, in the sixteenth-seventeenth centuries took upon itself the task of maintaining *vyākaraṇa* texts at great risk and in penury. Gradually the whole education system came to be disrupted, various schools disappeared one by one, and new objects of knowledge replaced this traditional knowledge.

The process continued with the British period. Dr. Bhattacharya has described the state of affairs and the attitude of Indians to their own learning:

> The introduction of English as the medium of instruction and the establishment of a large number of schools and colleges on the Western style led to the virtual closure of 'Tols and Patthashalas'. After the quelling of the Mutiny a feeling of desperation took possession of the Indian mind. It was feared that the old Indian literature, old Indian culture, old Indian sciences and arts 'would perish at no distant future. Manuscripts were perishing in heaps in the houses of Pandits or were being carried to all parts of Europe'. A Pandit in the early years of the 19th century considered his manuscripts to be his best treasures. 'His son who had learnt A B C' saw no good in the manuscripts and removed them from the best room of his house, first to the kitchen. 'The housewife' took the wooden-board covers and utilized them for fuel. The leaves got intermixed for want of board and string [and] in the course of a year or so were thrown to the kitchen garden to rot. — 54-55

The situation of ignorance came to such a pass that we could no longer read Aśoka's inscriptions (Princep had to do it for us), the Nawāb of Bhopal offered the Vidiśā sculptures to be taken away and had to be told by the British resident that he did not know what he was saying, and Jagat Singh, the general of the Rājā of Benāras pulled down the *stūpa* of Sārnāth to provide bricks/materials for the Rājā's new palace. As Swami Nirvedananda says:

> . . . young minds began to swallow queer cultural shibboleths, such as India has no culture worth the name, that her entire past was (one big error best forgotten) a foolish quest after false ideals, that if she wanted to live seriously, she would have to re-mould herself.
>
> Thoroughly in the mould of European civilization, these incantations lulled the self-awareness of the Indians into sleep. —653

Not just young minds, but India as a people grew ashamed. As noted elsewhere:

> It is perhaps not difficult for us even today to reconstruct the Hindu mood of deep despondency in the last decades of the nineteenth century '[And then subsequently] Marathas had been defeated in 1818, the Sikhs in 1839, the revolt of the Hindi heartland put down in 1857' [it was a case of people having lost] their voice [a case of] subjugation of the discourse — a whole lexis de-invigorated [dropped], rendered meaningless.
>
> — Kapoor, *Rebirth of a Language*, 100

We get a glimpse of the psychological state of the people in Swami Vivekananda's address also where he said: "It has been one of the principles of my life not to be ashamed of my ancestors. The more I have studied the past more and more has this pride come to me." He went on to link this mood to the submerging of India's thought and literature, and referred to the recurrence of this phenomenon and the repeated re-emergence of this thought in India's long history:

> Sect after sect arose in India, seeming to shake the religion of the Vedas to its very depths, but like the waters of the sea-shore in a tremendous earthquake it receded 'only to return in an all-absorbing flood.'[21]

VI

It is in this perspective that we have to see the renewal — the recovery and reconstitution — of texts in the modern times from the eighteenth century onwards, due to the "happy" accident of the British rule in India. It is the European scholars, particularly the Germans, who set in motion the process of recovery — of both the texts and the self-respect of the people.

It is not out of place to note chronologically the work of major contributors here as recorded by Dr. Bhattacharya (52-54). Warren Hastings, nominated Governor-General of India in 1773, commissioned the first law-book compiled by Sanskrit scholars. This was published subsequently, in 1776, in English translation as *A Code of Gentoo Law*. Later Charles Wilkins translated the *Bhagavad-Gītā* and *Hitopadeśa* into English. However, for really opening Indian literature to Europe credit goes, as is well-known, to Sir William Jones who founded the Asiatic Society, which printed editions of numerous Indian texts in a series known as *Bibliotheca Indica*. He himself translated *Śakuntalā* and *Manu-Smṛti* into English. Colebrooke continued this work and initiated Indian Philology. He introduced the *Ṛgveda* to Europe in 1805. H.H. Wilson next translated the *Ṛgveda*. Alexander Hamilton, another Englishman, learnt Sanskrit. On his way back from India he was detained in Paris. There, Fredrich Schlegel the German

21. From his Chicago Address, paragraph 1. This address was delivered on 11 September 1893 at the World Parliament of Religions.

scholar learnt that language from him and published his studies in German. His talented brother followed him and became the first professor of Sanskrit in Germany and settled in Bonn in 1818. Franz Bopp was a contemporary of Schlegel and became the founder of the new science of Comparative Philology.

Sanskrit studies grew more and more influential in Europe and a large number of scholars took to Sanskrit studies. Some of those who made significant contributions, apart from Max-Müller, are — Roth, Burnouf, Aufrecht, Lassen, Böhtlingk, Weber, Senart, Sylvain Levi, Foucher, and others. The long line ends in such giants at the turn of the twentieth century as Ferdinand de Saussure, the father of structuralism, who was a professor of Sanskrit at Geneva, had done his doctorate on the genitive case in Sanskrit and published papers in the area of Sanskrit poetics and metres; Roman Jakobson, the formalist, linguist and literary theorist who worked on Vedic mythology; and Trubetzkoy, the structural phonologist who had worked on the *Ṛgveda* for his doctoral degree. Sanskrit studies took root in America as well and a number of eminent scholars were associated with it — Lenman, Edgerton, Norman Brown, Whitney, Clarke and the two eminent contemporary scholars, D.D. Ingalls and George Cardona, whose works have, ironically, added respectability to Sanskrit Studies and promoted their acceptability in the Indian academy. This *sahasranāma* is auspicious and should be enounced by all those who study or revere this tradition.[22]

As Shri Kamalakar Tiwari appropriately observes we owe a deep debt of gratitude to these European and British scholars — they renewed a whole tradition afresh by reconstituting

22. We obviously disagree with "anti-imperialists" and so-called "Orientalists."

the texts and gave them respectability by making them the object of serious study in the mainstream education of Europe. It is through the medium of Sanskrit scholars, Shri Tiwari writes, that:

> We are getting to know our brightness/fairness. In this matter we shall ever remain grateful to the Western scholars who gave us the kind of sight (*dṛṣṭi*) that makes it possible for us to see our own past. —11

While William Jones did draw the attention of Europe to the Sanskrit language and its beauty through his translations of *Śakuntalā* and *Manu-Smṛti*, his scholarly efforts remained focused on post-Buddhist literature and Vedic literature remained a closed book. Colebrooke also did not realize the value of his work related to the *Ṛgveda*. H.H. Wilson also remained mostly interested in later Sanskrit literature. At this point, Burnouf published a comparative grammar of Zend and Vedic Sanskrit and initiated an intellectual revolution in Europe for the next twenty-five years from 1826 to 1852.

VII

Burnouf's two disciples, Roth and Max Müller, continued his work of foregrounding the intellectual strength of Vedic literature. Max Müller's contribution in this recovery/renewal cycle is unequalled.

As Max Müller declared, it was his "chief object 'to try to remove [a most unhappy misconception] that [while Sanskrit texts may be pretty, quaint and curious] Sanskrit texts' either teach us nothing or teach what we do not care to know" (*India: What Can It Teach Us* 4). He therefore took it upon himself to defend the tradition and articulate it as intellectual, and not fanciful, and in the process, the reconstruction of texts became his major work. The tasks were interrelated — as by constructing an authentic edition of the *Ṛgveda*, with Sāyaṇa's commentary, he both defended and articulated the Indian intellectual tradition.

However, it is important to note that in his seven lectures he explicitly devoted himself to the articulation and defence of the tradition.[23]

Max Müller offers a reasoned defence, in sequence, against the charge that

(i) Sanskrit literature has no serious thought content (4);

(ii) Indians lack truthfulness of character (33);

(iii) Sanskrit is a "dead" language (52);

(iv) Sanskrit literature is an artificial literature (54);

(v) Indians are impractical, therefore, failures in the material sense (61);

(vi) Vedic hymns are "irrational" outpourings (68);

(vii) Brāhmaṇas withheld knowledge from people (92);

(viii) The Vedas are purely fictitious (105) and primitive (31);

(ix) Vedic literature does not have the antiquity that is claimed for it (131);

(x) Modern India is in complete disjunction with its Vedic past (134);

(xi) Indian Vedic literature developed under the "foreign" influences of Babylonia, China, Persia, etc. (89)

It is not necessary to go into the details of his arguments against these postulates; suffice it to say that he argues from facts and uses reason. As he says in the context of the oral tradition: "we are not dealing with theories, but with facts, which anybody may verify" (131).

---

23. And this needs to be remembered by those who focus only on his "Christian" or "Imperialist" stance.

As for the articulation of the intellectual content of the tradition, we should note Max Müller's exposition, the first of its kind, of the rationality, the substance and the purpose of the Vedas, *Brāhmaṇas*, *Āraṇyakas*, Upaniṣads, *Sūtragranthas*, *Prātiśākhyas* and Vedānta. His exposition became the desiderata for subsequent research in Indian studies. In this expository discourse, Max Müller defends Indian character and thought. He gives evidence of his profound insight into Indian life and thought and asserts that India has contributed in a major way to the "global" repository of knowledge and values. To give some examples:

(i) He claims that India has a place in "the history of the human mind" and his argument comes from the Sanskrit language. He cites the verb root $\sqrt{as}$ as:

> . . . no language [he says,] could ever produce at once so empty, or, if you like so general a root as $\sqrt{as}$, 'to be' and this root $\sqrt{as}$, to breathe has to lose all signs of its original material character, before it could convey that purely abstract meaning of existence, without any qualification, which has rendered to the higher operations of thought the same service which the naught, likewise the invention of Indian genius, has to render in mathematics. Who will say how long the friction lasted which changed $\sqrt{\bar{a}s}$, to breathe, into $\sqrt{as}$, to be? (17)

(ii) After having talked of "the parallel columns of numerals, pronouns, and verbs in Sanskrit, Greek and Latin written on the blackboard, one felt in the presence of facts, before which no one has to bow," he underlines the consequence of this knowledge of affinity between India and Europe in these insightful terms:

> . . . the concept of the European man has been changed and widely extended by our acquaintance with India, and we know now that we are something different from what we thought we were many thousand years ago, we were something that had not developed into Englishman, or a Saxon, or a Greek, or a Hindu either and this is not all, it [the attested Sanskrit literature] has imparted to the whole ancient history of man a reality which it never possessed before. (18-19)

(iii) Reacting to Mill's critique of the average Indian character, Max Müller quotes Sleeman to make the observation that to know an Indian, he has to know him in the village community and then makes his own generalized point that "the political unit or the social cell in India has always been, and, in spite of repeated foreign conquests, is still the village community 'we hear of the circles of 84 villages, the so called Chourasees'" (31).

(iv) Reacting again to Mill's charge, Max Müller cites so many travellers and administrators to testify to the Hindus' reverence for truth and then cites etymological proof — "Their very word for truth is full of meaning. It is *sat* or *satya, sat* being the participle of the verb *as*, to be. Truth, therefore, was with them simply *that which is*" (41).

(v) He disputes the assertion that Sanskrit is a dead language and cites several facts to show that though Sanskrit had ceased to exist "as a language spoken by the people at large in the third century BC" yet such is the marvellous continuity between the past and the present in India that in spite of repeated social convulsions, religious reforms, and foreign invasions, Sanskrit may be said to be still the only language that is spoken over the whole extent of the vast country. He calls this the "third prejudice" and says that:

> . . . even after a century of English rule and teaching 'Sanskrit is more widely understood in India than Latin was in Europe at the time of Dante.' But even if Sanskrit were more of a dead language than it really is, all the living languages of India, both Aryan and Draviḍian draw their very life and soul from Sanskrit [literature].
>
> — 51-53

(vi) Talking of the range and the extent of Sanskrit *vāṅamaya,* he says that the examination of the manuscripts show that more than ten thousand "separate works" (texts in different domains of knowledge) are in existence. Saying that not all are of exemplary sophistication or excellence, he gives a parameter for judgement — judge an intellectual community by the best it has to offer:

> . . . there runs through the whole history of India, its three or four thousand years, a high road. 'It may have been trodden by a few solitary wanderers.' But to the historians of the human mind, those few solitary wanderers are after all the true representatives of India. Do not let us be deceived. The true history of the world must always be the history of the few; and just as we measure the Himalayas by the height of Mount Everest, we must take the true measure of India from the poets of the Vedas, the sages of the Upaniṣads, the founders of the Vedanta and Samkhya philosophies and the authors of the oldest law-books. — 54-55

(vii) Contrasting the Indian meditative philosophy of life with the activism of the West, he pleads to see some value in reflection and then posits: "two hemispheres in human nature, both worth developing — the active, combative and political on the side, the passive meditative and the philosophical on the other."

He later sets up an analogous opposition between "the northern Aryan and the southern Aryan" and asks why should we not be "satisfied with a little less of work, and a little less of pleasure, but a little more thought, and a little more of rest." And then in the spirit of the *Bhagavad-Gītā*, he adds as a clincher: "For short as our life is, we are not mere Mayflies that are born in the morning to die at night." (61, 64)

(viii) Nilakantha Shastri says that while Müller's theories of "Renaissance" in third century AD no longer find acceptance, the differences he noted between Vedic literature and later classical Sanskrit still hold good (73).

(ix) Müller boldly rejects the theory that brāhmaṇas "withheld their sacred literature from any but their own caste." Far from withholding it, they have been striving to make its study obligatory for the other castes. He also cites the reception his *R̥gveda* has received from the brāhmaṇas (92).

(x) In the progressive structuring of the gods in the Vedas, he observes with great insight "the gradual advance from the material to the spiritual, from the sensuous to the super-sensuous, from the human to the super-human and divine" (101).

(xi) Finally, his exposition of Vedic poetry, Vedic gods and domestic rituals enabled all subsequent research in these areas. Later scholars had only to pick up a sentence or a phrase from Max Müller and elaborate upon it to shed light on the whole domain.[24] To see the strength of these first enunciations, one has only to cite Max Müller's statement on the oral tradition of India (131-34), which is still informative in nature,[25] and his statement on Vedānta, a case of subtle interpretation (152-56). The following must be acknowledged as a rare right insight into this philosophical system, one worthy of our best seers:

> Much that was not dear, that had seemed for a time their very self, had to be surrendered before they could see the self of selves 'a subject independent of all personality' then the highest knowledge began to dawn, the self within (*pratyagātman*) was drawn towards the Highest Self (*Paramātman*) 'the oneness of the subjective with the objective self was recognized as underlying all reality.' —155

He adds that the leading tenets of the Vedānta are known to some extent in every village in India. And then he makes a remark that shows his great understanding of how the average Indian behaves (even today!):

> In India notwithstanding the indifference to religious matters so often paraded before the world by the Indians themselves, religion and philosophy too, are great powers still. —154

24. Work in Vedic mythology by later scholars like Roman Jakobson may be cited as an example.
25. He calls those who have memorized the texts, "living libraries" (132).

VIII

If we revert now to what we had said about the Vyāsa-institution and its functions, it is clear that after the great disruption, a number of the Western scholars worked hard to re-constitute and re-establish and defend Indian thought. Of all these scholars, Max Müller stands out for his life-long work.

Like a visionary, aware that all thought is human before it is Eastern or Western, he conceived, initiated and implemented, in large measure, an unrivalled, massive fifty-volume project of translations. Translation, as has been noted above, is a major instrument of dissemination and renewal of Indian texts. The act of translation is a very complex act — purpose, situations, format/nature and effect and function differ widely.[26]

First of all, inter-translatability is a philosophical problem as it involves "inter-cultural understanding, trans-cultural interpretation and trans-cultural evaluation" (Matilal 120). It also assumes a state of mind, a certain psychology of translation. There is in each act of translation, an attitude towards the source language and a certain assessment of the target language — it is a recognition of the intellectual strength of the source and of a vacuum or gap in the target language/culture. Translations from classical into modern languages may be done within the same culture and tradition or across cultures.

The first case is a real possibility. There are instances of some Buddhist texts having been retranslated into Sanskrit in modern times. These are cases of translations within the same overall intellectual tradition — a kind of special case of

26. For further details, see Kapil Kapoor, "Philosophy of Translation: Subordinating or Subordination."

renewal, one of the three functional parameters of translations, diffusion and borrowing being the other two. Similarly, when a text is translated into a modern language in the same tradition, it is also to be considered as a case of renewal — the text becomes accessible once again in a widely spoken and used language. The text is recomposed in a way, and in the process it is reinterpreted and made intelligible to a much larger readership. It also becomes pertinent — once again it begins to function as an explanatory construct for contemporary realities. Translations of classical texts of literary theory, philosophy and grammar such as *Nāṭyaśāstra*, *Mīmāṁsā-Sūtra* and *Aṣṭādhyāyī*, among others, into modern Indian languages are some recent examples of renewal.

When a text is translated into a modern language of another tradition/culture, it is a case of diffusion. Diffusion as a horizontal concept is a special case of renewal — a text not only gets activated, it also spreads beyond its earlier boundaries. The most recent example is the translation of Pāṇini's *Aṣṭādhyāyī* into German, French and English in the nineteenth/twentieth centuries which made this proto-grammar available to a whole new world of European and Anglo-Saxon scholarship. In such inter-cultural transfers, the parameter of borrowing is also present. This is the most recent renewal of a text, which in the history of Indian thought has been renewed again and again through various processes of abridgement, recension, reordering and adaptation, besides translation.

But in recent times, the overwhelming trend has been of translations from European languages into modern Indian languages and these too chiefly from English. This is virtually a unidirectional flow — as the few translations of texts into English (or, other European languages) are meant not for the European audiences but for the Indian readers. Apart from the self-evident problems of translating between such distant languages, there is in this process an implicit but characteristic one-way intellectual relationship, in other words, a recipient-donor equation. In the last hundred years or so, the Indian languages have been placed in the role of a recipient, with European languages, particularly English, as the donor. As we said above, there is in this an implicit recognition of the source language as the intellectual reservoir, and of the relatively impoverished state of the target language. This could be just a state of mind nurtured by quite extraneous reasons in the translators who are, almost all of them, Indians. There are three presuppositions in this one-way traffic: that all the worthwhile things are being said by the speakers of other languages, that what is being said is worthwhile, and that we have nothing worthwhile to say in return. This state of mind is a part of the general attitude of uncritical subordination to Western ideas.

There is, on the other hand, another kind of translation activity — equally pervasive and for its intellectual merit and wide usefulness much more significant — that has a long history and has also been going on in a big way in recent times. We are talking of the translations of classical Sanskrit texts, technical as well as literary, into modern European languages mostly by European scholars and also by modern Indian scholars. Sanskrit is the donor intellectual tradition in this transaction. Sanskrit has, in fact, always been a donor language for translations into Asian and European languages.

In the early centuries of the Christian era, Buddhist texts were translated into Chinese and later into Tibetan. Apart from this Northern connection, as attested by the Arab sources, there was considerable interaction between the Hindus and the pre-Islam Arabs on their west. Not much direct evidence remains but it is acknowledged that Hindu mathematics, astronomy, and philosophy travelled to the West in this phase. Even after the advent of Islam, on Alberuni's testimony, the relationship of give and take continued. From the eleventh century onwards, with the rise of modern Indian languages, Sanskrit (technical/cultural) texts began to be translated into those languages (Assamese, Marāṭhī, Kannaḍa, Telugu, etc.) as a method of preserving these texts through diffusion. At the same time, translations began to be made into Persian. Zain-ul-Abedin (1420-70), the enlightened ruler of Kashmir, established a translation bureau for bilateral renderings between Sanskrit and Persian. Dara Shikoh's Persian translations of the Upaniṣads and Mulla Ahmad's rendition of the *Mahābhārata* are among the major islands in this stream. In the seventeenth-eighteenth century, the great Sikh Guru, Guru Gobind Singhji, set up a bureau and had a large number of Sanskrit texts translated into Punjabi.

In the late eighteenth and nineteenth centuries, the encounter with the West resulted in a complex, bilateral, cultural-intellectual relationship. In the fields of science, engineering, and in the new disciplines such as politics and economics, English became the donor language for translations into Indian languages. In the fields of philosophy, religion, linguistics and literary theory, Sanskrit renewed its role as a donor language for translations into English and other European languages. In fact, in the nineteenth century, Europe discovered India as much as India discovered Europe and the mutual influence was perhaps equal. By 1820, all the major universities of Europe had chairs in Sanskrit, and Sanskrit studies had come to enjoy immense prestige. As the century progressed, Sanskrit studies increasingly shaped the European mind, and, as already noted, almost all the major European minds of the nineteenth century were either Sanskritists or, of their own admission, been deeply involved in Indian thought. In 1839-40, Otto Böhtlingk brought out an edition of Pāṇini's *Aṣṭādhyāyī* with German comments on rules and an index of technical terms with glosses. In 1841, N.L. Westergaard brought out an edition of the *Dhātupāṭha* (enumeration of Sanskrit verb roots) with Latin gloss and references. In 1858, Albrecht Weber published a German translation of the Vājasaneyī *Prātiśākhya*. In 1862, W.D. Whitney brought out his English translation of the *Atharvaveda Prātiśākhya*. In 1874, Lorenz Franz Kielhorn published a translation into English of Nāgojībhaṭṭa's *Paribhāṣenduśekhara*. This list of examples, restricted to grammatical texts, is illustrative of Europe's interest in Sanskrit technical literature. This engagement with Sanskrit literature continues. Europe was equally, if not more, interested in the philosophical literature in Sanskrit. It has been noted that as a result of these translations,

> . . . Goethe and many other writers of the early nineteenth century read all they could of ancient Indian literature in translation. From Goethe onwards most of the great German philosophers knew something of Indian philosophy. Schopenhauer, whose influence on literature and psychology has been so considerable, indeed openly admitted his debt, and his outlook was virtually that of Buddhism. The monism of Fichte and Hegel might never have taken the forms they did if it had not been for Anquetil-Duperron's translation of the Upaniṣads and the work of other pioneer Indologists. In the English speaking world the strongest Indian influence was felt in America, where Emerson, Thoreau and other New England writers avidly studied much Indian religious literature in translation, and exerted immense influence on their contemporaries and successors, notably Walt Whitman. Through Carlyle and others the German philosophers in their turn made their

> mark on England as did the Americans through many late 19th century writers. . . . — Basham 486-87

Interaction with Sanskrit thought proved very fruitful intellectually for the Western tradition. Merely by translating an alien text into one's language one does not ensure the transfer of knowledge — knowledge assimilates knowledge. European scholars remained rooted firmly in their own intellectual tradition even while "translating" Indian thought — making possible a very constructive interaction, which produced, as we have already noted, a number of highly original thinkers. Besides, a whole new discipline developed — Historical and Comparative Linguistics — which extended the methods of philology to the classical languages other than Latin and Greek. And most importantly, these studies generated a new and very powerful conceptual system, structuralism, which in itself and in its later *avatāra*s and alterities has continued to be the dominant intellectual construct of the twentieth century. Ferdinand de Saussure, the father of structuralism, was a professor and a scholar of Sanskrit. His phonocentrism, his conception of language as speech, is an insight founded on the classical Indian theory of language. (The three Indian words for language, *vāṇī, bhāṣā, vāk*, mean respectively "speech," "sound," "statement.") Saussure was a scholar of Sanskrit grammar and at the time of his death was working on the symmetries in the *Ṛgveda*.

This was an exemplary interaction between two intellectual traditions, the kind of interaction that the Indian scholars failed to achieve in modern times because having abandoned their own intellectual tradition they did not have the requisite frame of knowledge to receive knowledge. Thus the enterprise of translation from the European into Indian languages has not proved fruitful at all because it was not conceived carefully as a part of any larger intellectual goal. It amounts to a willing acceptance of the recipient's role. The effect of these translations has been to increasingly marginalize the native traditions of thought. This trend has been countered only by the translations from Sanskrit into the modern languages, particularly European. The European translations foregrounded these texts and the prestige and importance that their ideas acquired in the West gained them the esteem of the Indian academia as well, thus putting them on the agenda of Indian scholarship once again. It is in the middle of the nineteenth century that in Europe the first translations of Indian texts began to be made. At the same time in India, major Sanskrit texts began to be translated into English. The motivation, no doubt, was a little different from that of the European work — the Indian translations were a part of a larger process of resistance to the alien domination, an expression of identity, a reassertion of the native self.[27]

Max Müller's project of translating the Sacred Books of the East has to be assessed in this perspective. This was the first planned programme for translating a series of texts of thought from six major cultures (Judaism was left out). In the Programme of Translation and in the Preface to the Series, the learned Professor dwells on the difficulties and problems in such a programme of translations and on his well-considered philosophy of translation:

> We must not expect, [he says,] that a translation of the sacred books of the ancients can ever be more than an approxi-

27. But, and this is important, this effort was supported by the British whose eclecticism and real love for scholarship must be recognized as not all the translations they commissioned or supported were a part of their administrative requirement.

> mation of our language to theirs, of our thought to theirs. The translator, however, if he has once gained the conviction that it is impossible to translate old thought into modern speech, without doing some violence either to the one or to the other, will hardly hesitate in his choice. 'He will prefer to do some violence to language.' — xxxvii

> I have thought it best therefore to keep as close as possible to the Sanskrit original and where I could not find an adequate term in English, I have often retained the Sanskrit word.
> — xxxii

He was negotiating a very difficult terrain in overcoming both prejudice and opposition to the whole project of introducing Eastern thought to the West with the firm conviction that,

> Here is in every one of the sacred books, something that could make man shrink from evil and incline to good, something to sustain him in the short journey through life, with its bright moments of happiness, and its long hours of terrible distress. — xxxviii

Of the forty-nine volumes, after excluding the Index volume, thirty-two are Vedic, Buddhist and Jain texts. Of these, Max-Müller personally translated the *Ṛgveda* and the Upaniṣads and was one of the three translators of the Buddhist Mahāyāna texts.

But his outstanding contribution was his reconstitution and translation of the *Ṛgveda* text with Sāyaṇa's commentary. This was the work of his mature years which followed his first translation of the selected hymns of the *Ṛgveda* (*Ṛgveda Saṁhitā*) for Sanskrit scholars only "explaining every word and sentence that seems to require elucidation, and carefully examining the opinions of early commentators, both native and European"(xliv). I had taken the liberty to suggest, to much opposition and some applause, in a seminar at Calcutta that as reconstituting the *Ṛgveda* seems to be the prime determinant of the Vyāsa status, we may recognize Max-Müller's place in the intellectual traditions as the thirty-third Vyāsa. We have recognized Yāska of the ninth century BC, as the thirty-first Vyāsa and Ādi Śaṅkara of seventh century AD as the thirty-second Vyāsa. True, there was a palpable contradiction in his own attitude to Eastern knowledge and texts, and he swung between adulation and disgust. But to assess his contribution, we should apply to his work the same parameter of the "Himālayas" that he had applied to the Indian texts.

Thus, around Max Müller, and inspired by him, the central texts of Indian culture were once again renewed and re-established in the nineteenth and twentieth centuries after a period of textual dispersal and neglect spread over eight centuries. In fact, it was through translations that these texts gained a large new readership. His *Sacred Books* inspired The Harvard Oriental Series. Of the first forty-seven texts that have been textually edited, translated and published in the Series, with Charles Rockwell as the General Editor to begin with, twenty-seven are Indian texts.[28] These two series renewed a large number of texts of Indian (Brāhmaṇa, Buddhist, Jain) thought and literature and enabled and strengthened Indian studies. They also motivated and inspired Indian scholars to undertake the study of their own tradition with Western methods.

---

28. *Jātakamālā; Vijñānabhikṣu; Buddhism in Translation: Passages Selected From the Buddhist Sacred Books; Karpūramañjarī; Bṛhaddevatā; Atharvaveda Saṁhitā* (2 vols.); *Vedic Concordance; Pañcatantra; Yoga System* (of Patañjali); *Veda of the Black Yajurveda School Entitled Taittirīya Saṁhitā* (2 vols.); *Ṛgveda Brāhmaṇas: The Aitareya and Kauśitakī Brāhmaṇas of the Ṛgveda; Buddhist legends: Dhammapada*
→

IX

This diffusion and dissemination across cultures has also created a new challenge for Indian scholars — the need to defend the texts and the tradition in the face of attacks from the materialists, the proponents of the "modernist" reading and the Hebraic anti-polytheists.

Some Western scholars and their Indian followers do what one may call meta-reading; they talk about the text and ask "why" before they ascertain "what." Their purpose is to undermine the traditional reverence for the texts. They do this by selecting parts and portions of texts and making original claims by applying questionable methods of interpretation to those bits and pieces. There is also the attitudinal difference in these modes of scholarship. Subversion of beliefs and values is acclaimed as originality and takes precedence over a total, unbiased interpretation of the text. Debunking is very dear and meaning becomes the instrument for some given social/political purpose.

Now that such readings of Indian texts are setting the goals and modes of reading in the mainstream institutions of learning in India, it is imperative that Indian scholars should revert to, and cultivate, the traditional Śāstra *paddhati*, the method of interpreting the texts. The methods of traditional scholarship should be replicated and the traditional institutions and scholars must be given total state support in a way that

---

→ *Commentary* (2 vols.); *The Religion and Philosophy of the Veda and Upaniṣads* (2 vols); *Ṛgveda* (4 vols.); *Materials for the Study of Navya-Nyāya Logic*; *Viśuddhimagga* (of Buddhaghoṣa); *Subhāṣitaratnakośa* (of Vidyākara); *Saundaryalahirī*; *Anthology of Sanskrit Court Poetry*; *Navya-Nyāya Doctrine of Negation: The Semantics and Ontology of Negative Statements in Navya-Nyāya Philosophy*; *Diṅnāga on Perception*.

does not subject them to the methods and limitations of the mainstream Macaulayan system. Only that will maintain, renew and keep relevant India's intellectual traditions and texts. Right now the pressures of "modernity" are proving too much and the *paṇḍits* are busy storing in the computer what they used to store in their minds. The whole philosophy of knowledge is thus shifting. From an interiorized, subject-centred knowledge formation and storage of Indian theory, we are fast moving towards an exteriorized, object-centred system. Smṛti (memory) has been accepted as the crucial first part of intellection apart from *vimarśa* (reflection/permutation) and *prayoga* (application) — unless we have something in our mind, what will we reflect on! The exteriorized, necessarily sequential, sensory mode of knowledge formation closes all possibilities of those kinds of knowledge that are born of deep inward reflection and a certain *ekāgratā* (one-pointedness, concentration). This can only inevitably have deleterious consequences for knowledge-creation. In such a scenario — of competition from the all-powerful Western model — the question that is of utmost importance now is: how do we maintain and sustain the Indian knowledge-tradition?

References

Basham, A.L., *The Wonder That Was India*, New York: Grove Press Inc., 1954.

Bhattacharya, B., *Sanskrit Culture in a Changing World*, Baroda: Good Companions, 1950.

Hattori, Masaaki, tr. and annotated, *Diṅnāga, on Perception*, Harvard Oriental Series 47, ed. Daniel H.H. Ingalls, Cambridge, Mass.: Harvard University Press, 1968.

Hayes, Richard P., "Diṅnāga on Interpretation of Signs," *Studies of Classical India*, vol. 9, London: Kluwer Academic Publishers, 1987.

Heimann, Betty, *Indian and Western Philosophy: A Study in Contrasts*, 1937, New Delhi: Aman Publishing Company, 1994.

Iyer, K.A. Subramania, *Bhartrihari*, Poona: Deccan College, 1969.

Jha, Ganganatha, tr., *Ślokavārttika*, rpt. New Delhi: Satguru Publications, 1983.

Kapoor, Kapil, "Knowledge, Individual and Society in the Indian Tradition." Endowment Lecture delivered at Punjab University, Chandigarh, December, 2001, to be published by Punjab University.

———, "Philosophy of Translation: Subordinating or Subordination — Translating Sanskrit Technical Texts," *Translation Theory and Practice*, ed. Shantha Ramakrishna, New Delhi: Pencraft, 1997.

———, "Rebirth of a Language: The Conceptual Structure of Vivekananda's Discourse," *Reflection on Swami Vivekananda: Hundred Years After Chicago*, ed. M. Sivaramakrishna and Sumta Roy, New Delhi: Sterling Publishers, 1993.

———, "Some Reflections on the Interpretation of Texts in the Indian Tradition," *Structures of Signification*, ed. H.S. Gill, vol. I, New Delhi: Wiley Eastern Limited, 1990.

———, "Texts of the Oral Tradition," *Language, Linguistics and Literature: The Indian Perspective*, New Delhi: Academic Foundation, 1994.

———, "*Vyāsa Paramparā*, Text Renewal Mechanisms, Max Müller and European Scholarship," *Max Müller and Contemporary European Scholarship*, Ramakrishna Mission, Kolkatta, 2000.

Matilal, B.K., *Word and World*, New Delhi: Motilal Banarsidass, 1990.

Müller, Max, *India: What Can It Teach Us*, Indian edn., New Delhi: Munshiram Manoharlal, 1991.

———, tr., *Ṛgveda Saṁhitā: The Sacred Hymns of the Brahmans*, vol. I, *Hymns to the Maruts or the Storm-Gods*, London, 1869.

———, Sacred Books of the East, 1879, rpt., New Delhi: Motilal Banarsidass, 1969.

Nirvedananda, Swami, *Cultural Heritage of India*, vol. II, Calcutta: Ramakrishna Institute of Culture, 1953.

Pargiter, F.E., *Ancient Indian Historical Tradition*, New Delhi: Motilal Banarsidass, 1962.

Shastri, Nilakantha, *History of India*, Madras, 1950.

Tiwari, Kamalakar, Translator's introd., *Hum Bharata se Kyā Sīkh Sakte Hain?* [*India: What Can It Teach Us* by Max Müller.], 2nd edn., Allahabad: Adarsh Hindi Pustakalaya, 1967.

Vyasashishya, Kunwarlal, *Arsha Yajna Vidya*, New Delhi: Itihasa Vidya Prakashan, 1988.

Appendix

Judgement of the Supreme Court of India Regarding Sanskrit

In the Supreme Court of India* Civil Original Jurisdiction

Writ petition © No. 299 of 1989 (along with

WP © Nos. 13-3189, 1184189, 601189, 571189 and 1041189)

Shri Santosh Kumar & Ors. etc. — Petitioners

Vs.

The Secretary

Ministry of Human Resources Development and Anr. — Respondents

Judgement

1. A professor of Cambridge University is deeply engrossed in his studies in his calm chamber: An agitated English soldier enters the study room and accuses the professor in not sharing the trauma of war which he and many others like him are facing while fighting Germans. The professor calmly asks the young soldier for whom he is fighting for. Quick comes the reply that it is to defend the country. The wise man wants to know what is that country to defend which he is prepared to shed his blood. The soldier replies it is the territory and its people. On further questioning

the soldier says it is not only this but the culture of the country which he wants to defend. The professor quietly states that he is contributing to that culture. The soldier calms down and bows in respect to the professor and vows to defend with more vigour the cultural heritage of his country.

2. This is what is said to have happened during the Second World War when England was fighting almost a last-ditch battle of survival and all Englishmen contributed in their own way to the ultimate victory of England.

3. The above shows the concern for culture evinced even by the Westerners. So far as "We, the people of India" are concerned, they have always held in high esteem the cultural heritage of this ancient land. And to foretell our views, learning of Sanskrit is undoubtedly necessary for protection of this heritage. The stream of our culture would get dried if we were to discourage the study of Sanskrit, and that too on the most untenable ground that if the Central Board of Secondary Education (for short "the Board") were to do so, it would have to make facilities available for learning of Arabic and Persian — these being also classical languages, which is the ground advanced by Addl. Solicitor General, Shri Tulsi, appearing for the Board, in it not being in a position to accept the prima facie view expressed by us on 19.7.94, when these cases had come up for hearing that Sanskrit should be included by the Board as one of the elective subjects in the syllabus along with Assamese, Bengali etc. which are the languages specified in the Eighth Schedule of our Constitution, mentioning about Sanskrit being also an Eighth Schedule language. The

desire to keep Sanskrit out does not stop here, as the submission also is that if Sanskrit comes, the Board shall have to bring in languages like French and German. This is not all, as it is contended by the Addl. Solicitor General that the Board feels that arrangement may have then to be made for imparting education even in Lepcha, a language whose name many of the Indians might not have even heard.

4. We fail to appreciate at all the stand taken by a responsible body like the Board, who has been entrusted with the onerous duty of educating the youths of this country "in whose hands quiver the destinies of the future," as the same is wholly untenable. Without the learning of Sanskrit it is not possible to decipher the Indian philosophy on which our culture and heritage are based.

5. The question raised being important requires us, to answer it appropriately, to first know what our policy makers have said about the importance of Sanskrit. We shall then apprise ourselves about the place of Sanskrit in our educational ethos and shall finally see whether teaching of Sanskrit is against secularism?

Our Education Policy qua Sanskrit

6. Being called upon to decide whether Sanskrit is required to be included in the syllabus of the Board as an elective subject so far as teaching in secondary school is concerned, may we say at the threshold a few words on the importance of education as such. This point is not required to be laboured by us in view of the Constitution Bench decision of this Court in Unnikrishnan's case, 1993 (1) SCC 645 in which the majority Judges well brought home the importance of

education. It would be enough to mention what Mohan, J. (as a majority Judge) stated in that judgement. According to the learned Judge, education is a preparation of living and for life here and hereafter and education is at once a social and political necessity. It was also observed that victories are gained, peace is preserved, progress is achieved, civilisation is built up and history is made, not in the battle fields but in educational institutions which are seed-beds of culture. Education was, therefore, regarded as enlightenment and one that lends dignity to a man.

7. As we are concerned in these cases with the teaching in the secondary schools, we may say something about the importance of education in its early stages. It has been well recognised that it is this education which lays the foundation for a full and intense life and so this education must carefully keep alive the spark of curiosity and fan it into a beautiful, bright flame whenever it comes. It has been stated that it is the education received in early stages, which widens the contacts of child or youth with the surroundings of the world; and with every new and fruitful contacts with the world of things, the world of men and the world of ideas, life of the young becomes richer and broader. It is early education which seeks to broaden the mind by exposing the learner to the world of thought and reflection, which can inspire him with lofty idealism by giving him the glimpses of a good life which a worthy education is capable of bringing.

8. We may now advert to the broad framework of our education policy as accepted by the Central Government. For our purpose it would be enough if we refer to the policies as formulated in 1968 and 1986.

Here again, we would confine our attention to what was stated in these policies regarding Sanskrit. In the 1968 policy the following found place qua this language:

"Considering the special importance of Sanskrit to the growth and development of Indian languages and its unique contribution to the cultural unity of the country facilities for its teaching at the school and university stages should be offered on a more liberal basis. Development of new methods of teaching the language should be encouraged, and the possibility explored of including the study of Sanskrit in those courses (such as modern Indian philosophy) at the first and second degree stages, where such knowledge is useful."

9. The 1986 policy has to say as below in this regard in para 5.33 :

"Research in Indology, the humanities and Social Sciences will receive adequate support. To fulfil the need for the synthesis of knowledge, inter-disciplinary research will be encouraged. Efforts will be made to delve into India's ancient fund of knowledge and to relate it to contemporary reality. This effort will imply the development of facilities for the intensive study of Sanskrit." (Emphasis supplied)

10. It would be of some interest to note that when Sir William Jones, one of the most brilliant men of eighteenth century, came to India in 1783 as a Judge of the then Supreme Court of Judicature at Fort Williams in Bengal, he got interested to learn Sanskrit and it grew so strong that within six years he not only

became the master of the language but translated Kālidāsa's *Śākuntalam*. After about two hundred years it has fallen to the Judges of the present Supreme Court to highlight the importance of Sanskrit and to see that it finds its due place into the niche of our national life.

Place of Sanskrit in our Educational Ethos

11. It is well known that Sanskrit is a mother of all Indo-Aryan languages and it is this language in which our Vedas, Purāṇas and Upaniṣads have been written and in which Kālīdāsa, Bhavabhūti, Bāṇabhaṭṭa and Dāṇḍī wrote their classics. Teachings of Śaṅkarācārya, Rāmānuja, Mādhavācārya, Nimbārka and Vallabhācārya would not have been woven into the fabric of Indian culture if Sanskrit would not have been available to them as a medium of expressing their thoughts.

12. The report of the Sanskrit Commission (set up by the Government of India) which was submitted in 1957 speaks eloquently about the importance of Sanskrit. We do not propose to burden this judgment with all that was said by the Commission in this regard. It would be enough for our purpose if we take note of some passages finding place in the report which highlight the quality, substance, content and strength of Sanskrit. At page 71 of the report it has been mentioned that Sanskrit is one of the greatest languages of the world and it is the classical language par excellence not only of India but of a good part of Asia as well. At page 73 the report states that the Indian people and the Indian civilisation were born, so to say, in the lap of Sanskrit and it went "hand-in-hand with the historical development of the Indian people,

and gave the noblest expression to their mind and culture which has come down to our day as an inheritance of priceless order for India, nay, for the entire world." The report further speaks at page 74 about the "great mental and spiritual link" of Sanskrit and of it being the elder sister of Greek and Latin, and cousin of English, French and Russian.

13. There is no need to dilate on the importance of Sanskrit further in our national ethos in view of what was stated by no less a person than the first Prime Minister of the country, Pandit Jawaharlal Nehru, in this regard, which is as below:

> "If I was asked what is the greatest treasure which India possesses and what is her finest heritage, I would answer unhesitatingly — it is the Sanskrit language and literature, and all that it contains. This is a magnificent inheritance, and so long as this endures and influences the life of our people, so long the basic genius of India will continue."

Is Teaching of Sanskrit Against Secularism?

14. Of the three objections mentioned by the Addl. Solicitor General regarding the inability of the Board in acting in accordance with the prima facie views expressed by us in our order dated 19.7.1994, the only objection which merits our close look is that if Sanskrit were to be included as an elective subject, Arabic and Persian shall also have to be so done. The two other objections, namely inclusion of French and German also in the syllabus and of language like Lepcha do not deserve any consideration for obvious reasons.

15. The first objection needs our consideration because in some quarter there may be a feeling that by conceding to Sanskrit alone as an elective subject, we would act against secularism, which has been accepted by a nine-judge Bench of this Court in S.R. Bommai Vs. Union of India, 1994 (3) SCC 1, as a basic structure of our constitution. It is apparent that we cannot give any direction about which it can be said that it is against the secularist requirement of our Constitution.

16. For the disposal of the cases at hand it is not necessary to elaborately discuss what are the basic requirements of secularism inasmuch as in Bommai's case this exercise has been well done by the learned Judges. It would be enough for our purpose to note what some of the learned judges said in this regard. Sawant J., with whom one of us (Kuldip Singh, J.) agreed, quoted in para 147 of the report what Shri M. C. Setalvad had stated on secularism in his Patel Memorial Lectures, 1965. One of the observations made by Setalvad was that secular state is not hostile to religion but holds itself neutral in matters of religion. The further observation in para 148 is that the State's tolerance of religion does not make it either a religious or a theocratic State. Ramaswami, J. stated in para 179 that secularism represents faiths born out of the exercise of rational faculties and it enables to see the imperative requirements for human progress in all aspects and cultural and social advancement and indeed for human survival itself.

17. It would be profitable to note that according to Justice H.R. Khanna secularism is neither anti-God nor pro-God; it treats alike the devout, the agnostic and the

atheist. According to him, secularism is not anti-thesis of religious devoutness. He would like to dispel the impression that if a person is devout Hindu or devout Muslim he ceases to be secular. This is illustrated by saying that Vivekananda and Gandhiji were the greatest Hindus yet their entire life and teachings embodied the essence of secularism (see his article "The Spirit of Secularism" as printed in "Secularism and India; Dilemmas and Challenges" edited by Shri M. M. Sankhdhar.)

18. We also propose to refer to what was said by the Sanskrit Commission on the subject of "Sanskrit and National Solidarity" in Chapter IV of its report. The Commission has, in this context first stated that Sanskrit is the "embodiment of Indian culture and civilisation." It then observes that the Indian people look upon Sanskrit as the binding force for the different people of this great country, which was described as the greatest discovery which the Commission made as it travelled from Kerala to Kashmir and from Kamarupa to Saurashtra. The commission, while so travelling, found that though the people of this country differed in a number of ways, they all were proud to regard themselves as participants in a common heritage and that heritage emphatically is the heritage of Sanskrit. According to the Commission one of the witnesses which appeared before it went to the length of suggesting that if the Sanskrit commission had come before the States Reorganisation Commission many of the recent bickering in our national life could have been avoided (pages 80 and 81).

19. From what has been stated above, we entertain no

doubt in our mind that teaching of Sanskrit alone as an elective subject can in no way be regarded as against secularism. Indeed, our constitution requires giving of fillip to Sanskrit because of what has been stated in Article 351. in which while dealing with the duty of the Union to promote the spread of Hindi, it has been provided that, it would draw, whenever necessary or desirable, for its vocabulary, primarily on Sanskrit. Encouragement to Sanskrit is also necessary because of it being one of the languages included in the Eighth Schedule.

20. We, therefore, conclude by saying that *in view of importance of Sanskrit for nurturing our cultural heritage, because of which even the official education policy has highlighted the need of study of Sanskrit, making of Sanskrit alone as an elective subject, while not conceding this status to Arabic and or Persian, would not in any way militate against the basic tenet of secularism*. (Emphasis supplied). There is thus no merit in the first objection raised by the Board.

21. In the aforesaid premises, we direct the Board to include Sanskrit as an elective subject in the syllabus under consideration. Necessary amendment in the syllabus shall be made within a period of three months from today.

22. The writ petitions are allowed accordingly. No order as to costs.

Sd / -	Sd/-
(Kuldip Singh)	**(B.L. Hansaria)**

New Delhi
4 October 1994

The Contributors

Professor George Cardona, University of Pennsylvania, Pennsylvania, USA.

Professor Lokesh Chandra, President, International Academy of Indian Culture, J-22, Hauz Khas, New Delhi – 110 016.

Professor R.P. Goldman, Director, Study Centre of the University of California 8, Sri Ram Road, Flat No. 17, Civil Lines, Delhi – 110 054.

Dr. Kalyani Gopal, Department of Computer Science and Automation, Indian Institute of Science, Bangalore – 560 012.

Professor Kapil Kapoor, Special Centre for Sanskrit Studies, Jawaharlal Nehru University, New Delhi – 110 067.

Dr. Shashiprabha Kumar, Associate Professor and Chairperson, Special Centre for Sanskrit Studies, Jawaharlal Nehru University, New Delhi – 110 067.

Dr. Rajnish Kumar Mishra, Assistant professor, Special Centre for Sanskrit Studies, Jawaharlal Nehru University, New Delhi – 110 067.

Professor K.T. Pandurangi, Vice-Chancellor, Purnaprajna Vidyapeetha, Bangalore.

Professor Makrand Paranjape, Chairperson, Centre of Linguistics and English, School of Language, Literature and

Culture Studies, Jawaharlal Nehru University, New Delhi – 110 067.

Dr. Upendra Rao, Reader, Sanskrit Deemed University, Puri.

Professor V.V.S. Sarma, Department of Computer Science and Automation, Indian Institute of Science, Bangalore – 560 012.

Professor Rama Nath Sharma, Prof. of Sanskrit, University of Hawaii at Manoa, Honolulu, Hawaii – 96822 (USA).

Dr. Randhir Singh, Ex. Vice Chancellor, Chaudhary Charan Singh University, Meerut, Karnal Road, Shamli (U.P.)

Index